# The Telegraph Goes to War

*The Personal Diary of David Homer Bates,*
*Lincoln's Telegraph Operator*

DAVID HOMER BATES
1865

*Courtesy of the Library of Congress*

# The Telegraph Goes to War

*The Personal Diary of David Homer Bates,*
*Lincoln's Telegraph Operator*

Edited by

## Donald E. Markle

Edmonston Publishing, Inc.
Hamilton, New York

Foreword, Preface, Acknowledgments, Introductory Chapters, Diary Chapter Introductions, Notes, Index, Appendices, Editing and Volume Arrangement Copyright © 2003 by Edmonston Publishing, Inc.
ISBN 1-892059-02-9
Printed in the United States of America on pH neutral paper.
∞
10 9 8 7 6 5 4 3 2 1

  Library of Congress Cataloging-in-Publication Data
  Bates, David Homer, b. 1843.
    The telegraph goes to war : the personal diary of David Homer Bates, Lincoln's telegraph operator / edited by Donald E. Markle.
      p. cm.
  Includes bibliographical references (p. ) and index.
   ISBN 1-892059-02-9
   1. Bates, David Homer, b. 1843—Diaries. 2. United States. Military Telegraph Corps—Biography. 3. United States—History—Civil War, 1861-1865—Communications. 4. Telegraphers—United States—Diaries. 5. Military telegraph—United States—History—19th century. 6. Lincoln, Abraham, 1809-1865. I. Markle, Donald E. II. Title.
   E608.B28A3 2003
   973.7'3—dc21

                                                        2003001740

# Dedicated To:

Mikel, Ian, Sara & Lea, The Markle Future

# Table of Contents

Foreword by B. Franklin Cooling. . . . . . . . . . . ix
Preface. . . . . . . . . . . . . . . . . . . . . . xiv
Acknowledgments. . . . . . . . . . . . . . . . xvi
The Military Telegraph. . . . . . . . . . . . . . . 1
David Homer Bates. . . . . . . . . . . . . . . . 23
Introduction to the Diary. . . . . . . . . . . . . 25
November, December 1863. . . . . . . . . . . . 28
January, February, March 1864. . . . . . . . . . 57
April, May, June 1864. . . . . . . . . . . . . . . 76
July, August, September 1864. . . . . . . . . . 116
October, November, December 1864. . . . . . . . 151
January, February, March 1865. . . . . . . . . . 180
April, May, June 1865. . . . . . . . . . . . . . . 201
Appendix A. . . . . . . . . . . . . . . . . . . . 229
Appendix B. . . . . . . . . . . . . . . . . . . . 236
Bibliography. . . . . . . . . . . . . . . . . . . 240
Index. . . . . . . . . . . . . . . . . . . . . . . 244

# Illustrations

David Homer Bates. . . . . . . . . . . . . . . . . ii
Early Morse Telegraph Instruments. . . . . . . . . . 2
Andrew Carnegie. . . . . . . . . . . . . . . . . . 5
First Four USMTC Operators. . . . . . . . . . . . . 9
Tactical Stringing of Wire. . . . . . . . . . . . . . 11
Map of Telegraph Line, City Point to Washington. . . . 15
Lt. Richard Montgomery, Union Agent. . . . . . . . 19
Bates's Handwritten Comments. . . . . . . . . . . 27

Confederate Cipher Letter. . . . . . . . . . . . . . . . 44
CSA Cipher Alphabet. . . . . . . . . . . . . . . . . . 48
U.S. Military Telegraph Construction Corps. . . . . . 70
Telegraph Battery Wagon. . . . . . . . . . . . . . . 84
Field Telegraph Station. . . . . . . . . . . . . . . . 87
Field Expedient. . . . . . . . . . . . . . . . . . . . . 126
Grant, Sheridan, Meade, & Others. . . . . . . . . . 133
Tapping a Wire. . . . . . . . . . . . . . . . . . . . . 140
Wire Tapping Equipment. . . . . . . . . . . . . . . 141
Sherman Communicates from Fort McAllister. . . . . 170
Lincoln's Last Telegram from City Point. . . . . . . 206
USMTC Construction Crew at Richmond. . . . . . 208
Message Announcing Lincoln's Assassination. . . . 216
GUARD Route Cipher & Code Word Page. . . . . . 231
Pigpen Cipher. . . . . . . . . . . . . . . . . . . . . 234
USMTC Plaque. . . . . . . . . . . . . . . . . . . . . 238
Eckert, Bates, Tinker & Chandler (1907). . . . . . . 239

# Foreword

For the past decade or so, the American military has been experiencing a so-called Revolution in Military Affairs. In keeping with the widely proclaimed Information Age, notions of an information technology-driven revolution are now deeply imbedded in American defense planning as well as a new American way of war. That is not to say that revolutions in military affairs are anything truly new or that the Industrial Age of the nineteenth and twentieth centuries was anything but technology-driven. Certainly the American Civil War provided the first full-scale war shaped by tools and weapons of the Industrial Revolution. Examples include the mechanization of farm and factory, steam-driven, ironclad warships, rifled firearms for the battlefield, and the unprecedented use of railroads coupled with the electromagnetic telegraph. All contributed to the war effort. Indeed if anything, the technology of rail and telegraph formed the unsung revolution of war-making in the 1860s—something European countries like Prussia quickly adopted both for strategic and tactical purposes. If nothing else, the telegraph married information and technology with speed as a prerequisite for military success. While an integrating thread through all accounts of Civil War specifics, the role of telegraphy remains greatly underplayed in our understanding of that conflict.[1]

In truth technology was the largest new factor in the warfare of the era. Telegraphy stood at the high end of that technology for communication; decision-making, logistical support, war management, and combat were all directly affected in pivotal ways. In addition to diplomacy, the telegraph provided a tool for interweaving political, military, economic and informational policies during that war. Men and supplies, infrastructure and conveyances could be collected and transported over long distances although not in the sophisticated fashion we know today. The crucial ingredient of intelligence was often gathered and reported via telegraph, then translated from cipher, sifted, studied, and communicated further to government and military officials. The telegraph was the invaluable middle partner in the process, supplemented of course by courier and dispatch rider at the field end of the spectrum.

Many military and civilian leaders at the time appreciated this application of technology—President Abraham Lincoln and his senior military leadership in particular. New rifled-firearm technology favored the defense on the battlefield, but the railroads and telegraph undergirded strategic offensive operations. Commanders could conduct more rapid operations thanks to those non-lethal weapons, although firepower dominance still ended most such operations in bloody slaughter. While today's governments and their militaries recognize the potential and the means of utilizing the benefits of technology based on science, it was more human ingenuity and imagination that attended the revolutionary military changes of the Civil War. As over 600,000 war dead attested, human comprehension of technological potential had its limitations.

Even telegraphic technology had its limitations. Telegraphy had been around for some decades before the Civil War and had fascinated the United States government since Samuel F. B. Morse patented the electromagnetic telegraph in 1840. Typical of government's role at the time, Washington subsidized scientific experiment and start-up, then stepped back to let private enterprise commercially exploit the new device for the public good. Proving itself absolutely indispensable to the operation of the nascent rail system of the country—running trains on single-track lines would not have been possible without it—as well as business activities of market and exchange, the telegraph also assisted various professional and other enterprises by exchanging data for more efficient and effective utilization. The miles of telegraph wires spread rapidly in the 1850s, both here and in Europe. Still, telegraph wires lined the railroad rights-of-way or so-called telegraph roads, that may have presaged the later major highways and interstates of the automobile age. Extension to home or business remained absent; this was a business enterprise, tightly controlled by 1860 by six major companies with transmittal and receipt of information at centralized locations.[2]

In short, suggests John E. Clark, Jr., railroads and the telegraph's instant communication "began to insinuate time as a factor into people's daily lives," thus raising "time value to prominence in business thinking." Amazingly, while such a technological advance brought isolated sections of the young nation into almost hourly contact, this level and intensity of communication exacerbated public awareness of the differences between north, south, and west. A boon for newspaper reporting of events, the sound bites of telegraphy may well have supplied the same gratification for information provided today by TV sensationalism, cell phone chatter, and e-mail snippets as grist for popular consumption. The telegraph itself could only expedite data exchange, not analyze it. It could provide raw facts but not educative deliberation, so in reality, the telegraph in and of itself did little to congeal national unity in this divisive age when sectionalism, slavery, and rebellion ultimately led to war as a final recourse.[3]

Militarily the electromagnetic telegraph found its first but limited use in the Crimea in the 1850s. Typically military commanders there (especially the French), resisted the innovation—principally because (as would be later proven in the American Civil War) the device threatened a commander's independence of action when linked so easily with home governments. Dictates from civilian authorities hardly coincided with what generals and admirals fancied as their professional prerogatives. So it was not without precedent that both Union and Confederate central governments quickly grasped the potential for war management not just of generals, but also of the public mind and collective will. "War is no less about mobilizing human minds and wills than about recruiting supplies, weapons, and manpower and deploying them in combat," writes Israeli communications professor Menahem Blondheim. And much of the story that follows through the observations of David Homer Bates in Mr. Lincoln's telegraph office provides a glimpse of the broader, grand strategic use of the telegraph, although the reader must search his diary jottings to glean such perspective. He does not pinpoint that message as would today's essayist.[4]

The story of the telegraph's contribution to a revolution in military affairs during the Civil War can be seen at two levels. So much that we know about the use of the telegraph in the field or with the armies comes from the priceless two volumes of veteran William R. Plum, *The Military Telegraph During the Civil War in the United States*. Telegrapher/cipherist Bates presented the second or headquarters view in his recollections, *Lincoln in the Telegraph Office*. Probably few users of the monumental published *Official Records* of the Army take time to appreciate how many of those documents were conveyed originally by telegraph. Possibly only historians study the nature, the benefits, and handicaps of that so-called "message traffic" for the sequence of events and the decision-process. Yet those are the kinds of things that we must bear in mind as we place Donald E. Markle's edition of David Homer Bates's diary beside these other resources for re-exploring the telegraphic technology of the Civil War. Markle's introduction and commentary will help with understanding the endeavor.

The Bates diary provides so much more however by showing the meaning of information received and appreciated. His diary is the raw material of reminiscence, companion comments on people and times in wartime Washington as well as on the larger scope of events. With renewed interest in Civil War reminiscences and diaries—largely of combatants or the gender/ethnic genre—*The Telegraph Goes To War* provides a wonderfully different perspective from the War Department, but with events filtered much as senior officials would have received the information over the telegraph.

Above all it must be no small irony that the Federal government first appropriated $30,000 for construction of a telegraph line to span the 40 miles between Washington and Baltimore in the very year that David Homer Bates was born—1843. Bates embraced this new technology for his life's work, starting as a Pennsylvania Railroad telegraph clerk, then seconded with a team to the War Department Telegraph Office. Here as his reminiscences and diaries tell us, he rubbed elbows with the greatest figure of his age—the sixteenth president of the United States. In the end it was Abraham Lincoln who took and understood how to use this revolutionary instrument to communicate both with his military and his nation in forging public will for the ultimate fate of the nation—survival. Bates was part of the action, a witness to history. For it was there in that telegraph office, Lincoln's personal secretary John Hay noted, that the president "like a backwoods Jupiter" wielded "the bolts of war and the machinery of government" with a firm and steady hand. Both Bates and Lincoln in their own way thereby contributed to the future, ensuring through victory that there would be other such American revolutions in the interest of information and technology for the preservation of democracy and the nation-state.[5]

B. Franklin Cooling<br>Industrial College of the Armed Forces<br>Washington, DC

## Notes

[1]Trenchant comments on the role of the telegraph for war-making in the Civil War period can be examined in various essays in: Jessup, John E. & Ketz, Louise B. (Eds.) (1994) *Encyclopedia of the American Military.* New York: Scribners. Pp. 12, 14, 1180-1181, 1228, 1256, 1421, 1474-1475; and Huston, James A. (1966) *The Sinews of War: Army Logistics 1775-1953.* [Army Historical Series] Washington, DC: Office of the Chief of Military History, United States Army. Pp. 164, 195.

[2]Ross, Charles.(2000) *Trial by Fire: Science, Technology and the Civil War.* Shippensburg, PA: White Mane. Chapter 6.
[3]Clark, John E., Jr. (2001) *Railroads in the Civil War: The Impact of Management on Victory and Defeat.* Baton Rouge: Louisiana State University. p. 10.
[4]Blondheim, Menahem. "Public Sentiment Is Everything": The Union's Public Communications Strategy and the Bogus Proclamation of 1864, *The Journal of American History,* December, 2002, 869-899, especially 869-871.
[5]Rawley, James A. (1995) Introduction in: Bates, David Homer. *Lincoln in the Telegraph Office: Recollections of the United States Military Telegraph Corps During the Civil War.* Omaha, NE: University of Nebraska. p. xxi. (Reprint of 1907 edition)

# Preface

The American Civil War is often called the first modern war. The use of the telegraph by both the Union and the Confederacy stands as an excellent example of the employment of new technology in the prosecution of the war. Prior to the outbreak of the war in 1861, the United States government was totally dependent upon commercial circuits to handle all governmental communications. Army installations beyond the reach of these circuits were virtually isolated from timely direction or support.

When the war started, the Union government almost immediately grasped the importance of the telegraph and created the United States Military Telegraph Corps (USMTC) that functioned in direct support of the Union forces. Blessed with the capability of manufacturing the necessary wire and other components, the Union was able to string wire as required to provide communications to the troops as they moved throughout the countryside. The Confederacy on the other hand had virtually no capability to create wire and was therefore largely dependent on commercial circuitry (much of which represented the southern routes of northern companies) for its communications.

To handle the multitude of circuits in operation adequately, the Union government established a Telegraph Office in the War Department building adjacent to the White House. This office provided what was then considered rapid communications to and from the various armies—a function that had previously never been accomplished in a tactical military environment anywhere in the world. It was a dramatic first and a new capability that did not go unnoticed by the foreign military observers of the American Civil War.

The Telegraph Office was manned by USMTC operators, one of whom was a young man from Steubenville, Ohio, David Homer Bates. This young man maintained a meticulous diary of the day-by-day happenings in that office (a common practice for telegraph operators). Although Bates was not well educated, the grammar in the diary is very clear and concise as well as correct. Also due to his telegraphic training—which included a requirement that all messages transcribed be readable and that legible handwriting be used—the handwriting in the diary is exceptionally clear. Among his entries can be found some valuable historical information such as the time of receipt of messages, reactions to events, creations of codes, activity levels on the lines, etc.—all a part of his daily routine. By reading the entries in chronological order, the reader can grasp a comprehensive picture of the role of the military telegraph in the war.

The Bates diary is held by the Library of Congress, having been purchased as part of the Alfred Whital Stern collection in 1962. Mr. Stern had previously purchased the diary through Mr. Alfred Neuman, owner of the Lincoln Bookshop, Chicago, Illinois. The seller of the diary was Mr. Charles T. White, the local editor of a newspaper in Hancock, New York. It is not known how or when Mr. White acquired the diary.

David Homer Bates probably kept a series of diaries throughout the war period, but all that remains in existence today covers the period from November 13, 1863, to early June of 1865. Interestingly when Bates wrote his 1907 book, *Lincoln in the Telegraph Office*, relating his wartime experiences, he included only diary entries recorded between these specific dates.

The present work contains Bates's previously unpublished diary and provides context with related material from his book and other sources. David Homer Bates was indeed in a unique position to observe and report on the birth of the telegraph into a military environment and its value to the Union cause.

Donald E. Markle
Gettysburg, Pennsylvania

# Acknowledgments

When I first started the editing process for the diary, I thought it would be a fairly easy job. The handwriting was amazingly clear; the subject was familiar; and the people and places well-known. I could not have been more mistaken. The diary identified many individuals by last names only, necessitating a search for first names and titles in many cases. In addition place names were often misspelled and in some cases designated locations that were nothing more than obscure crossroads intersections in remote areas.

The assistance of a large network of local historical societies was invaluable. Without their willing help the editing process would have been a great deal slower and the finished product not nearly as accurate. Very special thanks must be given to the William F. Friedman Crytologic Collection, in the George C. Marshall Research Library, Virginia Military Institute, Lexington, Virginia; the Historical Society of Washington, DC; the Historical Society of Western Pennsylvania, Pittsburgh, Pennsylvania; the Lynchburg, Virginia, Museum System; the Maryland Historical Society, Baltimore, Maryland; the Morse Telegraph Club, Normal, Illinois; the Pittsburgh, Pennsylvania, Historical Society; the State Historical Society of Delaware, Wilmington, Delaware; the New York Historical Society, New York, New York; and the Decatur, Alabama, Historical Society.

In addition to historical societies, various individuals in the academic field provided me not only with information but guidance and support. These include Dr. T. Alford, Northern Virginia Community College, Fairfax, Virginia; Mrs. Louise Arnold-Friend, the Library of the U.S. Army Military Institute, Carlisle Barracks, Carlisle, Pennsylvania; Dr. Gabor Boritt, Gettysburg College, Gettysburg, Pennsylvania; Mr. James O. Hall, noted Civil War historian, McLean, Virginia; and Dr. Steven Miller of the University of Maryland, College Park, Maryland.

I am indebted also to various libraries that provided assistance as requested, including: the Rare Book Collection at the Library of Congress, Washington, DC; the Adams County Public Library System, Gettysburg, Pennsylvania; the Pennsylvania Inter-State Library Loan System; the Gettysburg Battlefield National Park Library, Gettysburg, Pennsylvania; Dr. Tom Perera of the W1TP Telegraph and Scientific Instrument Museums, Montclair State University, Upper Montclair, New Jersey; the Musselman Library at Gettysburg College, Gettysburg, Pennsylvania; the National Archives, Washington, DC; and the New York Public Library, New York, New York.

A special acknowledgment is due a very unique individual who volunteered to assist me with this project, Mr. Arthur Thimsen. Mr. Thimsen is a "detail man," who initially provided me with his expertise in developing the extensive index for the diary and later helped in all aspects of putting the final touches on the work. Without his help and keen eye the project would not have come to fruition nearly as quickly as it has. Over the course of the project, I came not only to respect Mr. Thimsen for his technical abilities but also to look upon him as a close friend and associate.

Lastly, very special recognition is due Geri, my wife, able proofreader and strong supporter of me in this project. Without her this book would not have been possible.

DEM

# The Military Telegraph

When the American Civil War began, the commercial telegraph was less than 20 years old. The use of the telegraph to transmit communications in the United States commercially began in 1843 when the United States Congress voted to fund the first telegraph line. The line ran between Baltimore and Washington along the Baltimore and Ohio Railroad bed. On the 24th of May 1844, the first telegraphic message was sent along this line to Washington, D.C. During the early days of the telegraph, it was normal practice to place telegraph lines adjacent to the railroad tracks as that area provided fairly level terrain as well as easy access in case repairs were needed.

At that time the telegraph operated with an embosser suspended above a moving roll of paper tape. The embosser marked the tape with dots and dashes depending on the electrical current received.[1] This was later replaced with an ink pen to mark the characters on the tape clearly. It was soon discovered that the operators were writing down the character sounds as they were being inked on the tape. This led in 1856 to the introduction of the sounder, which relied completely on acoustic signals and thus required the operators to have an accurate knowledge of all the Morse Code equivalents. The introduction of the sounder increased the speed of transmission from 20 to about 35 words per minute for a good operator and provided a very flexible and smaller piece of equipment for the operator to carry. Telegraph wire was made of copper (when available) or iron and usually insulated with gutta-percha (India Rubber). All of these early developments between 1843 and 1861 were driven by private companies, which viewed the military merely as one of their paying subscribers.

By the advent of the Mexican War in 1846, New York and Boston were connected telegraphically, and the first war news transmitted over the line consisted of accounts of the Battles of Palo Alto and Resaca de la Palma.[2] Continuous reporting of the American victories in Mexico coupled with the news of the presidential campaign of 1846 made the American people aware of the value of the telegraph, and it was hereafter looked upon as the prime source of the latest information. Military reports were passed on commercial circuits, as military networks were not in existence at that time.

Morse Canvas
Stretcher Receiver, 1842

*(Courtesy of the Smithsonian
Institution, Neg. 13,366)*

Civil War Key and Sounder,
Charles Wilson (Boston)

*(Courtesy of W1TP Telegraph and
Scientific Instrument Museum)*

Civil War Morse Telegraph Key

*(Courtesy of the Smithsonian Institution, Neg. 27,979)*

Early Morse Telegraph Instruments

Throughout the early 1850's the militaries of Austria, Britain, France, and Spain experimented with the use of the telegraph with only limited success. The first successful use of the telegraphic system of communications for military purposes was conducted by the British, French, and Turkish forces during the Crimean War (1854-1855). They used the telegraph only to connect their principal headquarters rather than employing it at the tactical level. This successful experiment led to the British military's establishment of the first military telegraph school for members of the Royal Engineers.[3]

An American observer present on the Crimean front was the future Union General, George B. McClellan, who later employed the telegraph in the American Civil War. Unlike the limited use of the telegraph in the Crimean War to connect only the higher echelon levels, McClellan initiated its usage down to the command levels of his tactical forces—a major advancement.

With the outbreak of the Civil War, the Federal Government quickly realized the importance of military telegraphic communications and established the United States Military Telegraph Corps (USMTC) in April of 1861. The USMTC was initially part of the U.S. Quartermaster Corps but later in January of 1862 was placed under the direct control of the Secretary of War as an independent corps. However it took time for the Corps to become fully operational, and initially the government placed civilian telegraph companies, such as the American Telegraph Company (ATC), under contract for the transmission of military communications.[4] ATC operated the majority of commercial lines running north and south in the eastern part of the United States while Western Union owned the lines running east and west. Early in the war on May 21, 1861, ATC severed all telegraph communications south of Washington, and its former network in the South became the Southern Telegraph Company. As the war progressed, ATC carried the majority of those Union military telegraphic communications which were transmitted on commercial lines. The usual procedure was to place military telegraph operators in commercial telegraph offices to ensure that military telegrams took priority over civilian messages and that the security of the military information transmitted was protected.

Relying on commercial companies proved to be very expensive. (The cost of a message was calculated by the formula: Total cost equals the number of words minus ten times .04 plus .50, or Total Cost = (Number of words - (10 x .04)) +.50. For example, the October 16, 1861, edition of the *New York Tribune* claimed that the Adjutant General had to pay about $1,400 per month for transmission while the Secretary of

War's monthly bill to commercial telegraph companies was over $5,000. Congress authorized the Federal Government to take control of the rail and telegraph lines in the Union for military purposes. While this move ensured priority handling of military telegrams, it did not solve the problem of large financial payments to the telegraph companies.

It became obvious that the government needed expert assistance in regulating and organizing both the railroad and the telegraph for efficient wartime operation. The two individuals initially called to Washington by Secretary of War Simon Cameron in the spring of 1861 were Thomas Scott, Vice-President of the Pennsylvania Railroad, and Andrew Carnegie, who had so successfully integrated the civilian use of the telegraph into the railroad business. It was Scott's task to set up a system giving the government priority use of the railroads. Carnegie, himself an ex-telegraph operator, was charged with the recruitment of operators and linemen for the newly established USMTC. Some of the recruited operators were women.

Thus from the very beginning, there was a governmental marriage forced between the railroad and the telegraph. The coordination of effort between the two proved throughout the war to be invaluable for military needs such as rapid troop movements. For example, in September of 1863, General William Rosecrans's army at Chattanooga was outnumbered and severely threatened by Confederate General Braxton Bragg. Initially the prevailing opinion in Lincoln's cabinet was that it would take 60 days to move reinforcements from the eastern theater to Chattanooga. But it was determined that with close coordination between the railroads and the telegraph, the troop movements could be accomplished in 15 days. In actuality the movements from Virginia to Tennessee, a distance by rail of 1,233 miles, were completed in 12 days.

Another assignment for Andrew Carnegie, in addition to overseeing the manpower needs of the USMTC, was funding for the new organization. Due to the budget cycle, there were no funds available initially. Carnegie went to the President of the ATC, Edward S. Sanford, and convinced him to fund the USMTC until Federal funds were forthcoming. When General Irwin McDowell and his troops advanced into Virginia in July of 1861 before the First Battle of Bull Run,[5] Carnegie was assigned to provide him with telegraphic communications; i.e., the stringing of wire and the placement of operators at critical junctures along the route. He accomplished his mission but suffered a heat stroke that severely impaired his health—ultimately forcing him to

Andrew Carnegie, 1861

*(Courtesy of the Library of Congress)*

leave the USMTC in the hands of John Strouse and return to private industry.

The importance with which the telegraph was viewed in this early engagement is evident in the account of telegraph operator, Charles W. Jaques, as follows:

"I was a boy of sixteen when the battle occurred and was stationed in Springfield, Virginia not far from the scene of action. I told the War Department office of the retreat of the Union Army, saying those who passed my office first were wounded soldiers, a few at a time, then squads of soldiers, followed later by companies and regiments. I added that I was going to close my office and go with the crowd. The following telegraph came back at once. 'War Department, Washington, to Jaques, operator, Springfield, If you keep your office open until you have permission to close it, you will be rewarded. If you close it without such permission, you will be shot. Thos. A. Scott [Asst. Secretary of War].' So I remained, giving the War Department all the information obtainable until the entire army, including wounded and stragglers had passed by. It was 8 a.m. Monday, July 22, when my office was closed and I left for Washington. My reward was a leave of absence for two weeks to visit my home in Ohio, with free transportation and three months' pay, all in twenty-dollar gold pieces."[6]

David Homer Bates's personal recollections of the First Battle of Bull Run, while not in the diary, have survived. They state:

Bull Run, July 1861

On Sunday, July 21, when the battle of Bull Run was fought, the military telegraph-line had reached Fairfax Court-House, and an improvised office had been opened at that point. Communication with General McDowell's headquarters at the front was maintained by means of a corps of mounted couriers, organized by Andrew Carnegie, under the immediate direction of William B. Wilson, who then served as manager. These couriers passed back and forth all day long between Fairfax and the front. Lincoln hardly left his seat in our office and waited with deep anxiety for each succeeding despatch. At times during the awful day, General Scott would confer with the President or Secretary Cameron for a short period, and then depart to put into effect some urgent measures for protecting the capital.

Bull Run, July 1861

All the morning and well along into the afternoon, McDowell's telegrams were more or less encouraging, and Lincoln and his advisers waited with eager hope, believing that Beauregard was being pushed back to Manassas Junction; but all at once the despatches ceased coming. At first this was taken to mean that McDowell was moving farther away from the telegraph, and then, as the silence became prolonged, a strange fear seized upon the assembled watchers that perhaps all was not well. Suddenly, the telegraph instrument became alive again, and the short sentence, 'Our army is retreating,' was spelled out in the Morse characters. This brief announcement was followed by meager details concerning the first great disaster that had befallen our troops and the panic that followed.[7]

The headquarters of the USMTC resided in the Telegraph Office which was situated in the War Department building, directly next to the White House. It provided the President with timely military reports and became the barometer for the status of ongoing military actions. If someone entered the room and found the operators idle, chances were that the activity level of the armies was low, but if the operators were heavily occupied, it indicated that news was coming in. The location of the office, adjacent to the office of the Secretary of War, allowed for virtually immediate access to both the Secretary and other senior government officials; e.g., General Henry Halleck. The location further provided a readily accessible transmitting facility between the authorities in Washington and the various generals in the field. During the early days of the war, the Telegraph Office staff consisted of four operators, but as the use of the telegraph increased, so did the staff which was composed mostly of young men under the age of 21. Eventually there were twelve day operators and two to three night operators—under the control of Major Thomas Eckert, who headed the office. The location and activities of the Telegraph Office were described by David Homer Bates:

"The office was first located in Chief Clerk Sanderson's room adjoining that of the Secretary of War, on the second floor of the building in the southwest corner; it was shifted to other locations in May and in October, and a final change was made soon after the *Monitor-Merrimac* fight in March of 1862 when Secretary of War Stanton directed the office be located in the old library room, on the second floor front, adjoining his own quarters. . . . Not long after the instruments had been moved to the library room, Secretary Stanton gave up the adjoining room for the use of the cipher operators. We remained in these quarters until after the close of the war.

"The War Department Telegraph [Office] was the scene of many vitally important conferences between Lincoln and members of his cabinet, leading generals, congressmen and others, who soon learned that when the President was not at the White House he could most likely be found in the Telegraph Office.

"During the entire war, the files of the War Department Telegraph Office were punctuated with short, pithy despatches from Lincoln, for instance on May 25, 1862, he sent ten or twelve to various generals, on May 23 as many more, and from one to a dozen on nearly every succeeding day for months. It is also worthy of remark that Lincoln's numerous telegrams were almost without exception, in his own handwriting, his copy being remarkably neat and legible, with seldom an erasure or correction."[8]

Telegraph operators were not in abundance in 1861. The 1860 census lists approximately 2,000 operators (of whom about 100 were women), but their importance had increased since the early days of the Morse system. When the USMTC began recruiting, close to half of the civilian operators joined the Corps, leaving a higher proportion of female operators on the civilian circuits. Almost without exception the operators and linemen who were recruited were very young men and women with limited education.

Once fully operational the Corps was in fact a complete telegraph company with linemen to construct new lines, repairmen to keep them operational, and operators knowledgeable in the employment of encryption techniques used to encipher and decipher communications. Operators were quickly assigned to field units with whom they traveled for the duration of the war. While female operators were recruited, they were normally not deployed to the forward tactical areas.

The members of the new USMTC were civilian throughout the war, and they were exempt from military service. However, their civilian status did not prevent them from being routinely placed with the military units on the battlefield as well as in strategic locations such as the Telegraph Office in Washington. When the war ended, the Corps was disbanded with operators denied government pensions for their war service. After the war Andrew Carnegie quietly supported the widows and families of USMTC personnel who had lost their lives or had been severely wounded in the war rendering them unable to work.

Unlike radio communications, a telegraph network cannot operate without physical lines for transmission. When initially formed, the USMTC did not have a dedicated network and the task of constructing a series of lines fell to the newly recruited linemen. They had the

From an ambrotype

Samuel M. Brown

David Strouse     Richard O'Brien

David Homer Bates

First four operators in the United States Military
Telegraph Corps, April, 1861

*(From Lincoln in the Telegraph Office, p. 17)*

daunting task of continually moving the telegraph lines as the armies moved. At the end of October of 1861, there were 50 telegraph stations and 280 miles of line in operation; by November 15, 1861, a few short weeks later there were 106 stations and 1,136 miles of telegraph line. The lines grew to 3,551 miles by the 1st of July of 1862 and to 5,326 miles by the 30th of June 1863. During the course of the war, the U.S. Military Telegraph Corps strung more than 15,000 miles of telegraph line at an average daily rate of 8 to 12 miles of new line per day (average cost equaled $75.00 per mile). In his 1865 Annual Report to the Quartermaster General, Anson Stager, Superintendent of the USMTC, stated that the total expenditures for the construction, maintenance, and operation of the United States Military Telegraph Corps during the period from May 1, 1861, to June 30, 1865, amounted to $2,655,000.[9]

The mileage of military telegraph line available in the various military departments during the war years gives an indication of the level of military activity in these departments. The total miles of lines available in 1865 are shown in the table below:

## Miles of Active Military Telegraph Lines in 1865[10]

| Department | Landline | Underwater Cable[11] |
|---|---|---|
| Department of the Gulf | 56.0 | 5.0 |
| Department of the South | 110.0 | 11.25 |
| Department of the Potomac | 1,824.5 | 53.5 |
| Department of WV | 303.0 | 0.5 |
| Department of KY, TN & MS | 2,127.0 | 1.5 |
| Department of MO, KS & AR | 1,702.0 | 1.5 |
| Total mileage active | 6,122.5 | 73.25[12] |

*Note: These figures are in addition to the commercial telegraph lines in each geographic area.*

Tactical Stringing of Wire

*(From Century Magazine, 38, 1889, p. 789)*

By the end of the war, the USMTC had active telegraphic communications to within 10 miles of the actual front, connecting for example General Grant at City Point, Virginia, with his field commanders as well as with President Lincoln in Washington. The Corps was able to set up its extensive lines of communication by using mules. As soon as the unit was settled down for the night or a stay, a spool of wire (weighing about 200 pounds) was placed on a mule's back. The mule then was led in the direction of another unit whose mule was making a similar trek from the opposite direction. When the mules met, the wires were connected providing communications between the tactical units as long as they remained in place. When the units moved, the wire was rewound and used again at a subsequent location.

The value of the telegraph in keeping army commanders in contact with headquarters even while operating at great distances was illustrated by Grant's usage of this technology when he launched his three-pronged attack on the Confederacy in 1864. Via telegraph he maintained communications with General George G. Meade in Virginia, General William T. Sherman in the Atlanta Theater, General George Crook in the Shenandoah Valley, and General Benjamin F. Butler in Virginia and the outer banks of North Carolina. Meade's military secretary, General Adam Badeau, wrote:

"Meade's Headquarters were near those of the General-in-Chief, and at night the two commanders discussed the plans of the morrow. While they were thus engaged, telegrams arrived, announcing that Sherman and Butler and Crook had all advanced. It had never happened in the history of war, that one man directed so completely four distinct armies, separated by thousands of miles and numbering more than a quarter of a million soldiers, ordering the operation of each for the same day, and receiving at night reports from each that his orders had been obeyed."[13]

Of equal importance was the use of the telegraph to keep the Union populace informed on the status of the war effort. With telegraphic communications newspaper reporting became more timely. Readers on the home front learned of the victories as well as the defeats of their armies almost as rapidly as their government leaders did. Local telegraph offices became the scenes of both joy and sorrow as the reports of the dead and wounded from a battle were received. For the first time the general population was caught up in the almost daily activity reports of the various armies.

General Nathaniel Banks later stressed the importance of the telegraph for sustaining wartime morale: "In our recent memorable struggle for the preservation of the Government, the Telegraph performed [an] important and patriotic part. It was the constant telegraph communications from the Government, and army, that re-assured the people, bound the loyal States together and stimulated civil and military authorities to greater exertion, by the almost limitless contributions of men and money to the cause of the Union. It was in truth, an electric nerve that united them, consolidated their power, inspired them with courage and hope and finally led them to victory. It was the chord of the national heart."[14]

The Union with its manufacturing capacity and access to raw materials had a far more extensive telegraph system than the Confederacy and utilized it to a higher degree. For example during the year of 1864, thousands of telegraphic messages were sent between Grant's Headquarters at City Point and the authorities in Washington. The Confederacy, in contrast, relied on commercial telegraph companies throughout the war and had only a very inadequate military telegraph network. The Southern Telegraph Company, which had broken off from ATC when the war started, had a very limited capability. The South had neither the manufacturing facilities nor the raw materials to create the necessary wire. In addition almost all of its commercial circuitry ran east and west along the railroad lines connecting the major ports to the cotton producing areas of the interior. In addition the major war zones were in Confederate territory where communications were subject to constant disruption by enemy actions. On the other hand, the USMTC constructed approximately 15,000 miles of telegraph lines, employed over 1,500 operators at an average monthly cost of $22,000 in 1862, which grew to $93,000 in 1864. The Confederacy, relying on commercial companies, had 211 miles of military telegraph lines in 1862, which grew to only 422 miles in 1864. The Southern military operator staff grew from 17 in 1861 to just 51 in 1864, at a monthly cost in the latter year of only $7,595 per month.[15]

Telegraphic communications during the war were not rapid by today's standards. The Bates diary mentions messages arriving in Washington three to four days—and in some cases up to nine days—after the date of transmission. Often this was due to the circuitous route that the message was forced to follow to avoid Confederate territory. For example the line between Washington and Fort Monroe, Virginia, was not direct. It followed a route from Washington to Baltimore to Wilmington (via commercial circuitry), then on by military circuits to Lewes, Delaware, Salisbury, Maryland, and Cape Charles, Virginia, then by 20 miles of underwater cable across the

Chesapeake Bay to Fort Monroe in Virginia—a total wire distance of 300 miles with transmission times varying from two to nine hours. Once Grant was operating in the area, the line was extended an additional 97 miles to his headquarters, for a total length of 397 miles. (See map and table showing geographic distances.)

## Washington to City Point Telegraphic Distance (Direct Routing Distance, 135 miles)

| Routing Employed | Miles |
|---|---|
| Washington to Baltimore | 30 |
| Baltimore to Wilmington (DE) | 60 |
| Wilmington to Dover (DE) | 40 |
| Dover to Lewes (DE) | 35 |
| Lewes to Salisbury (MD) | 35 |
| Salisbury to Cape Charles (VA) | 80 |
| Cape Charles to Fort Monroe (VA) | 20 (underwater cable) |
| Fort Monroe to Williamsburg (VA) | 25 |
| Williamsburg to Jamestown Island (VA) | 5 (underwater cable) |
| Jamestown Island to West Point (VA) | 25 |
| West Point to White House (VA) | 18 |
| White House to City Point (VA) | 24 |
| Total actual miles | 397 |

*Note: Of the total of 397 miles, only 90 miles (from Washington to Wilmington) was available on commercial circuits; the remainder was constructed by the USMTC.*

For Sherman in Atlanta to communicate with Washington or with Grant in Virginia, the communication had to go along the railroad lines controlled by the Union to Cairo, Illinois, and then east to

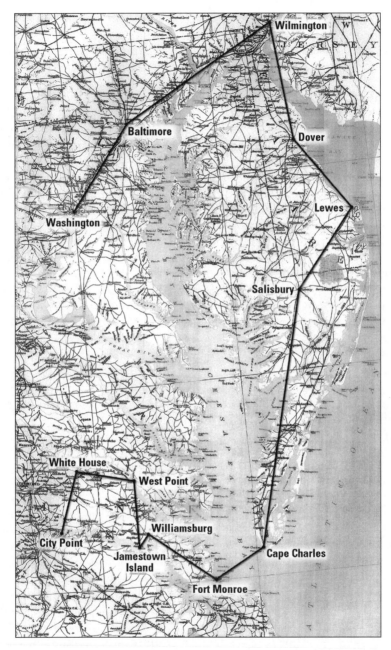

Map of Telegraph Line from City Point, Virginia, to Washington, DC

*(Based on details in the Diary of David Homer Bates and
The Military Telegraph During the Civil War in the United States)*

Washington, normally via Pittsburgh. Washington then relayed the message for Grant by way of the commercial and military lines through Fort Monroe. The Shenandoah Campaign communications for Grant were also relayed through Washington; the Telegraph Office had in fact become a command center.

Lines of these lengths and complexity were not always operational. The wire was not well-insulated and was therefore affected by adverse weather and unless guarded was often cut by the enemy or even by a Union soldier who wanted to send a piece home as a souvenir. For Civil War messages the date of origin was not necessarily the date of receipt, which may help to explain some of the field decisions made. Bates mentions in his diary a message from New Orleans that arrived in Washington nine days after the date of origin. But even with the built-in delays, the telegraph still represented a major advance in the sending and receiving of critical military information.

The use of non-military telegraph lines posed a problem as messages might be read by civilian operators not necessarily loyal to the Union. This security concern along with potential wiretaps on the military lines led to attempts to encipher the more important messages prior to transmission.

An early effort to secure military telegraphic communications was the use by General John C. Frémont's staff of the Hungarian language in transmission. Fortuitously General Alexander S. Asboth, Frémont's Chief of Staff, was a native Hungarian speaker as was Colonel Gustav Waagner, Chief of Artillery for General Grant, thereby providing a Hungarian language capability on both terminals of the circuit. Since very few Hungarian immigrants were in the country in the 1860's, the system provided a reasonable degree of security.[16]

When Anson Stager, the General Superintendent of Western Union, became Superintendent of the USMTC in 1862, he was responsible for the creation of enciphering systems to be used by the Union. Prior to the war he had developed a cipher system for Governor William Dennison of Ohio and decided to use a variant of that system, called the Route System, for high-level communications. To use this system, the operator copied the original message into a matrix, putting the first word in column 1, line 1, the second into column 2, line 1, and so forth until the matrix was filled. To encipher the message, words were extracted from the matrix up and down the columns; e.g., up column 1, down column 3, up column 5, down column 2, etc., and written out in the jumbled sequence obtained. Different routes up and down the columns were used at different times, hence the name, Route System.

Instructions for different sequences of enciphering and deciphering were the content of cipher (code) books. (See Appendix A.)

The code books were all created by hand by the operators in the Telegraph Office. (See illustration.) The Route System cipher was never broken by the enemy although many Union messages were intercepted in various wiretap operations; this failure deprived the Confederacy of important intelligence.

In addition to the Route System, other systems were employed by the telegraph operators for the passing of less sensitive material. Bates described a system created by the operators that President Lincoln is reputed to have enjoyed using. He cited as an example a message sent between two operators on April 3, 1865:

Headquarters, Armies of the U.S., City Point, (VA)
8:30, April 3, 1865

To: Charles Tinker, War Dept., Washington, D.C.

A. Lincoln its in fume a in hymn to start I army treating there possible if of cut too forward pushing is He is so all Richmond aunt confide is Andy evacuated Petersburg reports Grant morning this Washington Secretary War.

(Signed) S. H. Beckwith[17]

The message appears to make no sense at first reading. But if it is read backwards, stressing the phonetics and not worrying about the spelling, the message becomes very clear:

To: Charles Tinker, War Dept., Washington, D.C.

Washington Sec'y War

This morning Grant reports Petersburg evacuated and is confident Richmond also. He is pushing forward to cut off if possible their retreating army. I start to him in a few minutes.

A. Lincoln[18]

Stager also realized the importance of the cipher clerks and the necessity to maintain tight control over their actions. He directed that all cipher officers and clerks be assigned to him, not to the units served. He required daily reporting of message totals (both sent and received) as well as ciphers used and thereby was able to maintain a central control over all cipher operations. This is one of the reasons that the USMTC was never integrated into the regular Union Army.

The Confederacy predated the Union in the establishment of a Signals Corps to handle all types of communications, but had no equivalent central control system for its cipher systems. In addition its high level cipher systems, the Vicksburg Square for telegraphic communications and the Pigpen System for written correspondence, were both broken during the course of the war, providing the Union with specific strategic intelligence. Unlike the Route System, which reorganized the sequence of words, the Vicksburg Square substituted one letter for another creating a ciphered alphabet which was used to spell out the words of the message. The Pigpen System substituted symbols for letters and spelled out the words of the message in these symbols. Many other systems were employed in the Confederacy, often on the basis of personal preference. For example, Jefferson Davis employed a dictionary code; it was also broken by the Union. To use a dictionary code, both the sender and the receiver had the same dictionary. To transmit a word, the sender merely found the word in his dictionary and then transmitted the page, column, and numerical placement of the word in the column. For example, the word *enemy* would be sent as 24-1-14, meaning: go to page 24, first column, 14th word. (See Appendix A.)

The use of ciphers by both the Union and the Confederacy led to efforts on both sides to break or read the text of intercepted enemy enciphered messages. An illustration of Union success in obtaining and decoding enemy messages was the interception of cipher letters between Confederate operatives in Canada and the government in Richmond. By October of 1864, these letters were being delivered regularly to the Telegraph Office in Washington by the Confederate courier, Richard Montgomery, on his way to and from Richmond. In the Telegraph Office, operators deciphered and copied the letters before carefully resealing them in envelopes purchased from England to match the originals. The courier, Lt. Montgomery, was in fact a Union Army officer who had served on garrison duty in Washington, became bored, and decided to become a spy. By some means to this day unknown, he traveled to Richmond and managed to become a Confederate courier between Richmond and the Confederates operating in Canada—regularly making an intermediate stop at the Telegraph Office in Washington, D.C.

The value of the intelligence derived from messages from Canada can be illustrated by Bates's remarks in his book. One particular intercepted message from the Confederates in Canada in late 1864 clearly showed that the Confederates were using Canada as a staging area for raids into U.S. border towns and that the Canadian govern-

Lt. Richard Montgomery, Union Agent who Couriered Letters
between Richmond, Virginia, and Toronto, Canada

*(Courtesy of the Library of Congress)*

ment knew of these raids. Secretary of War Stanton wanted to keep the original message, signed by Clement C. Clay (prominent former Confederate Senator from Alabama), as evidence to support Union demands for damages from Great Britain for providing asylum to Union enemies. Lincoln, while aware of the importance of the message, did not want to expose the courier. A plan to deceive the Confederates was developed whereby the courier was arrested and taken to Old Capital Prison, where the message was discovered in a search. The courier was allowed to escape and continue his journey to Richmond, unsuspected by the Confederate government of duplicity. In the escape the courier was shot in the arm, further allaying any Confederate suspicions.[19]

The Union was fortunate to have three young USMTC operators in Washington, David Homer Bates, Albert Chandler, and Charles Tinker, known as the Sacred Three, who were experts in deciphering Confederate messages, both written and telegraphic. President Lincoln, aware of their cryptanalytic skills, gave orders that they were never to be disturbed while working on a Confederate message. A cipher message had to be sent to Washington for decryption and then back to the Command, a time-consuming process which rendered deciphered messages of little use for tactical support. The efforts of the Sacred Three, however, did provide valuable strategic information.

Late in the war these three operators took turns being assigned to Grant's command for extended periods, and all three stated that they did not engage in telegraphic duties while there. Perhaps Grant used them to provide on-the-spot cryptanalysis much as had been employed by George Washington in the Revolutionary War.[20]

Throughout the war Western Union continued to grow to the west free of disrupting military operations. By 1864 it had a coast-to-coast telegraphic capacity and surpassed in size its chief competitor, ATC. By 1865 three major commercial telegraph companies remained; in order of magnitude, they were: Western Union, American Telegraph Company, and U.S. Telegraph Company.[21]

The United States Military Telegraph Corps remained in existence until 1866 when it was incorporated into the United States Signal Corps, which had been responsible for non-telegraphic communications throughout the war. With the incorporation of the USMTC into the United States Signal Corps, the latter became the sole communications authority for the U.S. Army. At this time the remaining

USMTC operators were fully integrated into the ranks of the military and no longer retained civilian status.

The American Civil War firmly established the value of the telegraph as a means of rapid communication for military purposes. General Sherman stated in his memoirs:

". . .the value of the magnetic telegraph in war cannot be exaggerated, as was illustrated by the perfect concert of action between the armies in Virginia, and Georgia during 1864. Hardly a day intervened when General Grant did not know the exact state of facts with me, more than fifteen hundred miles away as the wires ran."[22]

## Notes

[1]Standage, Tom, *Victorian Internet*, p. 3.

[2]Thompson, Robert L., *Wiring a Continent*, p. 217.

[3]Bristwhistle, A. C., *75 Years of Service: Royal Engineers*, p. 3.

[4]Thompson, *Wiring a Continent*, p. 385.

[5]On the 16th of July, 1861, Union General Irvin McDowell, a West Point graduate, left Washington, DC with 35,000 men and began his march in the general direction of Centreville and Manassas, Virginia. On the 21st of July the Union forces engaged the Confederates near Bull Run, VA, and suffered a major defeat. Later, on the 29th and 30th of August of 1862, the Union Army under General John Pope again suffered a major defeat at Bull Run, VA. General McDowell was a Corps Commander at the Second Battle of Bull Run.

[6]Bates, David Homer, *Lincoln in the Telegraph Office*, p. 93.

[7]Bates, David Homer, Personal papers, Stern Collection, Rare Book Room, Library of Congress, Washington, DC.

[8]Bates, *Lincoln in the Telegraph Office*, Pp. 38, 42, 123.

[9]Plum, William, *The Military Telegraph during the Civil War in the United States*, Volume II, Appendix, p. 375.

[10]*Ibid.*, p. 371.

[11]The majority of the underwater cable laid during the Civil War was salvaged cable from the 1858 attempt to connect the U.S. to Europe telegraphically. That cable failed shortly after connection. The cable used was #22 copper wire with three layers of gutta-percha wound in hemp yarn. The cable was 5/8" thick and weighted one ton per mile. (Thompson, *Wiring a Continent*, p. 221.)

[12]Plum, *The Military Telegraph during the Civil War in the United States*, Volume II, p. 93.

[13]*Ibid.*, p 255.

[14]Speech given at the Morse Memorial reception in New York on June 10, 1871.

[15]Thompson, *Wiring a Continent*, p. 405.

[16]Perret, Geoffrey, *Ulysses S. Grant*, p. 139.

[17]Samuel H. Beckwith of Hamilton, NY, was General Grant's operator. He is reputed to have initiated the code word procedure utilized by the Union Army. For example, Lincoln's code word was Adam.

[18]Bates, *Lincoln in the Telegraph Office,* p. 63.

[19]*Ibid.,* p. 81-83.

[20]During the Revolutionary War, James Lovell, a member of the Continental Congress and Professor of Mathematics at Yale, was able to break the British cipher system. He subsequently trained a cadre of codebreakers who traveled with Washington's army. When a British message was acquired, it could be read on the spot. The system was instrumental in the defeat of Cornwallis at the Battle of Yorktown. (Kahn, David, *The Codebreakers,* p. 182.)

[21]The U.S. Telegraph Company had been formed in 1864 by a merger of smaller companies. (Thompson, *Wiring a Continent,* p. 405.)

[22]Sherman, William T., *Memoirs of General Sherman,* p. 889.

# David Homer Bates

When the Civil War broke out, David Homer Bates was a 17 year-old lad from Steubenville, Ohio, working as a telegraph operator. He was assigned to Altoona, Pennsylvania, as part of the Pittsburgh division of the Pennsylvania Railroad. His career took a major turn in the latter part of April 1861 as the result of the following telegraphic exchange between Andrew Carnegie in Washington and David McCargo, Superintendent of the Pittsburgh Telegraph Office:

Washington, D.C., April 22, 1861

David McCargo,

Send four of your best operators to Washington, D.C. at once. Prepared to enter Government service for the War.
(Signed) Andrew Carnegie

And in return:

Altoona, Pa., April 23, 1861

Andrew Carnegie, War Department, Washington, D.C.

Message received. Strouse from Mifflin, Brown from Pittsburgh, O'Brien from Greensburg, and Bates from Altoona will start for Washington immediately.
(Signed) David McCargo
Supt. Telegraph[1]

Thus began the career of David Homer Bates in the United States Military Telegraph Corps. Bates's initial assignment was to the telegraph office at the U.S. Navy Yard in Washington, D.C., followed by a short tour in Annapolis, Maryland. Soon thereafter he was assigned to the Telegraph Office in the War Department in Washington, where he remained until he left the USMTC as the Head Operator of the Telegraph Office on August 31, 1866.

Bates was not only an excellent telegraph operator, he also expanded his skills to include codes and ciphers—producing the cipher books for Union use as well as breaking the ciphers used by the Confederates. He worked with Colonel Anson Stager in the further development of the Route Cipher System. (See Appendix A.) More importantly he became very proficient at deciphering the most complicated of the Confederate enciphered traffic—both telegraphic and written.

After the war one of Bates's duties was to assist in reconnecting the Southern and Northern states telegraphically. On July 31, 1866, the Office of the USMTC awarded David Homer Bates, Charles A. Tinker, and Albert B. Chandler, and others silver watches for their "meritorious and valuable services."

David Homer Bates left the USMTC on August of 1866. He became a major spokesperson for the USMTC and the contributions of its members to the war effort. Well into the 20th Century he served as Secretary and Treasurer of the Society of the USMTC, actively maintaining contact with his fellow USMTC members and working unsuccessfully to convince the government to provide them with pensions.

After he moved to life in the private sector, Bates married Sallie J. Raphael Kenny on May 15, 1867. Only one of their three children David Homer, born in 1879, survived to adulthood, but he died in early manhood. Bates's civilian career in telegraphy flourished first with Western Union and later as President of the Baltimore and Ohio Telegraph Company. He was also an executive with the Willcox and Gibbs Sewing Machine Co.

After the war ended, David Homer Bates was frequently asked to speak on the subject of President Lincoln's association with the Telegraph Office. He also wrote a series of articles for *Century Magazine,* recounting his wartime experiences. The popularity of these articles plus his frequent lectures led to the writing of his book, *Lincoln in the Telegraph Office,* which was published in 1907 by the Century Company in New York. Unlike his diary the book does not contain extensive day-by-day accounts of the activities of the Telegraph Office but does provide a great deal of information regarding the activities of senior officials in Washington as they affected or were affected by the Telegraph Office. It clearly describes their use of the information received from the field via the telegraph.

Having outlived all of his contemporaries in the Telegraph Office, David Homer Bates died June 15, 1926, in New York City. While he was justly proud of his business accomplishments, it was his service in the wartime Telegraph Office as a member of the United States Military Telegraph Corps, including his association with President Lincoln, that represented the pinnacle experience of his life.

Note

[1]Bates, David Homer, *Lincoln in the Telegraph Office,* Pp. 14-15.

# Introduction to the Diary

The Bates diary, starting on November 13, 1863, and ending on June 4, 1865, is presented here with the entries divided into sections, each covering a three-month period—with the exception of the first and last sections, which cover a time period closer to two months in length. Each section of diary entries is preceded by a summary of events to provide historical context and perspective. The initial part of each summary highlights the telegraphic activity of the time period to be covered while the second part focuses on the political and military events of the period.

The frequent diary entries reflecting on Bates's personal life rather than his professional duties are only rarely included in the following transcription. An exception was the decision to leave in his comments and descriptions of the weather, as weather conditions were very relevant to the functioning of the telegraph.

Only minor punctuation and spelling changes have been made to aid in consistency and understandability. Abbreviations used by Bates are explained at the time of first mention, where necessary for clarity. The diary is annotated to provide factual and contextual information, with notes placed at the end of each diary section as endnotes.

The full names of individuals, both Union and Confederate, are identified in endnotes at the time of first appearance. For civilian entries, identification consists of the individual's full name and position, if known. For military personnel, identification includes full name, rank, and position. Once identified, subsequent re-identification appears for an individual when there is a change in status; *e.g.*, command, promotion, wounding, or death. Where names were misspelled in the diary, the correct spelling appears in brackets at first mention.

Geographic place names are also shown as they were originally written in the diary with the correct spelling of a specific location appearing in brackets. In cases where place names are mentioned without giving the state in which they were located, the state names are added in brackets unless the information is obvious from the text. Wherever possible, specific battles with dates are given in the endnotes.

In a few instances where David Homer Bates had pasted newspaper clippings into his diary, the clippings are reproduced and inserted into the transcription in the appropriate places. The photographs included in this work were not in the original diary. They are provided because of their relation to specific diary entries and to add to the reader's understanding of the telegraph and its use in the Civil War.

Memo. by D H Bates.

On the night of June 30. 1863 two operators — Ten Eyck H. Fonda and Luther A. Rose — started by different routes from Frederick Md to deliver to Genl Meade at Gettysburg Secy Stanton's dispatch telling of Longstreets whereabouts enroute to join Lee's army. They both arrived about dawn July 1. and the news enabled Meade to attack Lee at once and to win the battle which otherwise he might have lost.

The news of Meade's great victory was sent by Sam Edwards and Ed Hall over the single wire via Hanover Junction and reached us in the War Dept about the same time that Grant's message came announcing his capture of Pemberton's army at Vicksburg.

David Homer Bates's Handwritten Comments
on the Battle of Gettysburg

*(Courtesy of the Stern Collection, Library of Congress)*

# November, December 1863

While we do not have Bates's diary for the earlier period of the war, it is apparent from the following entries that the use of the telegraph by the Union Army had made some major improvements. When the war began, the military was totally dependent upon commercial circuits for transmitting its communications. These circuits were by their nature stationary and therefore of limited value to troops that were constantly on the move. The November/December 1863 entries by Bates clearly show that by that time the U.S. military was no longer dependent on stationary civilian telegraph facilities. It now had its own capabilities thanks to the efforts of the United States Military Telegraph Corps' linemen and construction crews that moved with the troops.

Bates reports on December 21, 1863, that he and his close associates, Charles Tinker and Albert Chandler, were developing a new skill, that of cryptanalysis. They had succeeded in deciphering several enciphered letters posted in New York and intended for delivery to Confederate authorities in Richmond, messages that proved to be strategically significant to the Union cause.

The military communications referred to in the Bates diary for November and December 1863 center on two areas, Virginia and Tennessee. In both cases the telegraph lines apparently functioned well, and messages flowed unimpeded in both directions. In the case of the Tennessee theater, there appears to have been about a 24 hour delay in receipt of messages in Washington, while from the Virginia theater receipt of news was more timely. In both cases Washington authorities were kept reasonably current on the status of the fighting. It is apparent from the diary entries that by this time the Telegraph Office was functioning well, and the telegraph operators gave much of the credit to Thomas Eckert, the head of the Office.

October 1863 saw the Confederate forces tightening their hold on the Union supply lines in and out of Chattanooga and placing the town under siege conditions. In early October General Joseph Hooker's force began to arrive in Bridgeport, Alabama, in an effort to reinforce the Union forces in Chattanooga. The 20,000 troops and 3,000 horses had traveled by rail over 1,100 miles in just over a week.

In mid-October General Grant was named to head the new Military Division of the Mississippi which included the Departments of the Cumberland, Ohio, and Tennessee, and General George H. Thomas succeeded General William S. Rosecrans as the Commander in Chattanooga. By the end of October the Union had succeeded in re-supplying its troops inside Chattanooga.

In November of 1863 the Confederate military transferred General James Longstreet and his Corps to Tennessee to reinforce the Confederate forces in the Knoxville area. He arrived in the Knoxville region on the 16th of November. At the same time the Union reinforced its forces in Chattanooga with General William T. Sherman's arrival with 27,000 troops on the 15th of November. In the ensuing battle of Chattanooga for the first time in the history of the war, one Union general (Grant) commanded elements of each of the three major Union Armies simultaneously. On the western military front Grant launched his counterattack at Chattanooga by attacking Lookout Mountain and Missionary Ridge on November 24 and 25. The Battle of Chattanooga raged on until the evening of the 25th of November when the Confederate forces retreated toward Ringgold, Georgia.

On the 29th of November, Longstreet launched an attack on Fort Loudon (Sanders) near Knoxville to dislodge General Ambrose Burnside, but due to a mishandled operation he was forced to retreat late in the day. This ended the Confederate efforts to dislodge the Union forces from Chattanooga and Knoxville. On the last day of November 1863, Confederate President Jefferson Davis accepted the resignation of General Braxton Bragg, Commander of the Army of Tennessee, defeated at Chattanooga. Confederate hopes of victory in the west had faded.

In December both the Union and Confederate Armies in the field settled down into winter quarters. The Union Army of the Potomac had failed at Mine Run in Virginia while the Confederate forces were defeated at Knoxville.

In the Confederacy on the 16th of December, President Davis appointed Joseph E. Johnston as the new commander of the Department of Tennessee. The end of year mood in the Confederacy was reflected in an article published in the *Richmond Examiner* on the 31st of December: "Today closes the gloomiest year of our struggle."

The troop movements and maneuverings of the military in Tennessee figured prominently in Bates's comments in the diary. General Grant's tactics as well as his emphasis on having adequate supplies before embarking on a military movement also received attention. Bates also described the mood of Washington officials regarding the lack of activity on the part of General Meade and the Army of the Potomac in December.                                    *Donald E. Markle*

*Friday, November 13, 1863*

General Meade[1] visits Washington today for consultation with the Prest [President] and Gen-in-Chief.[2] His Head Qrs. are now at Rappahannock Station. The Railroad is finished only to Bealeton[3] from which place supplies are wagoned. The rails are down beyond that point but the road is not ballasted & not capable of supporting heavy trains.

The *Massachusetts*[4] has just arrived at Ft. Monroe 48 hours from Charleston. She reports Ft. Sumter is a pile of sand. All the Monitors[5] will be ready for Naval operations in a few days. The people of Florida are driving their cattle East of St. John's river to prevent Bragg's[6] army from getting them.

*Saturday, November 14, 1863*

Information recd today from the west indicates that Burnside[7] will soon be attacked at Knoxville.[8] It is said that Longstreet[9] is advancing towards Loudon [TN] from the direction of Bragg's Army with from twenty to forty thousand men. Gen. Grant[10] has been advised to have Gen. Thomas[11] attack the communications of Longstreet northwest of Chattanooga & compel him to fall back.

*Sunday, November 15, 1863*

It has rained since 6 o'clock this morning very heavily.[12] At this time (10 a.m.) the sky has cleared & the sun is almost vainly trying to show his face. Genl. Meade telegraphs that from deserters & scouts he is induced to believe that Lee's entire army is falling back & he has ordered strong reconnaissance to be made in the morning.

*Monday, November 16, 1863*

Burnside has ordered his forces of the 9th Corps to make an attack on the advance of Longstreet's troops near Loudon. He will if not successful retreat by way of Cumberland Gap [TN], destroying all property which cannot be carried off. In the meantime Gen. Grant is to advance on Missionary Ridge from the North with a portion of Gen. Sherman's[13] troops which have arrived at Bridgeport [AL] & some of Thomas's. The balance of Sherman's troops will go by Whiteside Stn. [TN] & occupy Trenton [GA]. Bragg will thus be compelled to fall back from his position and Longstreet will be cut off from his base.

The Railroad is now running to Culpepper & W.Va.[14] & Gen. Meade will evidently make some demonstration against Lee.[15]

*Tuesday, November 17, 1863*

Weather clear and pretty cold. Gen. Grant telegraphs that he is pushing everything to give Gen. Burnside early aid & that he has impressed upon him in the strongest terms the necessity of holding on to his position. Genl. Sherman's troops marched today from Bridgeport [AL] & a strong column will be thrown between Bragg & Longstreet as soon as possible.

Gen. Burnside telegraphs that Longstreet crossed the Tenn [River] on Saturday at Huff's Ferry [TN] six miles below Loudon with about 15,000 men. His advance was resisted until our position was turned by superior cover & Burnside then retired in good order. His force is all within the lines of Knoxville.

Longstreet attacked our forces yesterday at Campbell's Station [TN] & fighting was kept up all day in which serious loss was inflicted on the enemy. Gen. Burnside thinks he will be able to hold his position. God grant that he may.

*Wednesday, November 18, 1863*

Today has been very pleasant indeed. Tomorrow occurs the dedication of the Gettysburg Cemetery. A grand time is expected.[16]

*Thursday, November 19, 1863*

Weather cold & pleasant day. Nothing heard from dedication of the National Cemetery. Prest. & suite will undoubtedly return tomorrow. Smithers is certainly cheated Representation in Delaware.[17] All plans are made for Sherman with 27,000 men to advance on Missionary Ridge while Hooker[18] attacks Lookout Mountain. Ewing[19] of Sherman's Corps will occupy Trenton Stn [GA] & a heavy force will be thrown on the front of the enemy's lines opposite Chattanooga. The whole movement will be culminated by Saturday. Great good is being done.

*Friday, November 20, 1863*

News from Burnside rec'd today is that he is surrounded by an overwhelming force. Fighting was going all day yesterday but no result known. Genl. Willcox[20] is on his way from Bull's Gap [TN] to Tazewell [TN] or Cumberland Gap [TN] with all of Burnside's army now concentrated at Knoxville. He will make good his position at Cumberland Gap.

*Saturday, November 21, 1863*

We have news from Gen. Willcox up to 4 p.m. [November] 20th. He was then at Tazewell, Tenn. His Cavalry had broken through the enemy's line of pickets on the Knoxville road & from prisoners learned that the enemy had assaulted Burnside on the 19th carrying two entrenchments but lost very heavily. Our men reserving their fire till the rebels were close upon them. Some firing was heard yesterday but not as heavily as the 19th. Gen. Grant's flank movement on Bragg has been delayed on account of Sherman's troops not being able to come up but it will be made soon.

Gold is at [$]154 today.[21] It rains here quite steadily.

Genl. Meade's preparations for an advance will all have been made today or tomorrow.

*Sunday, November 22, 1863*

My cold is a great deal better today. The air is clear this morning & the weather perfectly delightful.

Gen. Willcox has reached Cumberland Gap. His latest news from direction of Knoxville was up to 10 a.m. [November] 21st when firing was still going on. Gen. Grant telegraphs that on account of bad roads & for want of horses, 4 miles, the proposed movement, cannot possibly be made before Monday (tomorrow) morning. God bless it.

*Monday, November 23, 1863*

Nothing later from Burnside. At last accounts he was still fighting the Enemy.

Gen. Grant telegraphs that Genl. Thomas's troops attacked the rebel's left at two p.m. today & carried the first line of rifle pits. They captured 200 prisoners besides killed & wounded, & they will entrench themselves & hold their position until daylight by which time Sherman's troops will be up & a general battle will be begun. Bragg is, from all information gained, falling back to protect his line of communications with Longstreet.[22]

Genl. Meade advances tomorrow morning, but do not know how far.

*Tuesday & Wednesday, [November 24 & 25, 1863]*

Kept very busy.

*Friday, November 27, 1863*

We are having beautiful weather now. I arrived in Washington from Balt[imore], where I had gone to spend my Thanksgiving with Mr. & Mrs. Brown. I worked hard all day on Wednesday to get cipher books for Ma[jor] Dana[23] ready & left the Office at 4:15 p.m. I left the city at 5 o'clock reaching Mrs. Brown's about 7. I found her & family all well & glad to see me. I rested well during the night arose in the morning about 7 o'clock. After partaking of a good breakfast, I sauntered down Baltimore St. & visited the American Tel. ofs [offices]. Saw Mr. Mattingly & Mr. Wilson the manager & asst manager & Gentry (W.D.) the Chief Op[erator]. The office was in good order & looked neat. Guthridge (Jules F.) & Stumm (F.A.) were still there. Stumm goes December 1 to take charge of the Independent Ofs [offices] at Cleveland.[24] Next went to Gen. Schenck's Hd Qrs.[25] Saw Sampson but not Baldwin.[26] Returned to Mrs. Brown's & ate a hearty Thanksgiving dinner. Mr. McKnight[27] was there.

Gen. Grant's operations have been perfectly successful. The Enemy evacuated Lookout Mountain & Missionary Ridge & were pressed by Hooker & Sherman. We have taken some 7,000 prisoners & 60 pieces of cannon besides vast quantities of meat & stores. The rout of the Rebels is complete. They burned bridges & stores & devastated everything they could. Their stragglers are left all along the different roads.

Gen. Sherman occupies today Red Clay Station [GA] on the Cleveland & Dalton RR[28] & this cuts communications between Bragg and Longstreet & the latter will be compelled to retreat from Knoxville to Western Virginia or be captured or annihilated. Gen. Grant will very likely press on to Atlanta, where the rebels have a large amount of stores collected together with about 2,000,000 bales of cotton, which they have not the time to remove. Grant's forces are in pursuit of Bragg's retreating column.

*Saturday, November 28, 1863*

A cloudy, rainy day, very unpleasant. Went to choir meeting this evening. Staid [stayed] half an hour & then came to the office.

Genl. Meade has in all probability fought a battle today near Orange C[ourt]H[ouse].[29] We have not heard the result.

*Sunday, November 29, 1863*

Today is clear & windy, not very cold. Lines all working except to Hd Qrs which is okay only to the Rappahannock [River]. Hd Qrs is beyond the Rapidan [River]. We can hear nothing of their movements.

Col. Crawford[30] arrived from Cumberland Gap from Knoxville at 4 p.m. yesterday. He left Gen. Burnside on Wednesday night. Burnside is almost entirely surrounded by the rebels who are in heavy force & are busy entrenching themselves. He can defend himself against any assault but for want of provisions may have to surrender.[31] Gen. Burnside says he can hold out six or eight days from that time. Gen. Granger[32] is two days on his way from Chattanooga to relieve him & Sherman will go to the Hiawassie [Hiwassee River] in his support. These forces cannot fail to relieve Genl. Burnside very soon. From prisoners taken at Knoxville it is thought that some of Ewell's[33] Corps would reinforce Longstreet. The systematic & deliberate manner in which the siege is conducted also leads to the same conclusion.

*Monday, November 30, 1863*

This morning is very cold indeed. We have had nothing from the Army of the Potomac since 7 a.m. on Saturday. Hd Qrs are near Robertson's Tavern [VA].[34] Nothing yet from Burnside. Everybody is anxious. Gen. Grant says that a forward advance from Chattanooga cannot be made until six months supplies are collected & that it will not take all his force to hold Chattanooga. He proposes to embark 35,000 men at Chattanooga ostensibly to return them to West Tenn. & Vicksburg. He thinks he can land them at New Orleans, or possibly at Pascagoula Bay [MS] & invest Mobile [AL] before the enemy gets wind of it. He will invest Mobile with a small force keeping the garrison imprisoned without any unnecessary fight whilst with the bulk of his force he marches towards Montgomery, Selma or whatsoever point invites attack. He thinks a vigorous winter campaign can be conducted there. He desires the sanction of the Government.

*Tuesday, December 1, 1863*

Another clear day. Winter has fairly set in. Heretofore he [winter] has been trifling in his weak attacks, now he boldly comes forth as if to assert his rightful supremacy after the milder season. The leaves are all gone and the air is dry and chilled and it taxes a person pretty severely whilst outdoors to keep comfortably warm.

We rec'd a cipher telegram today dated Knoxville, Nov. 28th from Genl. Burnside. He had not been assaulted vigorously yet. He had repulsed the enemy in all his attacks, inflicting upon him severe loss. He felt himself fully able to hold out against any form that had yet made its appearance. He had ample supplies and his troops were in excellent spirits.

The siege of Charleston [Ft. Sumter, SC] still progresses. Occasionally a shell is thrown into the city, but little damage appears to be done.[35] Nothing yet from Genl. Meade's Army. The rebel Genl. Morgan who escaped last week from Columbus is rumored to be at Toronto, Canada. He will be a powerful leader for the conspirators there.[36]

The following is the official despatch giving the details of Gen. Grant's late battles: [The following newspaper article was pasted in the diary.]

*Detailed Official Dispatch*
*Headquarters, Cumberland, Nov. 30, 1863*

Edwin M. Stanton, Secretary of War:

Sir: On the 23d instant, at 11:30 a.m., General Grant ordered a demonstration against Missionary Ridge, to develop the force holding it. The troops marched out, formed in order, advanced in line of battle, as if on parade. The rebels watched the formation and movement from their picket lines and rifle-pits, and from the summits of Missionary Ridge, 500 feet above us, and thought it was a review and drill, so openly, so deliberately, so regularly was it all done.

As the line advanced, preceded by skirmishers, and at 2 p.m. reached our picket lines, they opened a rattling volley upon the rebel pickets, which replied and ran into their advanced line of rifle-pits. After them went our skirmishers, and into them, along the center of the line of 25,000 troops, which General Thomas had so quickly displayed, and we opened fire.

Prisoners assert that they thought the whole movement was a review and general drill, and then it was too late to send to their camps for reinforcements, and they were overwhelmed by force of numbers. It was a surprise in open daylight.

At 3 p.m. the important advanced position of Orchard Knob[37] and the lines right and left were in our possession, and arrangements were ordered for holding them during the night. The next day at daylight General Sherman had 5,000 men across the Tennessee, established on its south bank and commenced the construction of a pontoon bridge about 6 miles above Chattanooga.

The rebel steamer *Dunbar*, repaired at the right moment, rendered effective aid in this crossing, ferrying over some 6,000 men. By nightfall General Sherman had seized the extremity of Missionary Ridge nearest the river, and was entrenching himself. General Howard,[38] with a brigade, opened communications with him from Chattanooga, on the south side of the river. Skirmishing and cannonading continued all day on the left and centre. General Hooker scaled the slopes of Lookout Mountain from the valley of Lookout Creek, drove the rebels around the point, captured some 2,000 prisoners, and established himself high up the mountain side, in full view of Chattanooga. This raised the blockade, and our steamers were ordered from Bridgeport to Chattanooga. They had run only to Kelley's Ferry,[39] whence 10 miles of hauling over mountain roads and twice crossing the Tennessee on pontoon bridges brought us our supplies.

All night the point of Missionary Ridge, on the extreme left, and the side of Lookout Mountain, on the extreme right, blazed with the campfires of loyal troops.

The day had been one of driving mists and rains, and much of Hooker's battle was fought above the clouds, which concealed him from our view, but from which his musketry was heard.[40]

At nightfall the sky cleared, and the full moon, the "hunter's moon," shone upon the beautiful scene. Till 1 a.m. twinkling sparks upon the mountain side showed that picket skirmishing was still going on; then it ceased. A brigade sent from Chattanooga crossed Chattanooga Creek, and opened communications with Hooker.

General Grant's headquarters during the afternoon of the 23d and the day of the 24th were in Woods's redoubt,[41] except when in the course of the day we rode along the advanced lines, visiting the headquarters of the several commanders in Chattanooga Valley.

At daylight on the 25th, the Stars and Stripes were discerned on the peak of Lookout. The rebels had evacuated the mountain.

Hooker moved to descend the mountain, and striking Missionary Ridge at the Rossville Gap, sweep it on both sides and on its summit. The rebel troops were seen as soon as it was light enough streaming by regiments and brigades along the narrow summit of Missionary Ridge, either concentrating on their right to overwhelm Sherman, or marching for the railroad and raising the siege. They had evacuated the Valley of Chattanooga; would they abandon that of the Chickamauga?

The twenty pounders and four and a quarter inch rifles of Woods's redoubt opened on Missionary Ridge. Orchard Knob sent its compliments to the ridge, which, with rifled Par-rotts,[42] answered, and the cannonade thus commenced continued all day. Shot and shell screamed from Orchard Knob to Missionary Ridge, from Missionary Ridge to Orchard Knob, and from Woods's redoubt, over the heads of General Grant and General Thomas and their staffs, who were with us in this favorable position, when the whole could be seen in an amphitheater. The Headquarters were under fire all day long.

Cannonading and musketry were heard from General Sherman. Howard marched the Eleventh Corps to join him.

Thomas sent out skirmishers, who drove in the rebel pickets, and even shook them in their entrenchments at the foot of Missionary Ridge. Sherman sent an assault against Bragg's right, entrenched on a high knob, next to that on which Sherman himself lay fortified. The assault was gallantly made.

Sherman reached the edge of the crest, held ground (it seemed to me) an hour; but was then bloodily repulsed by reserves.

A general advance was ordered, a strong line of skirmishers, followed by a deployed line of battle some 2 miles in length. At the signal of the leaders from the headquarters on Orchard Knob, the line moved rapidly and orderly forward. The rebel pickets discharged their muskets and ran into their rifle-pits; our skirmishers followed on their heels; the line of battle was not far behind; and we saw the gray rebels swarm out of the ledge line of rifle-pits in numbers which surprised us, and over the base of the hill. A few turned and fired their pieces, but the greater number collected into the various roads which creep obliquely up its steep face, and went on to the top. Some regiments pressed on and began to swarm up the steep sides of the ridge. Here and there a color was advanced beyond the line. The attempt appeared most dangerous; but the advance was supported, and the whole line ordered to storm the heights, upon which not less than forty pieces of artillery, and no one knew how many muskets, stood ready to slaughter the assailants. With cheers answering to cheers the men swarmed upward. They gathered to the lines of least difficult ascent and the line was broken. Color after color was planted on the summit, while musketry and cannon vomited their thunder upon them.

A well-directed shot from Orchard Knob exploded a rebel caisson on the summit. A gun was seen galloping to the right, its driver lashing his horses. A party of our soldiers intercepted him, and the gun was captured with cheers.

A fierce musketry fight broke out to the left, where, between Thomas and Sherman, a mile or two of the ridge was still occupied by the rebels. Bragg left the house in which he had held his Headquarters and rode to the rear as our troops crowned the hill on each side of him.

General Grant proceeded to the summit, and then only did we know its height. Some of the captured artillery was put into position, artillerists were sent for to work the guns, caissons were searched for ammunition.

The rebel log breastworks were torn to pieces, and carried to the other side of the ridge and used in forming barricades across it.

A strong line of infantry was formed in the rear of Baird's[43] line, hotly engaged in a musketry contest with the rebels to the left, and a secure lodgment was soon effected.

The other assault to the right of our center gained the summit, and the rebels threw down their arms and fled.

Hooker, coming in from Rossville, swept the right of the ridge and captured many prisoners.

Bragg's remaining troops left early in the night and the battle of Chattanooga, after three days of maneuvering and fighting, was won. The strength of the rebellion in the center was broken; Burnside relieved from danger in East Tennessee; Kentucky and Tennessee redeemed; Georgia and the Southeast threatened in the rear; and another victory added to the caplet of Unconditional Surrender Grant.[44]

Tonight the estimate of captures is several thousand prisoners and thirty pieces of artillery.

Our loss for so great a victory not severe.[45]

Bragg is firing the railroad as he retreats toward Dalton [GA]; Sherman is in hot pursuit.

To-day I viewed the battlefield, which extends for 6 miles along Missionary Ridge and for several miles on Lookout Mountain.

Probably not so well-directed, so well ordered a battle has been delivered during the war. But one assault was repulsed, but that assault, by calling to that point the reserves, prevented their repulsing any of the others.

A few days since Bragg sent to General Grant a flag of truce to advise him, that it would be prudent to remove any non-combatants who might be still in Chattanooga.

No reply has been returned but the combatants having been removed from this vicinity, it is probable that the non-combatants can remain without imprudence.

M.C. Meigs, Quartermaster-General[46]

*Wednesday, December 2, 1863*

A clear pleasant day, not so cold as yesterday. Am feeling very well and hearty. Lines all working well. Offices opened morning at Brandy Station [VA].[47] The Army having returned there. The rebels were not attacked. This fine weather is being wasted and nothing is being done. The winter is lost to us.

We have intelligence from Burnside up to Monday night. He and his troops were then in excellent spirits amply supplied and confident of holding out. On Saturday night Longstreet with a selected force attacked desperately Fort Sanders. He was bloodily repulsed losing 1,000 men, 200 of whom were killed and wounded. Scouts who have come in to Tazewell [TN] where Gen. Foster[48] is with a force of 5,000 report that heavy firing was heard at Knoxville, from 3 p.m. yesterday up to the time they left the front last night. This is supposed to be Genl. Granger with his relieving column who left Chattanooga on Saturday. It is believed that Longstreet is retreating by way of Abingdon, Western Virginia.

*Thursday, December 3, 1863*

A very pleasant day. Lines all working well. Army of Potomac is back again to its position on the North side of the Rappahannock. Nothing whatever was accomplished in the recent movements across the Rapidan. Our loss altogether was 1,000 killed and wounded.

A Lieut. Col.[49] and 125 men and officers reached Tazewell Farm this morning. They left Knoxville at 10 a.m. Tuesday. They report everything favorable. Nothing new.

Col. Graham[50] Comdg Cavlry Brigade skirmished yesterday with Wheeler's[51] and Jones's[52] Cavalry force. He was driven back to the Infantry supports on the Clinch River [in TN] where all attempts by the rebels to force a passage were repulsed. Genl. Sherman's force left Charleston on the Tenn side of the Hiawassie River on the morning of the 2nd. Granger passed the mouth of the Hiawassie the day before. They will reach Knoxville today or tomorrow.

Gen. Foster reports that Wheeler's Cavly had been repulsed and were moving towards Knoxville and a Union citizen reports that a large body of Infy and Cavly (probably Ransom's[53] Rebel Div) passed Bean Station [TN] enroute for Knoxville this morning.

### Friday, December 4, 1863

Another beautiful day. The air is balmy and as pleasant as spring. Lines all working very well.

Genl. Foster reports that enemy's Cavalry retired yesterday towards Knoxville closely followed by our Cavly. Our scouts went 4 miles beyond Maynardsville, Tenn. They report that heavy firing was heard all day yesterday at Knoxville (probably Granger). Foster has ordered a Cavalry force to blockade the road from Spring House to Bean Station, on which it is supposed Longstreet will retreat.

Nothing new from the Army of the Potomac. All is quiet. It is rumored that Gen. Meade is to be superseded by Gen. Sedgwick.[54] His inaction demands it.[55]

### Saturday, December 5, 1863

Nothing new in any of the Armies. From Rebel newspapers we learn that Bragg has been superseded by Hardee.[56]

### Sunday, December 6, 1863

Today has been very pleasant.

Gen. Foster telegraphs from Tazewell, Tenn under date of noon today that his scouts have returned from Blain's Cross Roads and report that a rebel column was passing all night from Knoxville to Blain's Cross Roads. They heard the men say that they were going to Virginia; that the Yankees had surrounded them, but they would fight their way through. Scouts on the top of Clinch Mountain [TN] say that large campfires were seen last night on the road from Blain's X [Cross] Roads to Rutledge [TN]. Gen. Foster says he has no doubt that Longstreet is retreating.

### Monday, December 7, 1863

Lines all are working well today. Weather clear and cold. My health continues excellent.

Nothing new from any point except Tazewell. The rebels are retreating towards Virginia from Knoxville on the south valley of the Holston River. Sherman arrived at Knoxville with his relieving column yesterday. It is to be hoped that he will not allow Longstreet to escape into West Virginia.

*Tuesday, December 8, 1863*

Am in excellent health. Congress assembled yesterday and elected Schuyler Colfax[57] of Indiana Speaker on first ballot. He rec'd 101 votes, 92 being necessary to a choice. The President's illness has delayed his message.[58] It is not yet out.

*Wednesday, December 9, 1863*

President's message was read today in Congress. It is not very lengthy. It was well received, and all concur in pronouncing it ably written.

It speaks of various matters connected with our and other nations of importance, but is mainly composed of affairs and questions occasioned by the war.[59]

The Secy of War's[60] report is about equal length with the message. He compliments the military telegraph very highly indeed. He says none have surpassed & few have equaled the diligence & faithfulness of the Telegraph operation.

On the first of July 1862 there were 3,551 miles of land & submarine line in working order. During the year 1,775 miles of land & submarine lines were constructed making the total number of miles in operation during the year 5,326. By a close estimate it appears that at least 1,200,000 telegrams have been sent and received over the military lines in operation during the fiscal year ending June 30, 1863, being at the rate of 3,300 per day. These telegrams varied in length from ten to one thousand words & upwards & generally were of urgent, most important character.

Nothing new from the Army of the Potomac. Genl. Grant says it will be impossible to pursue Longstreet farther than Bristol, Va. as the supplies cannot be easily got there.

It is feared that Longstreet will get into Western Va. with most of his army.

*Thursday, December 10, 1863*

The following is a copy of a telegram sent by President Lincoln to Gen. Grant on the 8 inst. It is a very excellent telegram & comes from the heart.

*Wash. D.C., Dec. 8, 1863*

Maj. Gen. U.S. Grant, Chattanooga, Tenn.

Understanding that your lodgment at Chattanooga and Knoxville is now secure I wish to tender you and all under your command my more than thanks—my profound gratitude—for the skill, courage and Perseverance with which you and they, over so great difficulties have effected that important object. God bless you all.

(signed) A. Lincoln

Nothing new from any point. Weather is very pleasant indeed. Major C. A. Dana reached Chattanooga today. He left Knoxville with Sherman on the 7th. Sherman has gone to Tellico Plains [TN] with 15th Corps, sending a Cavly Div about 1,000 strong to Murphy, N.C. to destroy a rebel wagon train & if practicable make a raid as far as Dahlonega [GA], at the same time Davis's[61] Division occupies Columbus & Denton & the 11th Corps Athens [TN] & Charleston [TN]. These forces will eat out the country & go to Chattanooga in about a week.

Granger grumbled and complained so much about the distribution of his troops that Gen. Burnside moved out on Monday morning with his own troops to pursue Longstreet, who is retreating in an orderly manner with all his artillery. His rear guard was at Strawberry Plains [TN] on afternoon of Sixth. Foster had not yet relieved Burnside, but he was expected to do so in a day or so & Burnside would go north via Cumberland Gap.

*Saturday, December 12, 1863*

On last Sunday the ironclad *Weehawken*[62] sunk whilst off Charleston [SC] in a severe gale. Some thirty odd persons were drowned.

The *Minna* an English steamer was captured on the 9th by the Steamer *Circassian*[63] when one day out from Charleston. The *Minna* was a blockade-runner & had a very valuable assorted cargo.

*Sunday, December 13, 1863*

A very pleasant day. It rained & stormed hard through the night, but it has cleared off & is now very delightful.

Lines opened to Warrenton Village [VA] today.

*Monday, December 14, 1863*

Genl. Burnside turned over the Command of the Army of the Ohio to Major Gen. Foster on the 11th & started north on the 12th.[64]

Longstreet is moving leisurely up the Valley, foraging as he goes. His rear is harassed by our Cavalry supported by our Infy which was at Rutledge [TN] on the 12th.

Gen. Butler[65] reports a successful expedition to Charles City [VA] by Gen. Wistar.[66] They captured the whole about 100 men besides horses & destroyed camp & equipments. Our loss 2 killed & 4 wounded.

The N.Y. Mounted Rifles[67] in 44 hours marched 76 miles & the 139th N.Y. Infy in 54 hours marched 64 miles mostly in a severe storm, walking day & night. Great gallantry & endurance were manifested by all engaged.

*Tuesday, December 15, 1863*

The weather has been pleasant today. Seems more like spring than Dec.

All lines working well. My health is very good.

*Wednesday, December 16, 1863*

Genl. J. Buford[68] died today of typhoid fever. He had been ill but a short time.

Lines all working well. Weather very pleasant.

*Thursday, December 17, 1863*

A dull raining day, very unpleasant.

Today the steamer *Chesapeake* was captured near Halifax by the *Ella & Annie*.[69] The *Chesapeake* was seized some weeks ago by some parties when a few days out from N.Y. The Engineer murdered & the Capt & crew put ashore. She had been cruising along the coast of Nova Scotia ever since until today trying to get supplies. She will be taken to the nearest colonial port of entry & the Naval Officer will there await the approval of the British authorities.

Was too busy to go to class this evening.[70]

*Friday, December 18, 1863*

It has rained none today but it is damp & cloudy & muddy.

Lines are all down west of Harrisburg [PA] today. Business for and from the West is consequently delayed. The People's Line Telegraph[71]

Confederate Cipher Letter

*(From Lincoln in the Telegraph Office, p. 73)*

intends to run a line to War Dept from their office here. This will give us additional facilities for prompt transmission of telegrams.

*Sunday, December 20, 1863*

Another week has passed and gone & Sunday, the day of rest, is again with us. The weather is very cold & piercing today & everything has a chilling aspect.

Major Gen. Jno Buford is to be buried this afternoon. He died last week of typhoid fever. He belonged to the Cavalry arm of the service & was a brave & courageous officer. He has been with the Army of the Potomac a long time & many a gallant charge has he led. All will mourn his loss.

*Monday, December 21, 1863*

The weather today has been very cold. Lines all working well.

A letter addressed to Mr. Keith, Halifax, N.S. & put in the post office at New York on 18 inst. was intercepted & found to be written in cipher. It was sent by Mr. Abraham Wakeman, Postmaster at N.Y. to the Secy. of War who gave it to his confidential clerk to translate. They studied at it all day Sunday & gave it up. They could not translate it. This morning it was sent into the telegraph office & given to [Charles] Tinker who sat down with [Albert] Chandler & me & we tried to work it out. After five minutes inspection I made out the words "before this." We then scrutinized it closely & between us we made all of it out. It proved to be of the highest importance being a letter from J. H. Cammack, N.Y.[72] to J. P. Benjamin, Richmond,[73] to go by way of Halifax & Bermuda. It was immediately copied and taken to the Secy. of War who acted upon the matter. Orders were sent to N.Y. to prevent all outwards bound vessels leaving, without a pass from Robt. Murray, N.Y. marshal, & directing every passenger to be closely watched & every article of baggage closely examined until further orders. Every exertion is being made to arrest the guilty parties & bring them to justice.

I will get a copy of the translated letter & the alphabet & insert them tomorrow or the next day.

*Tuesday, December 22, 1863*

Today has been damp & unpleasant but very cold. A little snow fell in the evening.

Genl. Corcoran[74] fell from his horse at Fairfax CH and hurt himself seriously. He is in a critical condition—later report says he died at 8:30 p.m.

*Wednesday, December 23, 1863*

Weather still very cold. Everybody is busy buying holiday presents for his friends. The stores are full of people. Charles Tinker & I went to a bookstore to select a present for Major Eckert[75] who has done us a great many favors & who we think deserves from us some slight acknowledgment of the esteem in which he is held. It will cost $19.10 & will be paid for by Chandler, Tinker & me.

We selected 3 books, Hood's, Moore's and Ben Johnson's works. They are very handsomely bound & will be given to the major on Christmas.

We have a telegram from Gen. Averell[76] tonight dated Elroy, Pocahontas Co., Va. Dec. 21st via Beverly, W. Va., 22nd. He had just reached that point having marched 310 miles since the 8th inst. He cut the Va. and Tenn. RR at Salem [VA] on 16th inst. & returned safely with his command, consisting of the 2nd, 3rd, 18th Va. Mtd Infy, 14th Pa., Hobson's[77] Brigade of Cavalry & Ewing's Battery. At Salem 3 depots were burned containing 21,000 bbls [barrels] flour, 1,000 bbls wheat, 100,000 bbls bus.[bushels] shelled corn, 50,000 bushels oats, 21,000 bbls meat, 1,000 sacks salt, 20 bales of cotton, 100 wagons, several cords of leather, shoes, saddles & harnesses, 31 boxes clothing & equipments of all kinds. The telegraph [lines] to Richmond were torn up for half a mile. Six bridges burned & at Salem the water station, turntable etc. The total amt of property destroyed will not fall short of $1,000,000 & will cramp the rebels very much for food, during the winter mos. At one time he was confronted by six different Genls. under Early, Jones, Fitzhugh Lee, Jackson, Imboden & Echols,[78] but Averell captured a messenger from Jones to Early from which he learned the exact positions of the separate commands. They had all the roads blockaded except one which was considered impracticable. He eluded them all & took this road & now has reached Elroy safely.

He lost 6 men drowned, 1 officer & 4 men missing, & captured 2,100 men but only brought in about 80 as the rest could not be conveyed. He also captured 150 horses. Altogether it is one of the most successful raids of the war & will be of incalculable service in case an advance is made against Longstreet.

*Thursday, December 24, 1863*

I was prevented from going to class this evening by the rect of another of the rebel cipher letters from N.Y.

The following are translated copies of the two [Confederate cipher] letters [intended for Judah Benjamin] and also the alphabet they use, as far as we have it.

*N.Y., Dec. 18, 1863*

A. Keith Esq., Halifax, N.S.

Please detach and forward on before and telegraph when return answer is rec'd, write as before.

J.H.C. [J.H. Cammack]

*Cypher—N.Y., Dec. 18, 1863*

Hon, J.P. Benjamin, Sec State Richmond, Va.

Willis is here. The two steamers will leave here about Christmas. Lamar and Bowers left here via Bermuda two weeks ago.[79] The 12,000 rifled muskets came duly to hand & were shipped to Halifax as instructed. We will be able to seize the other two steamers as per programmed.

Trowbridge[80] has followed the President's orders. We will have Briggs[81] under arrest before this reaches you—cost $2,000. We want more money, how shall we draw? Bills all forwarded to Slidell[82] and receipt rec'd, write as before. J.H.C.

*Cypher—N.Y. Dec. 22, 1863*

To: Hon Benj. H. Hill[83] Richmond Va.

Dear Sir:
Say to Memminger[84] that Hilton[85] will have the machine all finished and dies all cut by first of January. The engraving of the plates is superb! They will be shipped via Halifax, and all according to instructions. The main part of the work has been under the immediate supervision of Hilton who will act in good faith in consequence of the large amount [he] has and will receive. The work is beautifully done and the paper is superb. A part has been shipped and the balance will be forwarded in a few days. Send some one to Nassau to receive, and take machine and paper through Florida. Write me at Halifax, I leave first week in January. Should Goodman[86] arrive please send word by your Agent that he is to await further instructions.

Yours truly, J. H. C.

*Friday, December 25, 1863*
Today has been clear and cold but very pleasant.

|   | 1 | 2 | 3 | 4 | 5 |   |   | 1 | 2 | 3 |
|---|---|---|---|---|---|---|---|---|---|---|
| A |   |   |   |   | X | | 0 | /// | \\\ | ≠ |
| B |   |   |   | oo | W | | 1 | S |   |   |
| C |   |   |   |   | Y | | 2 | B |   |   |
| D |   |   |   |   | Z | | 3 | 8 |   |   |
| E |   |   |   | ---- | U | | 4 |   |   |   |
| F |   |   |   | --- | V | | 5 |   |   |   |
| G |   |   |   | -- | S | | 6 |   |   |   |
| H |   |   | I | ··· | T | | 7 |   |   |   |
| I |   |   |   | ···· | Q | | 8 |   |   |   |
| J |   |   |   |   | R | | 9 |   |   |   |
| K |   |   |   |   | 0 |
| L |   |   |   | ·· | P |
| M |   | ✝ | | + | M |
| N |   | ⊕ |   | -- | K |
| O |   |   |   | -K | N |
| P |   |   |   |   | L |
| Q |   |   |
| R |   | = |   | ···· | I |
| S |   | ·· |   | € | E |
| T |   |   |   |   | g |
| U |   |   |   | --- | H |
| V |   |   |   |   | F |
| W |   | ·= |   | -·- | C |
| X |   |   |   | ※ |   |
| Y |   | -- |   |   | B |
| Z |

CSA Cipher Alphabet

*(From the Diary of David Homer Bates)*

This morning before Major Eckert got up Albert placed the books we had purchased for him on the table before his door. When he came to the office he shook hands with us all, and said in a hearty manner that he could not have been pleased better in the selection of books for him, and expressed himself very much gratified not so much at the mere value of the present as at the sentiment of the note accompanying it. The following is a copy of the note.

*Washington, D.C., Dec. 25, 1863*

Dear Sir:

Please accept these volumes of literary worth as a modest token of our appreciative regard for one whom for his sterling integrity & generous heart we have learned to love as a friend & companion and to serve with profound respect, and whose unvarying kindness will ever be cherished with feelings of deepest gratitude. We tender them, a "Christmas Gift" and with it an earnest prayer for the future welfare and prosperity of yourself and pleasant family. A Merry Christmas to you all.

Chas. A. Tinker, D. Homer Bates, Albert D. Chandler

Major Eckert told Charlie, Albert and me today that our salaries would be $150.00 a month & as a Christmas gift, it should commence December 1st.[87]

This increase is given in return for our having translated the rebel cipher letters and we are deeply sensible of the kindness. May we ever deserve it.

From the rebel actions contained in the two letters several arrests have been made in N.Y. and one Dr. Lugur[88] offered Ben Franklin,[89] the detective, $12,000 if he would hush the matter up. Several steamers have also been seized, containing arms, ammunition etc., & it is expected that other seizures will occur.

*Saturday, December 26, 1863*

Weather clear & cold.

Nothing new in any of the Armies. Gen. Grant has gone to Knoxville himself to drive Longstreet from East Tennessee. He will have to leave now with Grant after him.

Bej Franklin telegraphs that he has arrested Dr. Lugur, J.E. Conant, G.F. Canty & Joseph Perez[90] & will send them to Ft. Lafayette[91] in the morning. Conant has made a full confession in writing.[92]

*Sunday, December 27, 1863*
It has drizzled rain all day. Sidewalks are muddy and slippery.

*Monday, December 28, 1863*
Rain still continues. Weather is very unpleasant. Nothing new in any of the Armies. My health keeps well.

*Tuesday, December 29, 1863*
Nothing new of importance. Major Dana telegraphs from N.Y. that he has this morning seen evidence which affords good ground for belief that Marshal [Robert] Murray of that city is in collusion with the rebels. From long personal knowledge of Murray, Dana has no doubt that he is capable of such treasonable conduct.

*Thursday, December 31, 1863*
Charlie Tinker was taken ill with diphtheria yesterday & is confined to his bed. This makes the office work rather heavy.
Marshal Murray telegraphs this evening that he has arrested Hilton & seized several millions of dollars worth of Confederate bonds & a large amount of Confederate 20's and 50's. He also arrested foreman & Hilton's partner, secured Treasury notes 5's, 10's, 20's and 50's. He also arrested the lithographer, printer, secured all of the plates, dies & machinery & will probably secure the man who made the machinery. This has all resulted from the translating of the rebel cipher letters, and the Secy & Mr. Watson,[93] Asst Secy, both said that we deserved great credit & compliment us very highly.

## Notes

[1]Union Major General George G. Meade, Commander of the Army of the Potomac.
[2]Union Major General Henry W. Halleck, General-in-Chief, United States Army.
[3]The Orange and Alexandria Railroad ran south from Alexandria, Virginia. Bealeton, Virginia, was located on the rail line about 45 miles southwest of Alexandria, Virginia.
[4]The *Massachusetts* was a Union naval screw steamer vessel weighing 765 tons.
[5]"Monitor" was the generic name for all Union ironclads.
[6]Confederate General Braxton Bragg, Commander, Army of Tennessee.
[7]Union Major General Ambrose E. Burnside, Commander, Department of the Ohio.

[8]The Confederate Knoxville Campaign began on November 14, 1863, and continued until December 13, 1863.

[9]Confederate Lieutenant General James Longstreet, Commander, Department of East Tennessee.

[10]Union Major General Ulysses S. Grant, Commander, Military District of the Mississippi.

[11]Union Major General George H. Thomas, Commander, Army of the Cumberland.

[12]Telegraph operators normally maintained daily accounts, and the day usually started with a statement about the weather conditions as they had a definite impact on the efficiency of the telegraph lines. Entries also frequently contained references to the status of the telegraph lines as well as the health of the operator.

[13]Union Major General William T. Sherman, Commander, Army and Department of the Tennessee.

[14]The railroad connection between Washington and West Virginia was the Baltimore and Ohio Railroad.

[15]Confederate General Robert E. Lee, Commander, Army of Northern Virginia.

[16]President Lincoln traveled to Gettysburg, Pennsylvania, on the 18th of November where the next day he delivered what has come to be known as the Gettysburg Address. The address, which Lincoln initially considered a failure was given only a passing reference in the Bates diary.

[17]Nathaniel B. Smithers, a Delaware Republican politician ran for the U.S. House of Representatives seat left vacant by the death of William Temple, a Democrat. Bates is probably referring to the Democrats' appeal to all voters in Delaware to boycott the election to protest the presence of Union troops sent to protect the polls and the returning of troops coming home to vote. It was the Democrats' hope that the election would be declared null and void. The actual result of the election was 7, 299 for the Republican candidate and only 13 for the Democratic candidate, Charles H. Brown. Smithers served in the House of Representatives until the 1866 election winners were seated.

[18]Union Major General Joseph Hooker, Commander, 11th and 12th Corps, Army of the Cumberland.

[19]Union Brigadier General Hugh B. Ewing, Commander, 4th Division, 15th Corps, Army of the Tennessee.

[20]Union Brigadier General Orlando B. Willcox, Commander, Left Wing Forces in East Tennessee, Department of the Ohio.

[21]The daily price of gold was reported each day on the telegraph. As there was much speculation in the purchase of gold, it became an item of interest to the telegraph operators.

[22]The Battle of Chattanooga, Tennessee, was fought from November 23-25, 1863.

[23]Union Major Charles A. Dana was the War Department troubleshooter. When Dana traveled for the President, he carried a separate series of the

Union cipher system. On January 28, 1864, he was named Assistant Secretary of War.

[24]Mr. Mattingly and Mr. Wilson were civilian employees of the American Telegraph Office. Gentry, Guthridge, and Stumm were all USMTC operators assigned to the American Telegraph Company. The Union had placed USMTC operators in all major telegraph offices to ensure that military telegraphs received priority handling and were kept secure.

[25]Union Major General Robert C. Schenck, Commander, 8th Corps, Middle Department.

[26]Military telegraph operators, J. T. Sampson and G. I. Baldwin were USMTC operators assigned to the staff of General Schenck's Headquarters.

[27]Mr. McKnight was not a USMTC operator. He is not further identified.

[28]The Cleveland and Dalton Railroad ran between Cleveland, Ohio, and Dalton, Georgia.

[29]The Battle of Mine Run was fought from November 26-December 2, 1863.

[30]Colonel Crawford not further identified.

[31]The Confederate assault on Ft. Sanders, Tennessee, November 29, 1863, was part of the Knoxville Campaign.

[32]Union Major General Gordon Granger, Commander, 4th Corps, Army of the Cumberland.

[33]Confederate Lieutenant General Richard S. Ewell, Commander, 2nd Corps, Army of Northern Virginia.

[34]A large Confederate field hospital had been established at Robertson's Tavern (also referred to as Robinson's Tavern in some contemporary references), located on the north side of the Orange Turnpike at the crossroads hamlet of Locust Grove.

[35]Fort Sumter had been under Union bombardment since November 28, 1863. The Fort is located in the harbor of Charleston, South Carolina.

[36]Confederate Brigadier General John H. Morgan, Division Commander in Major General Joseph Wheeler's Cavalry, had been imprisoned at the State Penitentiary in Columbus, Ohio, after being captured on July 26, 1863, in a raid on Cincinnati. Morgan and six of his officers escaped via a self-dug tunnel on the night of November 27th. He did not head to Canada, but returned to the Confederacy by Christmas of 1863. The Confederate spy operation in Toronto, Canada, headed by Jacob Thompson, had among its functions the providing of safe haven and passage south for escaping Confederate prisoners of war, hence the assumption that Morgan went north.

[37]The Union Army of the Cumberland moved forward with two divisions from Fort Wood toward Orchard Knob, a Confederate holding in front of Missionary Ridge. It represented the initial phase of the Battle of Missionary Ridge, Tennessee.

[38]Union Major General Oliver O. Howard, Commander, 11th Corps, Army of the Cumberland.

[39]Kelley's Ferry, Tennessee, was the first link in what was dubbed the "Crackerline" to supply Union forces in Chattanooga.

[40]The Battle of Lookout Mountain on November 24, 1863, was also called the Battle above the Clouds.

[41]Referring to the temporary fortifications of the force of Union General Charles R. Woods, Commander, 1st Brigade, 1st Division, 15th Corps, Army of the Tennessee.

[42]Parrott guns were invented by Captain Robert Parker Parrott in 1860 while he was Superintendent of the West Point Foundry. The guns were made of wrought iron with a reinforced band around the breech end. The guns were cheaper than the bronze Napoleons and became very popular with both the Confederate and the Union forces.

[43]Union Colonel Absalom Baird, Commander, 3rd Division, 14th Corps, Army of the Cumberland.

[44]General Grant's initials, "U.S.," gave rise to several nicknames. At West Point he was called "Uncle Sam" by his classmate William T. Sherman. He earned the name "Unconditional Surrender" at the Battle of Fort Donelson, when the Confederates, on February 16, 1862, asked for the terms of surrender, and he responded with a demand for unconditional surrender.

[45]The losses for the Union at Missionary Ridge were 753 killed, 4,722 wounded, and 349 missing.

[46]Union Brigadier General Montgomery C. Meigs, Quartermaster General of the Union Army.

[47]Brandy Station (also known as Fleetwood, Virginia) became important as a telegraph site for the Union army as it advanced across the Rappahannock River in Virginia.

[48]Union Major General John G. Foster, Commander, Department of Ohio.

[49]Not further identified.

[50]Union Colonel Alexander Graham, 13th New York Cavalry, Commander, Brigade of Cavalry Corps, Army of the Potomac.

[51]Confederate Major General Joseph Wheeler, Commander of Cavalry Corps of the Army of Tennessee.

[52]Confederate Brigadier General William E. Jones, Commander, Cavalry Brigade, Ransom's Division.

[53]Confederate Major General Robert Ransom, Commander, Division, Department of West Virginia and East Tennessee.

[54]Union Major General John Sedgwick, Commander, 6th Corps, Army of the Potomac.

[55]The rumors proved unfounded. General Meade remained in command of the Army of the Potomac.

[56]Confederate General Braxton Bragg resigned command of the Confederate Army of Tennessee on November 30, 1863, and was temporarily succeeded by Lieutenant General William J. Hardee. Bragg became the Military Advisor to President Davis.

[57]Schuyler Colfax of Indiana was first elected to Congress in 1855. He later served as Vice President during the first term of President Grant.

[58]President Lincoln had developed a slight case of smallpox upon his return from Gettysburg. He remained in the White House under quarantine for three weeks. (Donald, David H., *Lincoln*, p. 467.)

[59]On the 9th of December, President Lincoln made his first major statement regarding the postwar period in his Proclamation on Amnesty. It included: full pardon to all Confederates, excepting government officials, high ranking army officers, those who resigned from the U.S. military to serve the Confederacy, and those who mistreated prisoners of war; pardons to be conditional on an oath of allegiance to the United States; restoration of all property except slaves; recognition of federal statehood for any seceded state in which one-tenth of the citizens swore allegiance to the U.S. and forswore slavery. (Foner, Eric, *Reconstruction: America's Unfinished Revolution, 1863-1877, p. 35.)*

[60]Edwin M. Stanton, Union Secretary of War.

[61]Union Brigadier General Jefferson C. Davis, Commander, 2nd Division, 14th Corps, Army of the Cumberland.

[62]The *USS Weehawken* was a 1,175-ton Union ironclad that sank while loading ammunition in rough seas. The cause was an open hatch.

[63]The *USS Circassian* was a 1,750-ton Union screw steamer.

[64]General Burnside turned over the command of the Army of the Ohio at his own request.

[65]Union Major General Benjamin F. Butler, Commander, 18th Corps and Department of North Carolina and Virginia.

[66]Union Brigadier General Isaac J. Wistar, Commander, U.S. Forces Yorktown, 18th Corps, Department of North Carolina and Virginia.

[67]The 4th New York Mounted Rifles, a black unit under the command of Colonel Samuel J. Duncan.

[68]Union Brigadier General John Buford, Commander, Division, Cavalry Corps, Army of the Potomac.

[69]The *Chesapeake* was a privately owned steamer, captured by a Confederate raiding party. The Union steamer *Ella and Annie* (later renamed the *USS Malvern*) recaptured the *Chesapeake* and returned it to its civilian owners.

[70]David Homer Bates had a limited education when he arrived in Washington. The classes were in all probability a continuation of his education at what would now be called high school.

[71]The People's Line Telegraph was a private telegraph company founded in 1845 with telegraph lines predominately to the areas of Kentucky and Tennessee. Its Washington office was located at 511 9th Street, Northwest, at the corner of Pennsylvania Avenue (about six blocks from the War Department Building).

[72]Confederate agent in New York City not further identified.

[73]Judah P. Benjamin, Confederate Secretary of State. He had previously served as Attorney General and Secretary of War in the Confederacy.

[74]Union Brigadier General Michael Corcoran, Division Commander, 22nd Corps, Department of Washington.

[75]Major Thomas T. Eckert, the first supervisor of the War Department Telegraph Office, became the president of Western Union after the war.

[76]Union Brigadier General William W. Averell, Commander, 4th Division, Department of West Virginia.

[77]Union Brigadier General Edward H. Hobson, Commander, District of South Central Kentucky, 1st Division, 23rd Corps, Department of the Ohio.

[78]Confederate Major General Jubal A. Early, Commander, Valley District, Department of Northern Virginia; Brigadier General William E. Jones, Commander, Cavalry Brigade, Ransom's Division, Department of West Virginia; Brigadier General Fitzhugh Lee (nephew of Robert E. Lee), Commander, Division Cavalry Corps, Army of Northern Virginia; Brigadier General William L. Jackson, Commander, Brigade, Lomax's Cavalry Division, Valley District, Department of Northern Virginia; Brigadier General John D. Imboden, Commander, Valley District, Department of Northern Virginia; and Brigadier General John Echols, Brigade Commander, Department of Western Virginia.

[79]Willis, Lamar, and Bowers were all Confederate agents not further identified.

[80]Trowbridge, probably a Confederate agent, is not further identified.

[81]Briggs is not further identified.

[82]John Slidell was a former U.S. Senator from Louisiana. He was in Paris as the Confederate representative to the French Government.

[83]Benjamin H. Hill was a member of the Confederate Senate from Georgia and member of the Senate Committee for Printing.

[84]Christopher G. Memminger was the Confederate government's Secretary of the Treasury until June 15, 1864, when he resigned.

[85]Hilton was probably an engraver.

[86]Confederate agent not further identified.

[87]The raise amounted to $25.00 a month.

[88]Dr. Luger is not further identified.

[89]Ben Franklin was a New York detective in the employ of the U.S. Marshall in New York City.

[90]Confederate agents J. E. Conant, G. F. Canty, and Joseph Perez were not further identified.

[91]Fort Lafayette was a Union prison in New York. In 1861 Maryland political prisoners were sent there. In 1862 Union General Charles P. Stone was incarcerated there for 189 days without charges.

[92]The National Bank Note Company in New York in 1861 printed currency for the Confederacy to be shipped to Montgomery, Alabama. The printing company then ceased immediately as it became apparent that the U.S. Government would seize and prosecute the firm for treason. The American Bank Note Company was also involved in printing money for the Confederacy. In the case of the 1863 action, based on the deciphered Confederate letter, there are some interesting ramifications. The diary states that the Confederate agents and the engraver were arrested and sent to Fort Lafayette in New York Harbor. However, no record exists of the arrests and the specific names

mentioned in the diary are unknown to scholars today. The Museum of the
Confederacy, the Money Museum, and the American Numismatic Association
have no information on the event. Further the U.S. Marshal's office in New
York, its National Headquarters in Washington, DC, and the *New York Times*
for the period, have no record of the arrests being made. This leads to
speculation that if the arrests were made public the Confederacy would soon
realize that its cipher system had been broken by the Union. The probable
scenario is that the suspension of the writ of *habeas corpus* was used, and the
arrests were never made public.

[93]Peter H. Watson, a Washington patent lawyer, was the Assistant Secretary of War.

# January, February, March 1864

The opening months of the year 1864 were quiet on the military front as most of the armies of both sides were in winter quarters. There was a new optimism on the part of the Union contrasted with a distinct air of pessimism in the Confederacy, where for the first time peace initiatives were openly discussed.

The diary during this period reflects the general activity level of the military. For example Bates spent the majority of the month of January away from Washington with no apparent feeling of urgency about his work. During February not only did the military activity pick up, but there are many references to the constant extension of the military telegraph lines into new areas of military operations, experimentation with new techniques for transmission of communications, and expanded cooperation between the military telegraph and the telegraph companies of the private sector. It is apparent from the diary entries that senior officials in Washington had by this time become very dependent on the telegraphic reports forwarded from the various armies in the field. There was also an increased use of the telegraph by military commanders in the field, not only to report to their seniors, but also to command their respective troops.

Communications to the Telegraph Office during this period emanated mainly from the Union forces in North Carolina, Virginia, and Florida in the East and from General Sherman during the Meridian Campaign. All telegraphic communications were considered timely, usually arriving the same day they were sent, except for the period when the cable was broken at Fort Monroe, thereby delaying messages on the Fort Monroe to Washington line.

The political situation in the Confederacy was becoming increasingly dire as inflation continued at a rampant pace, food became very scarce, and anti-draft riots occurred in states such as North Carolina. On January 4th for the first time, President Davis issued an authorization for General Lee to commandeer food from the population in Virginia to feed his troops who were desperately in need of supplies. The Confederate Congress also banned the import of all luxury items and ordered that half of all food shipments were for government use. These actions were not well received by the populace, who now fully comprehended the basic weaknesses in the Confederate supply system. Demand was out of proportion to supply.

On the 21st of January pro-Union citizens of Tennessee announced plans to call a constitutional convention that would establish a constitution abolishing slavery in the state. On the 3rd of February President Davis recommended to the Confederate Congress a suspension of the writ of *habeas corpus* for deserters. It was quickly adopted by the Congress.

Bowing to continued criticism of his meddling in military affairs, Davis, on the 24th of February, named Braxton Bragg to handle military matters; *i.e*, the Chief of Staff of the Confederate Army. While the creation of the post was taken positively by the military, the choice of Bragg to fill the position was seen as a mere political ploy.

In the Union political activity was beginning to be directed to the postwar period. On the 13th of January President Lincoln urged Union generals in occupied Florida and Louisiana to move quickly to set up loyal state governments. On March 18th voters in Arkansas ratified a pro-Union constitution—one that abolished slavery forever. Other areas in the South under Union control were moving in the same direction.

Not to be lulled into a false sense of security, Lincoln called for a 500,000 men draft on the 1st of February to augment the Union forces. He also began the necessary actions to promote Grant to the rank of Lieutenant General. The rank was officially approved by Congress on the 24th of February and the commission presented on the 8th of March. Grant's headquarters, however, did not remain in Washington but located with the Army of the Potomac.

President Lincoln's problems with Secretary of the Treasury, Salmon P. Chase, came to a head during this period with the Secretary's implication in the *Pomeroy Circular*—a document signed by Senator Samuel C. Pomeroy of Kansas espousing Chase as the Republican Presidential candidate *in lieu of* Lincoln for the 1864 election. Controversy over the circular led to Chase's eventual resignation from the Cabinet. In another political move Andrew Johnson was appointed the Military Governor of Tennessee on the 4th of March.

On the military front, activity began to increase in February with the opening of the Meridian Campaign in Mississippi on the 3rd; the mass breakout of Union prisoners from Libby Prison in Richmond on the 9th (109 escaped but 48 were recaptured); the sinking of the Union vessel, the *Housatonic,* by the Confederate submarine *H. L. Hunley* on the 17th; the Battle of Olustee in Florida on the 20th; and the arrival of the first Union prisoners of war at Andersonville Prison in Georgia on the 27th.

On the 28th of February President Lincoln and Secretary of War Stanton approved a plan to conduct a raid on the Confederate capital of Richmond. The raid, to be led by General Hugh Judson Kilpatrick,[1] was designed to free the Union prisoners of war in Libby Prison, seize the Confederate capital city of Richmond, and to distribute amnesty proclamations to the population. The raid was initiated on the 1st of March but immediately ran into trouble; the Confederates knew it was coming. In the ensuing battle Union Colonel Ulrec Dahlgren was killed, and the documents found on his body indicating an assassination plot against Jefferson Davis caused a political storm.

The period ended with a new feeling of optimism in the North with Grant in command. The Union was becoming more unified in its quest for unconditional surrender, and public opinion appeared to be with Lincoln.                                         *Donald E. Markle*

*Friday, January 1, 1864*

New Year's Day! It seems strange to me that the last year has passed away so quickly. It has been to me an eventful year. I have been greatly blessed in many ways, and my heart would be cold indeed did it not render thanks unto Him who giveth all good gifts unto men. I am deeply grateful for His mercies, and I pray that they may bring my heart nearer to Him.

Major Eckert was made the recipient this morning of a very beautiful gold headed cane costing $50 from the employees of this office. The orderlies also gave him a handsome present consisting of an embroidered cigar case & box of cigars costing $20. He feels very grateful for our notice of him.

The weather has changed very much. It has turned quite cold & the wind blows fiercely & shrilly.

*Saturday, January 2, 1864*

Tinker sick & we are very busy.

*Sunday, January 3, 1864*

Very busy at the Office today. Toward noon I became very sick & was obliged to go home to bed. I had a violent headache and disordered stomach. Mrs. Eckert doctored me and toward evening I felt better.

*Monday, January 4, 1864*

I came to office today, tho I should not have done so. Am weak & have a slight fever. I hope I will soon get well. Charlie Tinker has Diphtheria badly & is confined to his bed.

*Tuesday, January 5, 1864*

Some snow fell yesterday & today it has frozen hard. The cold is intense throughout the west. Thermometer in many places far below zero. Roads all blocked with snow & rivers are frozen up. The Mississippi above Cairo [IL] is frozen over.

*Wednesday, January 6, 1864*

Snow still on the ground & weather pretty cold.

*Sunday, January 10, 1864*

Feeling a deal better today, went to Office after breakfast & staid till 2 p.m. when I went to dinner.

*Monday, January 11, 1864*

Came to the Office this morning feeling splendidly. I hope that my sickness is now over. Weather very pleasant. Clear and cold.

*Wednesday, January 13, 1864*

Genl. Grant arrived at Nashville today from Knoxville. Lines all working well.

*Friday, January 15, 1864*

Col. Stager arrived here this morning from New York to remain about a week. He looks very well.

*Friday, January 29, 1864*

Nothing new has transpired today. Stoneman[2] is on his way to relieve Foster. Gen. Meade is sick in Philad[elphia]. Sedgwick is in command of the Army of the Potomac in his absence. Grant is in Louisville visiting his family some of whom are ill.

*Saturday, January 30, 1864*

The weather for last 3 days has been perfectly splendid. The air has been warm & balmy as spring. Today it has clouded up and it rains.

The Prest. has today ordered a draft for 500,000 men on March 10th (Order dated Feb. 1st, 1864). This is virtually a call for 200,000 men besides the 300,000 called for in Oct. most of which have been furnished.

*Monday, February 1, 1864*

It has been damp & unpleasant today. Mr. Adamson, one of the boarders at Mrs. Danenhower's,[3] has the varioloid[4] & some of the boarders are leaving. The Dr. has had him moved into the 4th story room & thinks there will be no danger to those in the house.

*Tuesday, February 2, 1864*

Weather still unpleasant. Lines are all working pretty well. Am working at No. 2[5] today. Will finish one copy by tomorrow morning.

The rebels are reported to have burned 2 bridges on the B & O RR, one over Patterson Creek & one 6 miles from Cumberland. It is expected they will attack New Creek & Cumberland tonight.[6] Troops & batteries are on the way from Balto & Wash.

*Wednesday, February 3, 1864*

The weather has changed very much. It is now clear, cold and windy. Lines all working well.

*Thursday, February 4, 1864*

Have not been very well today, having caught a severe cold which has settled in my side & back. Weather very fine, clear & cold.

Chandler & I have decided to leave Mrs. Danenhower's until Adamson gets well at least. We go to Mrs. Gonsalves, 31 13th Street, above "L."

Lines all working well.

*Friday, February 5, 1864*

We have reports from Genl. Butler that Newberne [New Berne, NC] has been besieged by a force of rebels 15,000 strong. On the morning of the 1st, the enemy advanced on the place & heavy skirmishing & hard fighting was kept up during the day. At night 15 launches came down the Neuse River & attacked the U.S. gunboat, *Underwriter*.[7] Killed & captured all on board except 5. The vessel was set on fire & about 6 o'clock on morning of 2nd, her magazine exploded opposite the town with terrible effect.

Skirmishing & shelling from Ft. Totten [NC] was continued through that day & about 4 p.m. Newport Barracks [NC] was taken. Communications with Beaufort [NC] was cut off. Every man at Newberne was in the field, the town was garrisoned by citizens & every Negro capable of bearing arms was shouldering a musket. Thus affairs stood at 8 p.m. of 2d.

Genl. Palmer[8] had rations for 6,000 men for 90 days. His force of troops amounted to 3,700 at Newberne. Genl. Butler is taking measure to relieve the force as soon as possible. The rebels that made the raid on the B&O RR have retreated by way of Moorefield [WV]. On the night of the 1st, Genl. Scammon[9] & 2 of his staff were captured by guerrillas, on board the str [steamer] *Levi* on the Ohio River some distance below Pt. Pleasant [WV]. Efforts are being made to retake the steamer & the Genl.

P.M. A telegram recd from Genl. Butler states that he has information from Newberne up to 3:00 of the 3d. The rebels were retiring towards Kinston & Newberne was relieved.

*Saturday, February 6, 1864*

The pistol factory of Samuel Colt, at Hartford, Ct., was burned yesterday morning. It is estimated that some 3,000,000 dollars worth of property was destroyed. Some of it will fall upon the Govt as there were large contracts for arms being filled.

The Engine *Vibbard*[10] ran into the North draw of Long Bridge [DC] this p.m. killing the Engineer & one soldier, who was just going home on a furlough. Have just recd a letter from home. All were very well & happy.

*Sunday, February 7, 1864*

Weather is clear & pleasant. It rained some during the night.

Genl. Sedgwick telegraphs that vigorous demonstrations were made yesterday on his extreme right. We lost at Morton's Ford [VA] last evening. 200 killed & wounded & took 60 prisoners. We punished the Enemy sharply. The operation is still going on. Sedgwick says one result of the movement has been to prove that it has spoilt the best chance we ever had for a successful attack on the Rapidan [River].

*Monday, February 8, 1864*

Today is a beautiful day. The air is mild and pleasant. The lines are working well.

*Tuesday, February 9, 1864*

Weather still fine. Genl. Butler's Expedition has returned to Williamsburg & Yorktown having been within ten miles of Richmond. They found all the fords and roads obstructed by fallen timbers & they were obliged to come back. The rebels it seems had obtained the news of our coming from a deserter from our lines and were fully prepared for us. Genl. Sedgwick's troops have also all returned to their old position on the Rapidan. Genl. Meade is still ill.

*Wednesday, February 10, 1864*

Weather is still very fine. Lines all working well. Am in good health.

*Thursday, February 11, 1864*

Last evening as I was leaving the office at 8:30 p.m. I heard the alarm of the fire from the grounds at the President's House. I ran back to the office & called up the Steam Fire Engine. The call was heard & the Engine was immediately started out. It proved to be the President's stable containing his carriage & six fine horses. There being a great deal of combustible material in the building it speedily became enveloped almost completely in flames. Nothing was saved except the bare walls. The carriage which was in was gotten out before being burned very much. The 3 span of horses were burned. The little pony, belonging to Willie,[11] the Prest's deceased son, was burned also.

Weather clear & pretty cold but pleasant.

*Friday, February 12, 1864*

Weather rather sultry today & air close. Lines all working well. Got the new relay sounder[12] to work on the People's Line[13] today. It is a really good idea & works admirably.

*Sunday, February 14, 1864*

Weather blustery & the air full of dust.

*Monday, February 15, 1864*

Weather unpleasant. Damp & chilly. Lines all working but AX2.[14] Have inserted 4.[15] My health is very good at present.

*Tuesday, February 16, 1864*

Very windy & blustery. Lines blown together a great deal, causing much trouble. About fifty Union Officers have escaped from Libby Prison & came into our lines,[16] among them Col. Streight (who was confined closely for a long time in retaliation for the rebel Genl. J. Morgan)[17] & several other Colonels, Lt. Colonels, Majors, etc. A great many got out but most were re-taken.[18]

*Wednesday, February 17, 1864*

It still remains extremely cold. Nothing new. Lines all working well.

*Friday, February 19, 1864*

Weather still cold. I am feeling very well now.

*Sunday, February 21, 1864*

Weather has moderated considerably. Information from Gen. Gillmore's[19] Dept is that he sent an expedition into Florida some weeks since which had been entirely successful.[20] Captured 8 guns & a large number of prisoners & supplies of all kinds. Our forces will remain in that region where we now have a permanent foothold.

*Monday, February 22, 1864*

Today is the anniversary of the birthday of Washington, our first President. Flags are floating from all the public buildings. The Depts are however not closed.

*Tuesday, February 23, 1864*

Weather extremely pleasant today & lines all working well. I am feeling very well.

Reports from rebel papers are that Gen. Sherman with 35,000 men has reached Quitman, Ala.[MS] on the Mobile Railroad & is tearing up bridges, track, etc. in his rear indicating that it is a permanent advance.[21]

Over 50 officers in all reached our lines of the 109 who escaped from Libby Prison in Richmond. The rest were retaken.

*Wednesday, February 24, 1864*

Nothing of importance today. Wind very high & streets very dusty. Lines all working.

*Friday, February 26, 1864*

Am feeling very well today. Will Gonsalves[22] who has been ill for some time was taken to Kalorama Hospital[23] yesterday broken out with small pox though not very bad.

*Saturday, February 27, 1864*

Weather very calm & pleasant. Prof. Dean[24] came to office this evening to experiment with Gauley Bridge,[25] a distance of nearly six hundred miles, worked with him very successfully. Exchanged signals 8 or 10 times each.

*Sunday, February 28, 1864*

I met Killingsworth[26] after Church & drove down with him to Giesboro Point & dined with him there. The Hd Qrs of the Cavalry Camp are situated at Giesboro.[27] The stables are very extensive & will accommodate a great number of horses. There are some 18,000 now there (sick & well). It is the only establishment of the kind in the world of such magnitude.

Did not go to Church this evening. Had to stay at office.

*Monday, February 29, 1864*

Gen. Kilpatrick started last evening from the Army of the Potomac with a large Cavly force to capture Richmond by a *coup de main*.[28] Gen. Butler will send to New Kent C.H. [VA] a force of 3,000 Infy & Artillery to meet them & assist them in every possible way.

Gen. Thomas's advance has reached a point near Buzzard's Roost[29] which is very close to Dalton [GA].[30] Nothing definite has occurred. The Enemy is in a strong position & it may be found impossible to dislodge him.

Cloudy with appearance of rain but lines all working well.

*Tuesday, March 1, 1864*

Today the first day of spring very wet & unpleasant. Sleet has fallen to some extent.

Genl. Kilpatrick has not yet been heard from though street rumors are plenty.

*Wednesday, March 2, 1864*

Cable to Ft. Monroe gave out during the night. There was a heavy storm on the bay, which is now over. Our business for Ft. Monroe being done by boat by Cherrystone.[31]

News from Gen. Meade is that Gen. Custer[32] has returned from his flank movement, having whipped the enemy severely, doing them great damage, & bringing in some 50 prisoners. Genl. Kilpatrick was at Spotsylvania C.H., on the way to Richmond with strong hopes of success.

### Thursday, March 3, 1864

The report from rebel sources is that Longstreet is retreating from East Tenn. into Va. Gen. Schofield[33] was at Morristown [TN][34] on the first. He could advance no farther then on account of supplies.

Gen. Thomas has returned to Ringgold [GA][35] to wait until the railroad is built to him there. Gen. Grant telegraphs that on February 23rd Gen. Sherman was at Meridian [MS] having divided Polk's[36] command following one part down toward Mobile some 30 miles, then returned & went East to Demopolis [AL][37] from which place he had just returned. Railroad communication has undoubtedly been cut for some distance on both the lines.

Maine has just passed a resolution in her Legislature recommending Prest. Lincoln for reelection & endorsing his administration. Ohio & Illinois have already passed similar acts.

Congress passed an act extending the time for extra bounty to the first of Apl.[38] The Lieut. General bill passed last week.[39] Gen. Grant was today ordered to report in person to the War Department. He will no doubt receive the appointment of Lieut. General & probably be made the General-in-Chief.

### Friday, March 4, 1864

Genl. Kilpatrick reached the lines of Genl. Butler at Williamsburg on yesterday afternoon. He did not succeed in the object of his Expedition, but he destroyed several bridges & the canal & a great deal of rebel property. He lost less than one hundred & fifty men, among whom was Col. Ulric Dahlgren son of the Admiral,[40] who is at present in the city. Gen. K[ilpatrick] will be returned by water transportation from Yorktown to Alexandria.

Weather pleasant. Lines are working well except Alexa[ndria] wires which have been unopened all day.

### Saturday, March 5, 1864

A party of rebel raiders attacked the Telegraph Office at Cherrystone [VA] this morning about 2 o'clock. They killed the horses belonging to the guard there & took the instruments, but Dunn[41] the operator afterwards got it from them slyly & pitched it into the Bay. He was paroled & came immediately to Eastville [VA] & gave the information. The rebels took possession of the Despatch boat there at the Point & started off with it, as they said, to capture the tug *McClellan* at work on the cable.

Gunboats were immediately sent down the Potomac from here in pursuit.

*Sunday, March 6, 1864*

Sheldon[42] arrived at Cherrystone this a.m. with cable boat & re-opened office there. We hear today that Col. Dahlgren with about 100 men has reached Kings and Queens C.H. Gen. Kilpatrick has sent some of his men to meet & assist them. When Gen. Kilpatrick left camp at Stevensburg [VA] he had 3,585 men, 6 guns, 8 caissons, 3 wagons, 6 ambulances. He now has without Col. Dahlgren's detachment 3,317 men, 3,590 horses, 6 guns, 8 caissons, 3 wagons, and 4 ambulances.

*Monday, March 7, 1864*

We have information this a.m. from rebel papers of 5th inst. that the rebels had a fight with about 100 of our men near Kings & Queens C.H. & that Col. Dahlgren was killed. We fear it is true.[43]

The commission of Genl. Grant as Lieut. General has been signed & he will be here this week to receive it. He thus becomes the General-in-Chief of the U.S. Army.[44]

*Tuesday, March 8, 1864*

It rained all day. Cleared up & sun came out about 5 p.m. Lines all working well.

*Wednesday, March 9, 1864*

I attended the President's Levee last night. The rooms of the White House were pretty well crowded. Saw the Prest. & shook hands with him. He asked me if I had any news, but of course, I told him "no."

About 10:00 p.m. Genl. Grant came in. Everybody crowded around him to shake hands with him. Secy. Seward[45] and Stanton were with him. For one hour he stood on a sofa & shook hands with the people. The enthusiasm was very great.

*Thursday, March 10, 1864*

Genl. Grant went to the Army of the Potomac this morning to visit Genl. Meade. Pursuant to the act of Congress approved Feb. 29, 1864, the President by Executive Order of this date, assigned Lieut. General U. S. Grant the command of all the Armies of the U.S.

*Friday, March 11, 1864*

It has rained for two days pretty constantly. Gen. Grant reached here today from the Army of the Potomac & left almost immediately for Tenn.

The Constitution State Convention of Va. (assembled at Alexandria) yesterday at noon passed an act abolishing slavery & involuntary servitude in the State forever.[46] 100 guns were immediately fired in honor thereof.

*Saturday, March 12, 1864*

Quite pleasant today. Rain has ceased. Gen. Sherman has returned to Memphis. His troops are near Vicksburg. They destroyed some 60 bridges in Ala. and Miss., tore up 100 miles or more of railroad,[47] brot. in some 8,000 Negroes & lost less than 500 men. His expedition was a complete success. He will now go to Shreveport [LA] & will also send a force to Alexandria [LA] to assist Genl. Banks on the Red River.[48]

Gen. Grant left yesterday for Tenn.

*Sunday, March 13, 1864*

Weather today is very changeable.

*Monday, March 14, 1864*

Weather pleasant today. Lines all working well. Palmer[49] started out this morning on the line to Point Lookout, Md. Expect the line will be done in about twenty days from now. No. 10 wire[50] is being used.

*Tuesday, March 15, 1864*

Weather pleasant today.

*Wednesday, March 16, 1864*

D. H. Darience, Chief Opr of Alexandria Railroad line, resigned today. He accepted a position as Despatcher at Alexandria.[51] There will be no one appointed to his place.

Weather cold & blustery. Line finished today as far down as Fort Washington [MD].

*Friday, March 18, 1864*

Gen. Grant leaves Nashville tomorrow morning for Washington.

Lines to Pt. Lookout [MD][52] finished nearly to Port Tobacco [MD].[53] It was broken 8 miles from there today, but was repaired by Connor.[54]

*Saturday, March 19, 1864*

We have circuit on line to Pt. Lookout today. The party reached Port Tobacco this evening. Line works splendidly. Emerick[55] came up from Headquarters today.

*Monday, March 21, 1864*

Nothing new today. Weather raw & chilly. Major Eckert goes to Phila a.m. tomorrow.

*Tuesday, March 22, 1864*

Gen. Grant leaves Phila this p.m. for Washn. His staff reached here today.

Cloudy & unpleasant.

*Wednesday, March 23, 1864*

Snow fell last night to the depth of 7 inches. It has mostly melted away however. At Chattanooga there were 12 inches.

There was a very heavy gale last night on the bay & the cable over the Chesapeake has failed to work since midnight.

*Thursday, March 24, 1864*

Gen. Grant was in town all day yesterday. He goes to the Army of the Potomac today. The 1st & 3d Corps are temporarily broken up & the troops composing those Corps are merged into 2nd, 5th & 6th Corps to be commanded respectively by Gen. Hancock,[56] Warren,[57] & Sedgwick. Gen. Sykes[58] is ordered to Ft. Leavenworth to report to Gen. Curtis,[59] Gen. French[60] is ordered to Cincinnati & Gen. Newton[61] to Phila to report by letter to the Adj. Gen. Gen. Pleasonton[62] goes to St. Louis to report to Gen. Rosecrans.[63] His place is supplied by Gen. P. H. Sheridan.[64] Until Gen. Sheridan reaches here, Brig. Gen. D. M. Gregg[65] will be in command.

*Friday, March 25, 1864*

Today is dull & cloudy.

Gen. Terry's brigade[66] of troops from Sandusky City O[H] is ordered to the Army of the Potomac, also Gen. Wheaton's Brigade[67] from Harper's Ferry. 3,000 men will be sent from the works around Washington.

*Saturday, March 26, 1864*

Weather dull and cloudy. Lines all working well. Palmer reached a point within a mile or two of Leonardstown, Md. He will get to Pt. Lookout by April 1st.

Major Eckert returns today from N.Y. Hon. Owen Lovejoy[68] is seriously ill. He is not expected to live.

U.S. Military Telegraph Construction Corps, April 1864

*(From Century Magazine, 38, 1889, p. 790)*

*Sunday, March 27, 1864*

Weather is clear & pleasant today.

The rebels under Forrest[69] about 6,000 strong attacked Paducah Ky. on Friday at 3 p.m. They fought till 10 p.m. We were assisted by two gunboats & made a desperate resistance. The rebels sent in two flags of truce demanding a surrender, saying that, if refused, they would give no quarter. They were both refused & our forces manfully held out. Rebels left at midnight of 25th. Our loss not very heavy. The enemy captured 500 of our men at Union City [TN].[70] Genl. Sherman is attending to [forcing] Forrest's return.

*Monday, March 28, 1864*

Weather pleasant. Lines all working well.

*Tuesday, March 29, 1864*

Blustery & chill today. Rain falling some. Lines blown together some.

*Wednesday, March 30, 1864*

Last night it rained very hard & blew a great streak. Gen. Grant will reach here from the Army of the Potomac today, on his way to Norfolk to inspect the works, etc.

*Thursday, March 31, 1864*

Nothing new today. Weather pleasant.

## Notes

[1] Union General Hugh Judson Kilpatrick, Commander of the 3rd Division, Cavalry Corps, Army of the Potomac.

[2] Union Major General George Stoneman was sent West to assume command of the Department of the Ohio to replace General John G. Foster, who had sustained an injury when his horse fell on him. Foster had been Commander, Department of the Ohio, since December of 1863.

[3] Mrs. Danenhower was the proprietress of the Washington boarding house where both Bates and Chandler boarded.

[4] Varioloid is the name given to an attack of smallpox after a person has received a vaccination.

[5] No. 2 was the position within the War Department Telegraph Office where the cipher books were created for use by the telegraph operators in the Union Army. The cipher routes and code words listed in the books were used to protect the security of the telegraphic messages between senior Union officers

and government officials. (Bates, David Homer, *Century Magazine*, Volume 74, Pp. 290-306.)

[6]Confederate General Early's raid into Maryland.

[7]The Union gunboat *Underwriter* was captured by the Confederates in the Neuse River on February 2, 1864. Union counterattacks made it necessary for the Confederates to deliberately set fire to the ship and escape. The Confederate movements against New Berne were an effort to recapture the town lost to the Union in March 1862.

[8]Union Brigadier General Innis N. Palmer, Commander, District of North Carolina, Department of Virginia and North Carolina.

[9]Union Brigadier General Eliakim P. Scammon, Commander, Department of West Virginia, was captured on February 3, 1863, and exchanged on August 3, 1863.

[10]The *Vibbard* was a locomotive engine.

[11]William Wallace (Willie) Lincoln was the third son of President and Mrs. Lincoln. He died in February of 1862 at the age of 11.

[12]A relay sounder was a device to convert electrical code impulses into sounds. Its main purpose was to amplify the sounds prior to being automatically relayed along the telegraphic lines.

[13]The People's Line Telegraph Company had offices in Washington, DC.

[14]"AX2" was the designation for a specific telegraphic line. The two letter digraph normally designated the other terminal, and in this case it probably stood for Alexandria, Virginia.

[15]"4" was the designation for the backup line substituted for the nonworking AX2 line. Commercial circuits did not normally carry the terminal digraph.

[16]The Libby Prison escape was via a tunnel engineered by Union Colonel Thomas E. Rose, a professional engineer.

[17]Union Colonel Abel D. Streight, Commander, Provisional Brigade, 14th Corps, Army of the Cumberland, had surrendered to CSA General Forrest on May 31, 1863, and was held in Libby Prison until his escape. He was not exchanged in retaliation for the Union imprisonment of General John Morgan. Colonel Streight resumed his old command after his escape.

[18]The Libby Prison breakout had actually occurred on February 9th. Bates had just learned of it on the 16th.

[19]Union Major General Quincy A. Gillmore, Commander of the Department of the South and the 10th Corps, Department of the South.

[20]Referring to the occupation of Jacksonville, Florida, the occupation of Gainesville, Florida, and the Battle of Olustee. At the Battle of Olustee on February 20, 1864, the Union troops broke at the opening of the battle, thereby allowing the Confederates to pursue the retreating troops. The Florida expedition was not the total success stated by General Gillmore.

[21]The Union's Meridian, Mississippi, campaign was from February 3-March 4, 1864.

[22]Probably a member of the Gonsalves family where Bates boarded.

[23]Civilian hospital located at 23rd and S Streets, Northwest, Washington, DC.

[24]Professor Dean is not further identified.

[25]Gauley Bridge is located southwest of Charleston, West Virginia, over the Gauley River.

[26]Killingsworth is not further identified.

[27]Giesboro Point located in the Southeast area of Washington, DC. It was the location of Camp Stoneman, a major Union Cavalry depot.

[28]*Coup-de-main* can be translated as "surprise attack."

[29]Buzzard Roost is located near the Okmulgee River in Georgia.

[30]Dalton, Georgia, was located at the juncture of the Western and Atlantic Railroad and the Tennessee and Georgia Railroad.

[31]Cherrystone, Virginia, was located at the mouth of the Planktank River and the junction of the Chesapeake Bay.

[32]Union Brigadier General George A. Custer, Brigade Commander, 3rd Cavalry Division, Army of the Potomac. Refers to Custer's raid into Albemarle County, Virginia, February 28-March 1, 1864.

[33]Union Major General John M. Schofield, Commander, Department of the Ohio.

[34]Morristown, Tennessee, was located on the East Tennessee and Virginia Railroad.

[35]Ringgold, Georgia, was located on the Western and Atlantic Railroad.

[36]Confederate General Leonidas Polk, Commander, Department of Alabama, Mississippi, and East Louisiana.

[37]Demopolis, Alabama, was located on the Alabama and Mississippi Railroad.

[38]Initially in July 1861, Congress voted $100 for three-year enlistments. The Enrollment Act of March 1863 established further financial payments to those entering the Army. The bounties ranged from $100 for conscripts and substitutes to $400 for a five-year enlistment. In February of 1864, the Amendatory Act extended the 1863 Act and provided additional bounty in order to meet the manpower requirements. (Geary, James W., *We Need Men*, Pp. 68-69.)

[39]This legislation re-established the military rank of Lieutenant General, a rank that had not been held by any U.S. Army Officer since George Washington held the rank in brevet.

[40]Union Colonel Ulric Dahlgren, the son of Union Rear Admiral John A. Dahlgren, had volunteered for the Kilpatrick raid.

[41]USMTC telegraph operator, William A. Dunn.

[42]USMTC telegraph operator, George D. Sheldon.

[43]Colonel Dahlgren was killed during the Kilpatrick raid. The Confederates found letters on his body that talked of burning Richmond and killing President Davis and his Cabinet. The discovery caused major indignation on the part of the CSA Government.

[44]Ulysses S. Grant received the rank of Lieutenant General in the Union Army and was assigned as the General-in-Chief of the entire Union Army.

His condition on accepting the General-in-Chief position was that he would locate with the Army of the Potomac and not remain in Washington, DC. General Order 98, dated March 12, 1864, Adjutant General's Office, Washington, DC, assigned Lieutenant General Grant to command the Union Armies. (*The War of the Rebellion: A Compilation of the Official Records of the Union and Confederate Armies,* Series 1, Volume 32, Part III, p. 58.)

[45]William H. Seward, Union Secretary of State.

[46]The Constitution State Convention of Virginia consisted of members from the areas of Virginia held by Union forces.

[47]The railroads damaged in the raid were the Mobile and Ohio Railroad and the New Orleans and Jackson Railroad.

[48]Union Major General Nathaniel P. Banks, Commander, Department of the Gulf, was in charge of the Red River Campaign in Louisiana, March 10-May 19, 1864.

[49]The USMTC consisted of two major divisions: (a) the telegraph operators, and (b) the construction crews who strung the wire for the military units as they moved. They normally strung wire from the units to a commercial line. The USMTC roster listed Solomen Palmer as the foreman of the builders and repairmen for the lines.

[50]Number 10 wire was the gauge of the "open" or non-insulated wire, used by local telegraph companies when stringing new lines.

[51]Alexandria, Virginia, located on the Potomac River, was one of the major railroad junctions for the movement of troops and matériel south.

[52]Point Lookout, Maryland, located at the mouth of the Potomac River and the Chesapeake Bay, was the site of a major Union prisoner of war camp.

[53]Port Tobacco, Maryland, was located on the Maryland side of the Potomac River.

[54]USMTC telegraph operator, Charles O. Connor.

[55]USMTC telegraph operator, J. H. Emerick.

[56]Union Major General Winfield S. Hancock, Commander, 2nd Corps, Army of the Potomac.

[57]Union Brigadier General Gouverneur K. Warren, Commander, 5th Corps, Army of the Potomac.

[58]Union Major General George Sykes was relieved as 5th Corps Commander, Army of the Potomac, and reassigned to the Department of Kansas.

[59]Union Major General Samuel R. Curtis, Commander, Department of Kansas.

[60]Union Major General William H. French, Commander of the 3rd Corps (de-activated in the reorganization), was considered a failure at the Battle of Mine Run and mustered out in May 1865.

[61]Union Major General John Newton, Commander, 1st Corps, (dissolved in the reorganization), was eventually sent west to General Sherman's Army.

[62]Union Major General Alfred Pleasonton, Commander of the Cavalry Corps, Army of the Potomac, was transferred to the Department of the Missouri.

[63]Union Major General William S. Rosecrans, Commander, Department of the Missouri.

[64]Union Major General Philip Henry Sheridan was transferred from Commander, 3rd Division of 20th Corps to that of Commander of the Cavalry of the Army of the Potomac, replacing General Pleasonton.

[65]Union Brigadier General David M. Gregg, Commander, 2nd Division, Cavalry Corps, Army of the Potomac.

[66]Union Brigadier General Henry D. Terry, Commander of the Union prison on Johnson's Island, Ohio.

[67]Union Brigadier General Frank Wheaton, Commander, 1st Brigade, 2nd Division, 6th Corps, Army of the Potomac.

[68]Owen Lovejoy was a member of the House of Representatives from Illinois, first elected in 1856. An early abolitionist he was given the honor of introducing the bill that abolished slavery in the territories.

[69]Confederate Major General Nathan B. Forrest, Commander, Cavalry Corps, Department of Mississippi and East Louisiana. After the Civil War he became a leader of the Ku Klux Klan.

[70]Confederate troops under General Forrest captured Union City, Tennessee, on March 24, 1864.

# April, May, June 1864

For the Union the spring months of 1864 were months of high hopes—it now had an aggressive General-in-Chief who was busy preparing his Grand Strategy for the winning of the war. Soon the Union armies would be on the move, and the Confederate armies would be crushed.

In developing his Grand Strategy, General Grant was well aware of the key role that would be played by the telegraph. It would provide him with a capability previously not known to a field commander; he could direct his armies at great distances from a central location. The telegraph operators understood Grant's reliance on them for this critical function, and they performed their roles with efficiency and devotion.

From entries in the Bates diary, it is apparent that the work load of the telegraph operators had increased. We find frequent entries of "too busy to attend class tonight" as well as "too busy to attend Church today." From the almost daily entries cited from each commander, it was clear that the strategic value of the telegraph for planning military operations as well as the reporting of outcomes had become firmly established. As the armies became more and more accustomed to the telegraph, its usage spread to lower and lower levels. For example on the 28th of April, Bates stated that "two operators are assigned to each Corps and will go with the Corps Hdqrs."

The telegraphic reports from Grant with the Army of the Potomac and Sherman in the West were generally written in the early evening after the events of the day. They were regularly received in Washington within 24 hours although on occasion receipt was delayed to 48 hours. When the activity level of an army increased, the reporting tended to be delayed. For example Grant's first report on the Battle of the Wilderness was not sent until 48 hours after the initiation of the battle. Communications from more remote military operations took a great deal more time to reach Washington; *e.g.*, Arkansas— seven days, Red River—five days, and New Orleans—six days. Unlike Grant and Sherman the generals in these areas had no direct route for telegraphic communications.

Tactically, the telegraph was now fully employed in lateral communications. As an example, on one day in 1864 General Grant telegraphed Sherman in Georgia as well as telegraphing Generals George Crook[1] in West Virginia, Franz Sigel[2] in the Shenandoah Valley and Benjamin Butler on the James River. As an indication of the efficiency of the telegraph system, General Grant had responses from all of these generals the same day.

The Army of the Potomac was constantly on the move during this period, and Bates's comments described both the reporting and the extensions of the telegraph lines to keep pace with the Headquarters as the army moved. Army movements which led to the Battle of the Wilderness were not simultaneous with the extension of the telegraph line. Bates stated that the initial report of the Battle of the Wilderness provided to Washington came from a *New York Tribune* correspondent on the 7th of May—two days after the commencement of the battle. The lack of telegraphic communications was soon corrected, and on the 3rd of June Bates reported that the line was complete to the Headquarters of the Army of the Potomac, approximately 10-15 miles behind the Army. It is also during this period that the Beardslee[3] telegraph equipments, belonging to Colonel Albert J. Myer, Chief Signal Corps Officer, were removed from the Army of the Potomac, leaving the USMTC as the sole telegraphic organization for the United States Army. Colonel Myer's signal troops now became the sole provider of the wigwag system for tactical communications.[4]

As the Union troops moved deeper and deeper into Confederate territory, diary entries began to report military movements gleaned from Richmond newspapers. This practice became more common, particularly as Sherman's Army moved away from Union telegraph lines.

On the political front, the abolition of slavery was the predominate issue, with actions occurring on both the state and national levels. In April Louisiana adopted a new constitution that abolished slavery in the state. On the 8th of April the U.S. Senate approved the 13th Amendment to the Constitution, abolishing slavery. It was more than a year later before the House of Representatives approved the amendment and sent it to the states for ratification.

The month of May opened with the House of Representatives passing the Wade-Davis Reconstruction Bill.[5] Lincoln felt the bill was too punitive in nature and later pocket-vetoed it.

During this same period political activities began that pertained to the upcoming presidential election. There was wide speculation and debate as to who would be running and even greater speculation about a possible candidate on the Republican ticket to replace Lincoln. A dissident group of Radical Republicans met in Cleveland, Ohio, on the

31st of May and nominated General John C. Frémont[6] for president. Frémont immediately resigned his commission to begin his political career. The following week, on the 7th of June, the National Union Convention, composed of most Republicans and some War Democrats, held their convention in Baltimore and the next day nominated Abraham Lincoln as their candidate for a second term as president. Andrew Johnson, the military governor of Tennessee, was nominated as his vice-presidential candidate. To close the political events of the period, Secretary of the Treasury Salmon P. Chase tendered his resignation again, and this time the President accepted it.

The military strategies of the Union and the Confederacy by the spring of 1864 had settled into two very different modes. The Confederacy realized that its forces were no longer strong enough to carry the war into the North, and came to rely on a war of attrition, hoping to wear the Union down (as the Americans had done to the British in the Revolutionary War). The Union military on the other hand carried the war into the Confederacy with the destruction of the Confederate armies as its goal—especially Lee's Army of Northern Virginia.

Early military events in April of 1864 centered on the Red River Campaign in Louisiana with battles at Mansfield on the 8th and Pleasant Hill on the 9th. Attention shifted to Tennessee on the 12th with the massacre of Union soldiers, predominately black troops, after their surrender at Fort Pillow, Tennessee, by troops of General Nathan Bedford Forrest. On the 17th of April General Grant turned down a Confederate offer to exchange prisoners of war—he knew he was harming the Union prisoners in the Confederacy but did not want to alleviate the severe manpower shortage in the South. In North Carolina the Battle of Plymouth took place from the 17th to the 20th of April.

The three prongs of Grant's Grand Strategy[7] commenced in early May with the Army of the Potomac, under General Meade, crossing the Rapidan River in Virginia on the 5th; the opening of the Atlanta Campaign by General Sherman on the 7th; and the initiation of cavalry raids in Virginia by General Sheridan on the 9th of May. All these movements were simultaneously controlled through the telegraph by General Grant who was with the Army of the Potomac.

For the Army of the Potomac, battle came quickly and intensely in Virginia with the Battle of the Wilderness on the 5th and 6th; the Battle of Spotsylvania on the 8th; the Battle of the North Anna River from the 23rd to the 26th of May; the Battle of Cold Harbor on the 1st of June; and finally, the Battle of Petersburg from the 15th to the 18th of June. The latter led to the siege of Petersburg, which lasted until the 2nd of April 1865. General Grant's strategy was to remain on the offensive.

Sherman's well-supplied troops left Chattanooga, Tennessee, on the 7th of May and met initial opposition on the 9th of May at Dalton, Georgia. This was followed by the Battles at Resaca, Georgia, on the 14th; New Hope Church, Georgia, from the 25th of May to the 4th of June; Brice's Cross Roads, Mississippi, on the 10th of June; skirmishing near Pine Mountain, Georgia, on the 14th of June; and the Battle of Kennesaw Mountain, Georgia, on the 27th of June. Sherman soon set a pattern of outflanking General Joseph Johnston's[8] troops and forcing his retreat on the other flank.

The third prong, that of General Sheridan, the newly appointed Head of Cavalry for the Army of the Potomac, went into action on the 9th and 10th of May in skirmishes near Beaver Dam Station in Virginia, followed by battles at Yellow Tavern, Virginia, on the 11th of May and at Trevilian Station, Virginia, on the 11th and 12th of June. By the end of June Sheridan was back with the Army of the Potomac at Petersburg, Virginia.

Simultaneously with the above actions, two additional Union military initiatives were undertaken. First, Benjamin Butler led a small Union army up the James River towards the southern approaches to Richmond. This advance was stopped on the 16th of May at the Battle of Drewry's Bluff, Virginia. And second, General Sigel led an Army into the Shenandoah Valley. Sigel's army suffered a defeat at the battle of New Market, Virginia, on the 15th of May, and he was replaced by General David Hunter.[9] The two forces met again at Piedmont, Virginia, on the 5th of June resulting in a Union victory. However later in the month, Hunter decided to retreat from the Valley due to the arrival of Confederate reinforcements.

Meanwhile the Red River campaign under General Banks had faltered, and his forces continued to retreat. By the 22nd of May the last of the Union troops successfully crossed the Atchafalaya River and escaped from General Richard Taylor's Confederate forces.[10] The month of June closed with Confederate General Jubal Early making his initial moves through the Shenandoah Valley in preparation for a planned raid on the Union capital.          *Donald E. Markle*

*Friday, April 1, 1864*

This morning opened very fine. The sun shone beautifully, but soon it was raining & has continued to do so ever since.

*Sunday, April 3, 1864*

The Govt took possession today of a wire between here and Louisville & we will in future send all our business direct to Pittsburgh or Cincinnati. Gen. Grant returned from Ft. Monroe today.

*Monday, April 4, 1864*

Raining again today. Lines working pretty well.

*Tuesday, April 5, 1864*

Rained all day.

*Wednesday, April 6, 1864*

Weather has changed for the better. Sun shines very clear & pleasant. Our new arrangement of working direct to Pittsburgh begins this morning. It is splendid. Our business goes off very rapidly & well & answers are recd perfectly.

*Thursday, April 7, 1864*

Geo. Low[11] took an instrument & went with repairs on line to Pt. Lookout this a.m. which is not working.
Very busy tonight. Did not go to class.

*Friday, April 8, 1864*

Murray[12] came in circuit at Leonardstown, Md. He is on his way to Washn. Gen. Burnside[13] went to Annapolis tonight. Weather pleasant.

*Saturday, April 9, 1864*

It has rained most of today again.

*Wednesday, April 13, 1864*

Mr. A. A. Lovett, Supt. of the People's Telegraph, died this evening very suddenly while standing in New York Office.

*Thursday, April 14, 1864*

Went to class this evening & then came back to office & have been kept busy ever since. Gold was up to [$]189 today.

*Friday, April 15, 1864*

Ft. Pillow on the Mississippi was attacked & captured by the rebels yesterday.[14] 50 white & 300 colored soldiers were killed. They also came to Columbus [KY][15] & demanded surrender of the place but it was refused and the rebels left after being repulsed once or twice. They also returned from Ft. Pillow toward Memphis. Gen. Burnside was here today. He is making big preparations. He will go up the James or York Rivers & cooperate with Meade.

*Saturday, April 16, 1864*

Raining all day. [Telegraph] line ordered to be extended to Winchester [VA] & towards Staunton [VA] by Gen. Sigel but Secy. of War has not yet approved it.

*Sunday, April 17, 1864*

Weather very changeable today. The afternoon however was pleasant. Was busy at the Office & could not get to Church. Took dinner at Maj. Eckert's. Mrs. William Chandler[16] is there on a visit.

I purchased from Col. Stager on the 14th two shares of Western Union Telegraph Stock at $200 per share. I paid half down & will pay the balance in 6 months with 7 per cent interest. It is valuable stock.

The Atlantic & Ohio Telegraph lines between Philad. & Pittsbg were consolidated on Friday with the W. U. [Western Union]. This will be a new source of revenue to that Company.

A report has just reached Ft. Monroe by flag of truce boat that a great battle has been fought near Shreveport [LA] by Kirby Smith[17] & Banks in which the latter is defeated with loss of 14,000 killed, wounded & captured. The hospitals at Baton Rouge [LA] & other points were being filled with the Federal wounded. This report is no doubt very much exaggerated.[18]

*Monday, April 18, 1864*

Nothing new today. Very busy in the office. Line to Pt. Lookout today began working. Operator having just reached there.

*Tuesday, April 19, 1864*

Sec. Chase[19] has been in N.Y. for last few days. His presence there has pushed gold down. It is [$]169 today.

*Wednesday, April 20, 1864*

Great preparations are being made for a vigorous campaign the latter part of the month. Operations will begin on or about the 24th of April.

*Thursday, April 21, 1864*

Too busy to attend class tonight. Despatches from Newberne, N.C. indicate that on the 19th the rebels attacked Plymouth, N.C. by land & with a ram by water. The *USS Miami* was disabled & Lt. Comdr. Flusser killed. Rebels have possession of the river & it is apprehended that Newberne will be attacked. There is great consternation. The gunboat *Southfield* was sunk by the ram.[20]
Gen. Burnside moves from Annapolis Saturday morning.

*Friday, April 22, 1864*

We have despatches from Texas. Genl. Banks loss was 4,000 men, 16 guns & 200 wagons. His army is much demoralized. His expedition to Mobile will thus be delayed or prevented altogether.[21]

*Saturday, April 23, 1864*

Gen. Burnside arrived here today. His troops will pass through the City tonight & tomorrow en route from Annapolis to Alexandria where they will embark on Monday for some point on the York River & strike the enemy's lines.

*Sunday, April 24, 1864*

Brevet Maj. Gen. J. C. Totten[22] died Saturday. He had been nominated by the Prest. for Bvt. Maj. Gen. & the Senate had just confirmed him, but before they could get word to him he was dead. He was Chief Engineer, USA.
We have news from Gen. Banks that he will be ready to move against Shreveport in concert with Gen. Steele[23] by 28th inst.

*Monday, April 25, 1864*

Gen. Burnside's troops passed through today from Annapolis, which place they left Saturday. They are mostly in Alexandria now where they will be organized tomorrow & leave Wednesday.

*Tuesday, April 26, 1864*

Gen. Meade today ordered the Signal Instruments[24] in the Department of the Potomac sent to the rear when they move. They have been a great expense to the Govt & I am heartily glad they will no longer burden us.[25]

*Wednesday, April 27, 1864*

Gen. Burnside's troops left Alexandria today & will march to Fairfax Station tonight & Manassas on tomorrow.

Gen. Sherman will collect all his troops ready to make a grand advance from Chattanooga by May 5th. Gen. Meade's troops will all be relieved by Gen. Burnside's tomorrow or next day.

*Thursday, April 28, 1864*

Military matters are fast coming to a point. Two operators are assigned to each Corps & will go with the Corps Hdqrs. Our new battery wagon works well & will be of great service to us.[26]

*Friday, April 29, 1864*

Gen. Burnside reached Catlett[27] today. He will be in his position by Sunday & the Army of the Potomac will in all probability move on Monday morning. Sherman will be ready to move on 5th prox.

Gen. Grant has telegraphed to Genl. Halleck[28] asking him if he can take command of the Mississippi Dept in person until someone can be assigned to it. He says he fully appreciates the importance of Gen. Halleck being in Wash, but it is more important to have a Commdr for the Trans Miss. Dept. Of the Genls. now there Steele is the best but there is none to take his place in Ark. & he could not be spared.

*Saturday, April 30, 1864*

The weather has changed. It is quite cool now & rains some. Genl. Burnside visited Gen. Grant at Culpeper [VA] today.

*Sunday, May 1, 1864*

We were very busy at the Office today. I did not get to Church at all.

*Monday, May 2, 1864*

Worked hard to get MacIntosh[29] & party off to Ft. Monroe but they failed to make the Train & so had to wait till Tuesday.

*Tuesday, May 3, 1864*

Gen. Grant telegraphs today that the Army of the Potomac will move tonight & will have possession of Germania [Germanna], Ely's

A Telegraph Battery Wagon near Petersburg, June 1864

*(From Century Magazine, 38, 1889, p. 791)*

& Culpeper fords [VA] by daylight. Butler,[30] Sigel & Sherman all move at the same time. God prosper them & give success to our cause. I think we will win this time.

### Wednesday, May 4, 1864

The Army of the Potomac moved last night across the Rapidan & are now moving on the enemy. They crossed at Ely's, Germania & Culpeper Fords. All of Gen. Burnside's troops are moving in the direction of Germania Ford where they will be by tomorrow.

### Thursday, May 5, 1864

Brandy Station [VA] & all stations between there & Devereux [VA] were evacuated last night & the operators came into Alexandria. One train went as far out as Rappahannock Stn & returned.

Gen. Sherman arrived at Ringgold, Ga. today. His lines were advanced 3 miles today. He will attack Tunnel Hill [GA] on Saturday & in meantime will occupy Johnston's whole attention.

We have no communications with the Army of the Potomac. Nothing yet heard from Gen. Grant. We don't know where he will come out.

### Friday, May 6, 1864

A telegram has been received from Gen. Steele dated Apl 28th in which he states that a train of 200 wagons with an escort of 1,600 Infy, 500 Cavy & 6 pieces of artillery were attacked on the 25th while a few miles out from Camden [AR] on the Washn road & after a desperate fight of three hours were captured with the exception of about 4,300 of the men who came in to Little Rock & Pine Bluff.[31]

Telegram just been recd from Gen. Butler dated City Point 1:30 a.m. May 6th stating that the Army made a successful landing at that place the evening before. There was no opposition seemingly a surprise. They found the *New York* flag of truce boat at the Wharf. She had not had time to deliver the prisoners. There were 400 rebels on board.

Genl. Kautz[32] with 3,000 Cavy left Suffolk this morning on special service. Nothing yet heard of Gen. Grant.

### Saturday, May 7, 1864

Special Correspondent of the *NY Tribune* reached Union Mills last night, having left the Army 5 a.m. yesterday. He reports that on Wednesday our forces fought the rebels in the "Wilderness" near Chancellorsville.[33] Warren's & Hancock's Corps principally engaged & that on Thursday morning the fight was renewed with no decisive results. Lee has a large army. Genl. Burnside with 30,000 fresh troops reached the scene of action yesterday & as the Correspondent left they were preparing for another day's conflict. Our heavy reinforcements will be very much in our favor. Asst. Sec. Dana went out with special train to Rappahannock Stn this morning with despatches for Gen. Grant. An operator went with [him] & has office open at Rappahannock Bridge now. We are anxiously awaiting additional news from the army.

### Sunday, May 8, 1864

A telegram from Gen. Ingalls[34] this morning via Rappahannock Station indicates that Lee is retreating, after three days fighting. About 10,000 wounded are being sent in by wagon train. Cars are on the way to Rappahannock to meet them. A large quantity of forage & supplies are also being forwarded to the Army. We have heard of the death of two General officers, Alex Hays of Pittsburgh & Jos.[James] S. Wadsworth of N.Y., Gen. Webb & one or two other Genls. wounded. Genl. Longstreet of the rebel Army was severely wounded on Thursday. Gen. Jones and Jenkins killed. Gen. Stafford severely wounded.[35] May recover. Genl. Butler is entrenching himself in his position in case of any incident to the Potomac Army.

### Monday, May 9, 1864

Sherman was to have attacked Johnston today at Dalton [GA]. McPherson[36] was at Villanow [GA] Saturday & would strike Resaca [GA] on the Railroad today. We expect to hear from him in the morning. A bearer of despatches from Gen. Grant reached us today. The telegrams left the HdQrs at Piney Branch Church at noon 8th. Lee has fallen back, defeated. Seven days rations were being opened to our men & an advance takes place immedy.

The wounded were being sent to Fredksburg. Gen. Grant would endeavor to form a junction with Butler.

### Tuesday, May 10, 1864

Genl. Butler telegraphs today under date of yesterday, that he sums up his operation as follows—a brigade of colored Infty came from direction of Williamsburg [VA], forced the Chickahominy [River] & came safely into his lines & are now the advanced pickets towards Richmond. Genl. Kautz left Suffolk [VA] the same day that Butler's movement took place & struck the railroad at Stony Creek [VA] & is now operating against Ricksford [VA] & Weldon [VA]. Beauregard's[37] forces were separated & by this act, the part which had arrived at

Field Telegraph Station

*(Courtesy of the Massachusetts Commandery Military Order of the Loyal Legion and the U.S. Army Military History Institute, Carlisle, Pennsylvania)*

Petersburg under Hill[38] were whipped on Sunday by Gen. Butler & some prisoners taken. No reinforcements from Beauregard are likely to reach Lee.

A despatch from Genl. Grant dated one p.m. 9th says that Lee is massing on his left with the intention of cutting our forces off from Fredericksburg, or of getting the inside track to Richmond. No attack would be made yesterday, but five days rations would be issued to the men & an advance take place today. Hd Qrs were 4 miles north of Spotsylvania C.H.[39]

Gen. J. Hobart Ward[40] is under arrest for deserting his command in the "Wilderness." All seems to be going well.

From Sherman we have a telegram dated 9 p.m. on the 9th. He had been fighting all day against precipices & mountain ranges to keep Johnston's attention from McPherson who was to be at Resaca before that time.[41]

From Newberne we have news the rebel ram *Albemarle* is captured after fighting seven of our gunboats.

Surely all this is good news.

*Wednesday, May 11, 1864*

Nothing of importance from the armies today. There was some fighting in the Army of the Potomac yesterday with what result is not known. Gen. McPherson reached Resaca but found it too strongly guarded & fortified to attempt its capture. He accordingly withdrew without breaking the railroads. Sherman will wait till he is in supporting distance & will attack Johnston.

*Thursday, May 12, 1864*

Gen. Grant sends a copy of a communication from Gen. Sheridan dated May 10. He was south of the South Anna River. He had destroyed ten miles of the Orange Railroad line. His presence has created great consternation among the citizens & every one said that Lee was beaten badly. Sheridan had recaptured 500 of our men.[42] Amongst them two colonels.

It has rained very heavily here today.

*Friday, May 13, 1864*

Gen. Grant sends a communication dated Spotsylvania C.H. 6 p.m. 12th in which he states that they have had another hard day's fight. The rebels fought desperately but were pushed so by Genl. Hancock that they had to fall back from some of their breast works.[43] The result of the day's operations is the capture of one entire Div (Edward

Johnson's) & part of Genl. Early's.[44] Major Gen. Johnson & Brig. Gen. Steuart are among the prisoners.[45] We took some 30 or 40 cannon. 6 p.m., a telegram recd via Belle Plain dated 8 a.m. from Asst. Secy. Dana says that Lee abandoned his works during the night & retreated, whether to assume a new position or to retreat to Richmond could not be determined. A division of Wright's[46] & one of Hancock's Corps are in pursuit & will soon ascertain. At 7:45 they had come upon the enemy's rearguard.

Genl. Butler is still pushing his forces toward Richmond & Petersburg & Genl. Kautz has gone to the Danville road [RR] & will evidently sever the connection between the rebel capital & the Southwest.

The rain has been very steady today. It will be good for the poor soldiers.

*Saturday, May 14, 1864*

Gen. Sherman telegraphs this p.m. that his flank movement on Resaca compelled Johnston to evacuate Dalton [GA]. Sherman's message dated today near Resaca. He is pushing forward as rapidly as possible.[47]

Our despatches from Gen. Grant are up to 7 p.m. yesterday. Lee had fallen back about 4 miles only & had taken up a new position. 7,000 rebel prisoners & 400 officers reached Belle Plain [VA] last night. They were sent to Pt. Lookout & Ft. Delaware[48] & other points north.

Gen. Grant asks that Gen. Butler be telegraphed to cut the Richmond & Danville RR if possible.

*Sunday, May 15, 1864*

Gen. Sheridan telegraphed last night from Bottom's Bridge [VA] that he reached there during the day. On the 9th inst. he left the Army of the Potomac & marched from our right to the rear of the enemy & reached the North Anna [River] that night without opposition. During the night he destroyed the Depot of supplies at Beaver Dam [VA] containing a million & a half of rations, 100 cars, and 3 fire engines. He destroyed the railroad[49] for ten miles including several culverts. On the tenth he resumed his march crossing at Grand Squirrel [River] Bridge [VA]. On the 10th he captured Ashland Station [VA] capturing & destroying a train of cars & eng. & several Govt buildings with a large amt. of supplies, also 6 culverts & about 6 miles of railroad. About 7 a.m. of the 11th he resumed his march towards Richmond & encountered J. E. B. Stuart[50] concentrated at Yellow Tavern [VA]. He attacked him & after an obstinate contest gained possession of the

Brook turnpike, took 2 pieces artly & drove his force back towards
Ashland & across the North Fork of the Chickahominy, a distance of
4 miles. At the same time a party charged down the Brook road &
captured the first line of works around Richmond. He demonstrated
on the second line of works but finding them too strong he determined
to recross the Chickahominy at Meadow Bridge. This bridge had been
partially destroyed by the rebels, but was rebuilt in about 3 hours,
under heavy fire from the enemy. He then returned to Bottom's Bridge
which place he reached in safety. His whole loss does not amt to more
than 350 men & 100 horses.

Genl. Butler telegraphs that his forces are around Ft. Darling [VA]
& that Smith[51] made a flank movement (on the 12th) on the enemy's
right & took his first line. Gen. Gillmore made a movement on the
morning of 13th, which resulted in the capturing of the first line of the
enemy's work on the right. Its speedy downfall is inevitable. Our
advices from the Army of the Potomac are up to 6:30 a.m.[on the] 14th.
The 5th & 6th Corps had moved to our left & were to attack Lee
yesterday morning, but as no sound of battle has been heard it was
judged that Lee had retreated during the night. He will be compelled
to go towards Lynchburg [VA] as all other avenues are closed. The
rebellion is fast falling to pieces. They have little left to hope for.

P.M. Gen. Sherman telegraphs from near Resaca under date of 8
p.m. May 14th, they had been fighting hard all day. Johnston partly
on the defensive. Resaca has several detached redoubts and an immense amount of rifle trenches. His forces have closed [with] the
enemy well in gaining ground slowly but surely all day. Howard's
Corps[52] followed the enemy down from Dalton & his right was then
joined to the main line & the forces were all united, the line extending
from the Oostanaula [River] above, to below the town. Stoneman's
Cavalry is on the east of the river & Garrard's[53] is sent around by the
right to cross the Oostanaula above Rome [GA] if possible & break the
railroad north of Kingston [GA]. Sherman would attack again today.

### Monday, May 16, 1864

Office at Mid Point opened today, will open at Belle Plain tonight
and Fdrckbg on Wednesday.[54]

Gen. Sherman telegraphs that Resaca was evacuated by Johnston
at midnight & is now occupied by our forces. The RR[55] will be O.K. to
that point today. He will pursue Johnston farther South.

Genl. Grant telegraphs that it has rained incessantly for five days
& the mud is very deep, so bad indeed that ambulances with wounded
can no longer run between Fredksburg & the Army. He assures the

Prest. & Sec. War that it is the rain only that keeps him inactive & not any weakness on his part. All offensive movements are impossible at this time. Gen. Sheridan is at Turkey Bend [VA] on the James River. Butler is still besieging Ft. Darling.[56]

### Tuesday, May 17, 1864

Gen. Sherman telegraphs from Resaca under date of this morning that his forces were closing well up & would be at Adamsville [TN] today. 8 guns & over 2,000 prisoners have been taken altogether. Johnston's troops are much disheartened & if they will not fight behind works of such strength as those at Resaca it is probable they will not fight at all. Sherman expects to be at Kingston [GA], on the railroad tomorrow.

We have despatches from Gen. Sigel up to May 16. He fought a severe battle on the 15th at New Market [VA] with the forces of Echols & Imboden under Gen. Breckinridge.[57] Our force was about 6,000, that of the enemy 9,000. We lost 650 in killed, wounded & missing. Our forces withdrew to Strasburg [VA] & Cedar Creek bringing off all wagons etc. & most of the wounded.

Genl. Butler telegraphs that he learns from the Richmond papers that Genl. Kautz had been at Coalfield Stn [VA] & had reached Appomattox Station. His orders are after destroying the Canal & railroad[58] to proceed to Wicksford, N.C. & cut the railroad there thus imprisoning the rolling stock which had been massed there when he cut the road at Stony Creek.

To enable Gen. Kautz to get well started Gen. Butler had concentrated his forces around Drewry's Bluff & Ft. Darling, but now that Kautz has been heard from Butler will probably withdraw as heavy reinforcements were rec'd at Ft. Darling & he could hope of doing little there.

### Wednesday, May 18, 1864

Gen. Hancock & Wright attacked the enemy this morning in their works on the left of our centre.

They drove the rebels from their first and second line & for a time it was believed we had struck their lair & had succeeded in whipping them, but it was discovered that they had an interior line of works which were very strong & were protected by an impassable abatis.[59] Genl. Grant at last ordered the attack to cease. Our troops now occupy their old posts.

*Thursday, May 19, 1864*

We have news this morning from Genl. Grant up to 8 a.m. Nothing new had taken place except that the remaining portion of the Cavalry under Gen. Torbert[60] went to Guinney's Station [VA] yesterday, drove out the rebels, burned Railroad Depot & Post Office, destroyed a small railroad bridge & small quantity of supplies. Weather still good.

Genl. Butler telegraphs that Genl. Kautz had returned from his raid on the Danville railroad. He had torn up the track in several places for two or three miles, burned one or two bridges. He destroyed two trains of cars & one engine & station house, water tanks at Coalfield, Powhattan & Thala stations on the Danville road & at Wilson, Wellville & Black & White Station on the Lynchburg railroad, then crossing he struck the Petersburg & Weldon road at Garrett's Station, tore up track, burnt station, house etc. During his expedition he destroyed a great deal of Comsy [Commissary] & other supplies. Altogether it was a very successful raid.

Genl. Sheridan has started for the Army of the Potomac via New Kent C.H. Gen. Sherman telegraphs under date of 6:30 p.m. yesterday that the heads of his 4 columns had reached the front of Kingston [GA] & gone into Camp. Johnston had fallen back to his entrenchments at that place & it was thought possible that he might fight there. Some 300 deserters came into our lines & gave themselves up.

*Friday, May 20, 1864*

Gen. Sherman telegraphs this morning that Johnston evacuated Kingston & his troops were then occupying it. Davis's Divn of the 14th Corps were in Rome, Ga. Railroad trains will run to Kingston today & Sherman will replenish his stores & make for the Chattahoochee [River]. The rebels are concentrated at Allatoona [GA], where the railroad[61] passes through a range of hills. Gen. S. does not intend to go through them but will strike for Atlanta or some point on the Chattahoochee in its rear. They will fight hard for Atlanta, as it is one of their largest supply depots & being on the railroad to the East, is a great strategic point.

Genl. Grant had determined to make a flank movement this morning to gain possession of Bowling Green [VA] & Milford Stn but yesterday afternoon Ewell's Corps made an attack on our extreme right.[62] He was promptly & handsomely repulsed by Birney's[63] & Tyler's[64] Divisions & part of Warren's troops who were on the extreme right. Some 300 pris. fell into our hands besides killed & wounded. Our loss will foot up to about 600 wounded & 150 killed & missing, but Grant says this may be overstated. The flank movement was postponed until the plans of the rebels are more developed.

No news from Gen. Butler today.

Genl. Hunter[65] left here today to take command of the Dept of W. Va. and relieve Sigel.[66]

Last news from Gen. Canby[67] was dated Vicksburg. Everything was quiet. He would take command of the Army [of Western Mississippi] at Alexandria [LA].

Day before yesterday a bogus proclamation appeared in the *N.Y. World* & the *N. Y. Journal of Commerce*, purporting to be issued by the Prest. appointing the 26th as a day of national humiliation, fasting & prayer & calling out an additional force of 400,000 men. By twelve o'clock a telegram was sent by the Secy. of State pronouncing it a bad & treasonable forgery. It appears that it was palmed off upon those papers by some scoundrel. The balance of the N.Y. papers failed to be sold [on this story and] did not publish it. A great excitement was created. Those two papers were ordered to be closed & as it was supposed to have been sent by telegraph on the Independent line,[68] the offices of that Co. in N.Y., Phila, Balto, Wash, Hbg [Harrisburg] & Pittsburgh were taken military possession of & the operators & clerks were arrested. They were released however on parole.

*Saturday, May 21, 1864*

Gen. Dix[69] yesterday arrested Jos. Howard former reporter of the *NY Times* who is the author of the bogus proclamation. He is frank in his confession, saying it was a stock jobbing operation. He has been sent to Ft. Lafayette, & *The World* & *Journal of Commerce* have been put in possession of their establishments again.[70]

The Independent Telegraph has been released also. Their business is being looked over at our office.

Genl. Butler telegraphs that there was fighting in his front all day yesterday with advantage on our side. We captured some prisoners, amongst them Genl. Walker[71] of Texas Brigade.

Nothing new from Sherman. He is getting up supplies ready for a march to the Chattahoochee to strike rear of Atlanta. Nothing new from Gen. Grant today. He is watching & waiting for Lee's movements & will make his flank movement for Bowling Green [VA] if Lee is quiet in a day or so.

Gen. D. Hunter took command today of the Dept of [West] Va. Hd Qrs near Woodstock. He has directed Gen. Crook[72] & Gen. Averill[73] to move directly to Staunton [VA] where he would meet them.

*Sunday, May 22, 1864*

Gen. Grant's army commenced moving from its positions around Spotsylvania C.H. night before last, toward Bowling Green & Milford Stn [VA], on the line of the Mattapony [River]. This position was reached with safety & our base of supplies will in future be Port Royal [VA] instead of Belle Plain. Our line is being built to that place now.

Lee has fallen back from his entrenchments South of the Po [River] to confront us on the Mattapony.

*Monday, May 23, 1864*

Genl. Grant telegraphs under date of 6:30 a.m. today that Lee has fallen back to the South bank of the North Anna. Our army extends from a point near the junction of the Po & Ny rivers, to Milford Stn, on a line nearly parallel with the Mattapony. Genl. Hancock holding the left, Gen. Wright & Burnside the centre & Gen. Warren the left. [Warren was actually on the right.] There has been no fighting of any consequence for several days. Our line from Rifes Pt. [VA] to Port Royal [VA] will be finished by noon tomorrow. The Depot at Belle Plain is being transferred to Pt. Royal.

*Tuesday, May 24, 1864*

Gen. Sherman left Kingston, Ga. on the 22nd Inst., to strike the Enemy's lines near Atlanta. He has 20 days rations & it will be a week before we hear from him again.

Lee has fallen back from his position on the North Anna & Grant is pursuing. Hancock had some fighting yesterday & drove the enemy from their works on the North Anna near Taylor's Bridge & Jericho Bridge, a great many were drowned & some captured. It is not known whether Lee means to fall back to Richmond or only to the South Bank of the South Anna. Grant will soon find out about this however.[74]

*Wednesday, May 25, 1864*

Maj. Gen. Fitz Hugh [Fitzhugh] Lee made an attack on Ft. Powhattan [VA] yesterday which was handsomely repulsed. When he first appeared with his force he sent a flag of truce to Gen. Wild,[75] Commanding, demanding the surrender of the place, stating that he had a large force & if they surrendered they would be treated as prisoners, but if he were compelled to assault & capture the place he would not be answerable for the consequences. Genl. Wild replied "We will try that." The rebels attacked us for several hours. The fight was very severe, but they finally retired leaving twenty-eight killed & a great many wounded in our hands. All the troops defending the fort were Negroes & Genl. Butler speaks in the highest terms of them.

It rained quite hard this evening.

*Thursday, May 26, 1864*

Gen. Grant telegraphed from Jericho Bridge dated noon yesterday that Gen. Hancock had a spirited engagement with the enemy this side of the South Anna on the 24th & half of a brigade was captured by the enemy. Lee seems to have a strong position in the shape of a "V" and he is defending it desperately. Gen. Butler is ordered to send Genl. Smith with 20,000 men to the White House on the Pamunkey River [and] march from there to reinforce the Army of the Potomac. They will be there in a few days & will help us very much.

Genl. Canby telegraphs from mouth of Red River [LA] under date of 21st that the Army is all across on the Mississippi side & that he will go to Memphis [TN] & Little Rock [AR] to arrange his campaign. Genl. J. Smith[76] had a spirited fight with rebel Gen. Plinac's [Polignac's] division.[77] Smith defeated them & drove them several miles capturing 300 prisoners. Gen. Steele telegraphs from Little Rock dated 21st that rebel Gen. Shelby[78] has crossed Arkansas with about 3,000 men & is marching north probably intending to go into Mo.

*Friday, May 27, 1864*

Have news from Gen. Grant recd up to 8 a.m. of 26th. HdQrs had moved to the north bank of the North Anna & orders for a southward movement issued last night. Gen. Wright's & Warren's Corps are to march in the night time toward Hanover Ferry [VA] on the Pamunkey River & today were to seize the ferry & crossings near there & march their troops across. They will be followed closely by Hancock & Burnside. The place occupied by Wright & Warren will be filled by other troops in such a manner that their absence will not be noticed by the rebels. It is hoped we will be able to get in the rear of Lee's army & march on Richmond.

*Saturday, May 28, 1864*

Genl. Sherman telegraphs from near Dallas, Ga. 6 a.m. today that the enemy had discovered his movement to flank Allatoona & had come out there to meet him. Their columns came together near Dallas & Sherman pushed the rebels back to the point at the forks of the roads from Atlanta & Marietta. Johnston has thrown up hasty but strong parapets of timber & earth & is disposed to fight. Sherman's right is [at] Dallas, centre about 3 miles north & he is gradually working round to the left so as to approach the Railroad near Acworth.[79]

Genl. Grant's Hd Qrs this a.m., at 7 o'clock were at Magahick Church 10 miles from Hanovertown [VA]. Everything going on finely, troops coming up rapidly & in good spirits, by noon today all our troops will be south of the Pamunkey [River].

White House will be the new base of supplies.

### Sunday, May 29, 1864

Gen. Smith with 15,000 men left City Pt. at dawn this morning enroute for White House from which place he will march to Gen. Grant. Our telegraph line will be completed to White House by Wednesday.

Gen. Hunter telegraphs from near Woodstock, Va. dated 12 noon yesterday that he had been delayed acct of [waiting for] shoes but they had arrived and he would start immedy to meet Crook at Staunton & move east on Gordonsville & Charlottesville [RR].

Gold went up to [$]190 yesterday, the highest point it has yet reached.

A man named Mullarkey,[80] an operator from Louisville called on me Saturday & asked me to make arrangements as follows. A stock broking firm in Louisville with a heavy capital would buy & sell gold according as I would direct & half the profits were to be divided between Mullarkey & me. I being in a position where I could get all the news, could tell exactly when to buy & sell. I told Mr. Mullarkey that I didn't desire to be a party to any such transaction, that I had earned a good position by my faithfulness & I didn't desire to compromise my character by any such action.

He gave me to understand that I could make $50,000 by the operation, but I declined accepting it. Before he commenced the conversation he asked me to promise faithfully that it should not be divulged to his discredit. Were it not for this promise I would have him arrested.

### Monday, May 30, 1864

Mr. Dana telegraphs from Gen. Grant's Hd Qrs at Hanovertown south side of the Pamunkey River dated 2 p.m. 29th. All the Army had got safely across the Pamunkey & held a strong position on the north of Totopotomoy Creek & extending to the Pamunkey River. At noon yesterday a division from each Corps was ordered out on a reconnaissance & were to be supported by the respective Corps to which they belong if necessary.

Gen. Grant thinks it probable that Lee has taken up a position back of the Chickahominy [River]. Sheridan had an engagement with the rebels Saturday afternoon at Hanover C.H. in which he lost 44 killed & 300 wounded. He drove the rebels some distance.

A telegram from Gen. Sherman dated Dallas, Ga. 7 a.m. 29th was recd last night.

Johnston had discovered his movement to the left & had come out of his breastworks & attacked McPherson who repulsed him handsomely, driving them back some three miles to their breastworks with little cost to us. Our loss was only 300 altogether. The enemy left his dead and wounded in our hands, some 2,500 besides 300 prisoners. We were protected by breastworks so that our loss was very slight. Sherman had given McPherson all day yesterday to bury the dead of both sides & the troops were to move last night to the left & try to approach Acworth [GA]. Gen. Blair[81] from Rome [GA] is ordered to Allatoona [GA] which is supposed to be garrisoned only by militia.

*Tuesday, May 31, 1864*

We have information from Genl. Grant up to 6 a.m. this a.m. He reports that Warren engaged Ewell's Corps yesterday & although attacked desperately he repulsed them & held his ground.[82] The rebels left their dead on the field. We captured a number of prisoners. To relieve Warren, Gen. Hancock was ordered to make an attack on the Enemy's left & drove them from a strong entrenched skirmish line & now holds it (6 a.m.). Gen. Smith with 17,000 reinforcements was to have been at New Castle today where he would be in easy supporting distance of Grant. Our line from Yorktown to White House is completed to within 10 miles of West Pt. on the Yorktown side & is all done from Wshn to White House. This ten miles to be done tomorrow p.m. when we will be working to within ten or 15 miles of the Army.

Gen. Sherman reports that he will not be able to do much until he hears from Blair at Allatoona Gap. If Blair succeeds in taking this place, Sherman will return to his railroad communications again.

*Wednesday, June 1, 1864*

We have news from Grant up to 4 p.m. of yesterday. Gen. Warren's losses in his skirmish of the 30th were 500 killed & wounded. Those of the enemy were much greater. Crawford[83] alone buried one hundred dead rebels. Yesterday our lines were pushed forward steadily. A prisoner was taken from Buckner's Divn,[84] who says his Div is now a part of Longstreet's Corps. He says the outside line of rebel entrenchments are north of the Chickahominy.

Gen. Grant is waiting for Wilson[85] to finish destroying the two railroads from Hanover Junc,[86] south as far as he can, and to allow Smith to get up with his force. He is delayed by his transportation & supplies & Gen. Grant directed him not to start till he was all ready.

An Officer on Gen. Stoneman's staff arrived yesterday at Kingston [GA] & reported that at 7:30 p.m. rebels attacked us & were repulsed. The action lasted till 10 a.m. when we had driven the enemy back & had reached the railroad at Marietta.

*Thursday, June 2, 1864*

We have recd a telegram from Sec. Dana dated 10 a.m. of the 1st in which he states that Genl. Sheridan perceived a column of rebel Cavalry which proved to be Fitz Lee at Cold Harbor. He attacked them about 5 p.m. (of the 31st) & after a hard fight routed them together with Clingman's Brigade[87] of Infy which had been sent to support Fitz Lee. Sheridan remains in possession of the place & the 6th Corps was immediately sent out to occupy it.[88] Gen. Smith was also ordered from New Castle to join Wright. Genl. Wilson had a sharp fight on the evening of 31st near Hanover C.H. with Young's Cavalry,[89] completely routing them, killing and capturing a great many.

Yesterday Sheridan successfully held his position at Cold Harbor, repulsed an assault of Longstreet's Corps. Gen. Wright's Corps reached Cold Harbor about 9 a.m. yesterday & Smith's forces soon after. At 5 p.m. an attack was ordered to be made on our left by Wright & Smith. The attack was made with great spirit & was successful. We carried the enemy's first line of works on Wright's front & also those of Smith's front, but those of the latter were found to be commanded by another line of works & were untenable. We captured a good number of pris. Griffin's Div[90] alone taking 500.

Gen. Lockwood[91] who was ordered to attack the enemy although he heard the firing both on his right & left unaccountably lost his way & was found 2 miles to the rear with his troops. He was relieved of his command & will be recommended by Gen. Grant for dismissal.

Gen. Sheridan was ordered to make an attack on the left early this morning. As soon as his guns were heard the other positions of the Army would also advance. We are anxiously waiting to hear from the front.

Our line to West Point was completed last night. Will be finished to White House tomorrow. We have been unavoidably delayed.[92]

*Friday, June 3, 1864*

A telegram from Gen. Sherman dated 7:30 p.m. 2d says that McPherson moved up on the 1st from Dallas [GA] to a point in front of the enemy's lines & Gens. Schofield & Hooker moved to the extreme left.[93] Yesterday they all pushed forward in the midst of a heavy rain & thunder storm and advanced about two miles towards Marietta. Gen. Stoneman's Cavly was sent direct to Allatoona & Garrard's to the Western End of the Pass, both of who[m] reached there safely and secured possession of the pass. The railroad will be immediately required to this point and Sherman will push around by the left till he reaches the railroad.

The possession of the pass at Allatoona is a great point gained by us.

A telegram from Gen. Crook dated Meadow Bluff, Va. May 31 is recd today. He says he will be in Staunton in about six days from that date. Hunter will meet him there.

*Saturday, June 4, 1864*

We have news from Gen. Grant up to 4 p.m. of yesterday. There had been no fighting of consequence on the second as the troops were much exhausted from their long marches & movements & Gen. Grant postponed the attack till 4:30 a.m. when all was in readiness.[94]

The attack yesterday was made with great vigor on all parts of our line. Gen. Warren spread his lines out too much, his front occupying 4 miles & Burnside also stretched his lines too great & did not succeed in accomplishing much. Hancock had the left, with Barlow's[95] and Gibbon's[96] in front & Birney as reserve. Wright was next & Warren on the right, with Burnside in his rear & right. We gained advantages here & there. Burnside carried the exterior line of entrenchments & took a few prisoners. Smith got very well forward to aid Wright. Barlow drove through a very strong line & held it some time with the guns, colors etc. but the work was commanded by an interior line & he was compelled to abandon it bringing off but a single color [enemy flag] & 22 prisoners as tokens of his brief success.

At noon we had fully developed the rebel lines & ascertained what was necessary to get through them. Hancock reported that in his front it could not be done. Wright was decidedly of opinion that a lodgment could be made in his front but it would be difficult to make much out of it unless Hancock & Smith could also advance. Smith thought he could carry the works in front of him but was not sanguine. Burnside also thought he could get through but Warren who was near him did not share this opinion. In this state of things Gen. Grant ordered the attack to be suspended. We hold all the positions gained except that which Barlow occupied temporarily. Gen. Grant estimates our loss at 3,000. Among the killed are Col. Porter, 8th N.Y. Heavy Arty, Col. Haskell, 36th Wis. & Col. Morris, 66th N.Y. Among the wounded are Gen. R. O. Tyler who loses a foot, Col. McMahon, 1st N.Y., Col. Brooke, 53rd Pa. & Col. Byrne, 28th Mass., probably mortally.[97]

The prisoners captured from Hancock were mainly from Breckenridge's Divn who is under Beauregard.

Weather was cool & pleasant. Showers had laid the dust. Gen. Jno. Frémont was nominated at Cleveland some days since by a radical wing of the Republicans for Prest. of the U.S. He has tendered his resignation as Maj. Gen. It was immediately accepted.

*Sunday, June 5, 1864*

We have information from Gen. Grant's Hd Qrs up to 8 a.m. yesterday. The telegram states that about 6 p.m. of the day before (Friday) the enemy suddenly attacked Smith's[98] Brigade of Gibbon's Division. They were unwaveringly repulsed. About 7 p.m., Gen. Wilson fell upon the rear of one of Heth's[99] brigades which Lee had thrown around apparently with the intention of enveloping Burnside & after a sharp but short conflict drove them in confusion from their rifle pits. Wilson had previously engaged & routed Gordon's Brigade of Cavalry.[100] He captured a few prisoners. We lost Col. Preston 1st Vt. Killed, Col. Benjamin 3rd [8th] N.Y. Cav. Gen. Stannard[101] serving with 18th Corps was severely wounded yesterday.

Gen. Sherman telegraphs under date of 3 p.m. yesterday 13 miles west of Marietta, Ga. that his left is well around to the railroad, covering all roads leading to the South. His Cavly had been to Acworth & he occupies in force Allatoona Pass. Later news from Gen. Grant is just recd. His Adjt. Genls. Office reports the total losses in the 3 days operation (1st, 2nd & 3rd of June) to be 7,500. Col. Cesnola[102] reached the Army on the 3d with 1,500 men, new & old regts, and stragglers about 4,000 reached there on the 2d so that the supply is equal to the losses.

There was no fighting in front of Richmond yesterday. The force of fighting men in the Army of the Potomac is now 115,000 men, this includes Cavalry. Lee's force is known to be 80,000 exclusive of what militia may be in Richmond. When Gen. Grant started from Culpeper one part of his plan was to destroy the Va. Central Railroad so effectively as to prevent its use for a long time, also the Fredksburg road from the Chickahominy to the North Anna. Gen. Grant expected before reaching the Chickahominy to have had a chance to crush his

[Lee's] army by fair fighting. This expectation has been foiled by Lee's success in avoiding battle upon any equal terms. Before proceeding any farther in the movement this expectation must be accomplished & Gen. Sheridan will move Monday for that purpose. If he fails in it the whole army will be swinging around, even if communications with the White House must be temporarily broken.

*Monday, June 6, 1864*

A telegram from Army of the Potomac dated 6 p.m. yesterday says the day passed off quietly with no fighting except an occasional rattle of musketry along the skirmish line and now & then a cannon shot. The 5th Corps was ordered to move out of position last night & mass itself in reserve in rear of Cold Harbor. The 9th Corps will move to the right of the 5th Corps. Two divisions of Cavalry are to be ready to move up the railroad on morning of 7th & destroy both roads from the nearest practicable point, to the South Anna thence the Cavalry moves to Charlottesville Stn [VA] & thence sends forward forces to communicate with Genl. Hunter & destroy railroad bridges southward. Genl. Hunter is ordered to return from his expedition to Lynchburg & joining Sheridan's Command aid in the thorough destruction of the Va. Centl RR moving along its line in this direction & having accomplished this work is to join the Army of the Potomac.

A later telegram (dated 7 a.m. today) says the 5th & 9th Corps took up their new positions without difficulty. About half past 3 o'clock last night the enemy made a sudden assault on Hancock's & Wright's lines. The firing lasted about twenty minutes & was very loud but amounted to nothing. Nobody was hurt. Sheridan moves tomorrow morning.

From Sherman we have news up to last night. He was ten miles from Allatoona on the railroad. McPherson was at Acworth. It had rained for three days & the roads were very bad. The railroad bridge over the Etowah [River] cannot be rebuilt for ten days but a pontoon bridge is being put down & as soon as his supplies are up Sherman will march on Marietta.

Dates [messages] from New Orleans to 30th Inst. are recd. On the 27th the stmr *Blackhawk*, Adm. Porter's Flag Ship[103] was caught fire & with 11 others of his vessels, gunboats etc. was burnt to the waters edge. Gen. Canby is concentrating his troops as much as possible & abandoning unimportant points & holding his forces ready for any emergency. (This report of burning of Admiral Porter's ships was after found to be incorrect. The vessels were private ones.)

*Tuesday, June 7, 1864*

Gen. Sherman telegraphs that Blair has passed Kingston & will soon be at Allatoona pass which will be fortified & made a strong point. Sherman's advance is within 6 miles of Marietta & he is getting up his supplies for a ten-day march. He will start forward on the morning of the 7th.

Gen. Grant & Lee yesterday & the day before had a correspondence in request to allowing each party to remove the dead & wounded after a battle is over. Gen. Grant in the last letter says that he can only express his regret that all his efforts to alleviate the sufferings of the wounded have been rendered negatory. Gen. Grant is preparing to move his army to the James river & will commence this movement in a few days. Sheridan started this morning on his expedition.

*Wednesday, June 8, 1864*

Nothing new from any direction today except the fact of John Morgan[104] having entered Kentucky. He has captured a railroad train & burnt it & cut up the railroad some distance.

The *Richmond Examiner* of the 7th recd by Gen. Grant says that Gen. W. E. Jones[105] was defeated by Genl. Hunter 12 miles beyond Staunton [VA] & Gen. Jones killed.[106] His successor had retired to the mountains between Charlottesville & Staunton. Our forces occupied Staunton.

*Thursday, June 9, 1864*

Morgan has captured Mt. Sterling, Cynthiana & several other places in Ky. & is creating a vast deal of excitement. Our forces are in pursuit of him & it is hoped he may be caught.

The Convention at Balto. yesterday nominated Abraham Lincoln for Prest. & Andrew Johnson of Tenn. for Vice Prest. by acclamation. Great enthusiasm prevailed.

*Friday, June 10, 1864*

Mr. Dana telegraphs that the army will probably commence its march towards the James River tonight or tomorrow sometime. Information recd from a deserter indicates great want prevails there, that there is a scarcity of meat & flour & all other necessaries of life.

News from Morgan today is that he has captured Falmouth, 30 miles from Cincinnati. Gen. Butler sent out on the night of the 8th a force under Gen. Gillmore to make a demonstration on Petersburg on the one side whilst Gen. Kautz attempted with his Cavalry to get in on the other. Gen. Gillmore returned having failed to force the fortifi-cations. Gen. Kautz is still out with orders to cut through.

*Saturday, June 11, 1864*

Gen. Butler telegraphs that his force under Gen. Kautz penetrated the works around Petersburg & entered the town but not receiving the expected support from Gen. Gillmore he was compelled to with-draw with forty prisoners & one cannon as his trophies. It is unfortu-nate that Gen. Gillmore did not wait till the Cavalry was heard from before retiring. Gen. Sherman has advanced from Acworth, Ga. to-ward Marietta & will attack in turn the enemy today. Johnston's Cavalry got in our rear & destroyed a train of cars & captured a few prisoners today. Telegraph line is all right again.

Preparations are being made to withdraw our base of supplies from White House & move to Bermuda Hundred. The movement will be made today and tomorrow.

*Sunday, June 12, 1864*

It is reported today that Gen. Hobson[107] has surrendered to Morgan & also that Genl. Burbridge[108] came up with Morgan near Cynthiana this morning & after a two hour fight completely broke him up. No particulars yet.

Gen. Grant's army is still in the same position. One Corps of his Army will be sent by water from White House to Bermuda Hundred & as soon as they are heard from the whole army will be moved to that place.

Gen. Hunter's official report of his battle of last Saturday was recd. It is dated Staunton, Va. June 8th. The battle was fought at Piedmont & after a fight of ten hours we routed the rebels, killing Gen. Wm. E. Jones the Comdg officer & taking 1,500 prisoners & 1,000 men & over 60 officers on the field & 3,000 stand of small arms, three cannon & many stores. Gen. Hunter had that day effected a junction with Genls Crook & Averell & would resume his march south on the 9th. He will have been reinforced by Gen. Sheridan's force by this time.

*Monday, June 13, 1864*

Gen. Sigel telegraphs that he has reliable information that Gen. Breckenridge with 7,000 men passed Gordonsville for Staunton last Wednesday & also has information not so reliable that Pickett's[109] force passed through the day before.

Gen. Hunter will have been reinforced by Sheridan's Cavalry before these troops can be of any avail against him [Breckenridge].

Gen. Grant's army is in motion for Bermuda Hundred via Jones' & Long Bridge. Weather fine & all going well.

In Gen. Burbridge's fight yesterday he completely routed the rebels & captured 700 besides killing and wounding three or 400.

### Tuesday, June 14, 1864

Cable across Chesapeake at Cherrystone is still broken. All business taken across by boat. The movement of the Army of the Potomac to the James river still progresses favorably & smoothly. A force will be left at the White House until the arrival of Genl. Hunter & Gen. Sheridan which will be this week.

Gen. Burbridge has arrived at Lexington, Ky. He says "In six days my command has marched over 200 miles, fought two severe battles, killing, wounding & capturing over three-fourths of Morgan's command. The remaining fourth is scattered & being pursued in all directions."

The success of Gen. Burbridge is very gratifying. On the other hand our forces in West Tenn. have been unfortunate. Gen. Sturgis[110] with a force of 3,000 Cavalry, 5,000 Infy & 16 pieces of artillery met Genl. Forrest near Guntown, Miss. on the 10th inst. in a large force of all arms.[111] The fight was very severe & the loss on our part very heavy, probably 5,000 men killed, wounded & captured. We were completely routed. Sturgis' rear at last accts was near Collierville, the enemy pursuing. The movement into Miss. by Sturgis was made by orders of Genl. Washburne[112] at Memphis, in accordance with directions from Gen. McPherson & Gen. Sherman who said that all of Polk's Corps was with Johnston in Ga. & Forrest was on his way there & that the best time to make the movement was then. It was very unfortunate at this time. Gen. Washburne has enough troops at present & will do all in his power to wipe out the disgrace.

A despatch boat just arrived at Cairo[113] reports a force under rebel Gen Marmaduke[114] near Vicksburg on the west side & one near Greenville on the east side of the Miss. It is expected these forces will unite & close the navigation on the river. Gen. Canby has his troops in hand however & will take care of these rebels in that direction.

### Wednesday, June 15, 1864

Gen. Grant telegraphs from Wilcox Whf on the James River dated 1 p.m. 14th that all is progressing well. Troops are reaching Bermuda Hundred rapidly. Nothing is known of Lee's movements. He has sent no troops south of Richmond yet. Gen. Sherman telegraphs from near Kennesaw that yesterday was the first clear day for two weeks. Roads are drying fast. He advanced his lines somewhat yesterday & captured a few prisoners.

Our Signal Corps have the rebel alphabet & have read several signals made by the rebels.[115] By this means they learned yesterday of the death of Lt. Gen. Polk.[116] His body was sent to the rear. Polk before the war was one of the Bishops of the Episcopalian Church but early joined the rebels.

*Thursday, June 16, 1864*

Gen. Sherman telegraphs from near Kennesaw at 9 p.m. last night that enemy abandoned his position on Pine Hill [GA] during the night, which was immediately occupied by Howard's Corps. Johnston held a position running from Kennesaw on the East to Lost Mtn [GA] on the South West. Pine Hill is the center of the two points.

Yesterday Gen. Schofield advanced on Lost Mountain taking the first line of the rebel works & a few prisoners. Gen. Thomas was pushed forward in the centre & when last heard from at sundown had advanced a mile and a half. At the same time McPherson was ordered to attack Kennesaw Mountain. He carried the first line of works left exposed by loss of Pine Hill, took prisoners the 14th Ala Regt entire 320 men. Gen. Sherman says Johnston will have to fight today on open ground or retire to the Chattahoochee, most probably the latter.

Gen. Grant's Hd Qrs were yesterday a.m. at Charles City C.H. They would be moved to City Pt. by noon. Gen. Smith's Corps was ordered to advance on Petersburg at daylight yesterday.[117] It would be immediately followed by Hancock's Corps. Nothing heard from there yet. Line is being constructed from Jamestown along to City Point. Will be done tomorrow.[118]

Wilson's Cavalry is along the line from White Oak Swamp to the James. From prisoners taken yesterday he learned that Hill[119] and Ewell were entrenching themselves between Malvern Hill & the Chickahominy. Lee evidently had no idea we were going to Bermuda Hundred.

6 p.m. Boat just in from Ft. Monroe with information from City Point up to 7:30 p.m. yesterday. Gen. Grant reports that the latest information from Gen. Smith was up to 4 p.m. He had then carried the first line of the enemy's works at Beatty's House near Petersburg, the colored troops assaulting & carrying the rifle pits with great gallantry. Smith expected to assault the main line just before dark. He describes the rebel artillery fire as very heavy. Hancock was within three miles of Smith.

Rebel papers state that Hunter was within 12 miles of Lynchburg on the 11th & had destroyed the bridge over the Rye River.

*Friday, June 17, 1864*

Gen. Smith took 16 guns in the works in front of Petersburg & about 500 prisoners. The rebels at last accounts held the town but it is of no use to them as our guns command the place. Genl. Butler reports that the rebels have evacuated their position in front of Bermuda Hundred. Our troops were engaged in tearing up the railroad between Petersburg & Richmond.[120] Obstructions have been sunk in the James near Trent's Reach which will prevent the rebel vessels from coming down & greatly strengthen our position at Bermuda Hundred & City Point.

*Saturday, June 18, 1864*

Gen. Hancock's Corps closely followed Gen. Smith's & took one of the enemy's forts on the west side of the City [Petersburg]. Gen. Burnside's troops were also brought up & captured some of the rebel works with 4 more guns & 500 prisoners. Gen. Butler reports that last evening the enemy formed in line of battle, drove in his pickets & re-occupied the line in front of Bermuda Hundred which they abandoned to us the day before.

Gen. Sherman reports that his lines have advanced some 3 miles today, the falling back from Lost Mountain leaving six miles of splendid field works in our possession. A few days will give us all the country down to the Chattahoochee.

The following is Gen. Grant's summing up of the recent movements. Our forces drew out from within 50 yards of the enemy's entrenchments at Cold Harbor [and] made a flank movement of about 55 miles march crossing the Chickahominy & James River, the latter 2,000 feet wide and 84 feet deep at point of crossing, surprised the rear of the enemy at Petersburg. This was done without the loss of a wagon or piece of artillery & only about 150 stragglers picked up by the enemy. In covering this move Warren's Corps & Wilson's Cavalry had frequent skirmishing with the rebels, each losing from 50 to 60 killed & wounded & inflicting an equal if not greater loss upon the enemy. The 18th Corps (Smith's) were transferred from White House to Bermuda Hundred by water, moved out near to Petersburg the night of their arrival (Wednesday) & captured the very strong works northeast of the town, before sufficient force could be got in there by the rebels to hold them. Smith was joined the night following by the 2d Corps which in turn captured more of the redoubts further south. This Corps was followed by the 9th which this morning (17th) carried two more redoubts, with 4 guns & 500 pris. Too much credit cannot be given the troops & their Commanders for the energy & fortitude displayed the last five days. Day & night has been the same & no delays allowed.

*Sunday, June 19, 1864*

Maj. Eckert has ordered me to the Army for a week or so to act as Cipher Clerk to Mr. Dana. I leave via Balto. at 3 p.m. today.[121]

*Monday, June 20, 1864*

Reached Balto. last evening. Will leave for Ft. Monroe at 5 p.m.

*Tuesday, June 21, 1864*

Left Balto. last ev'g. The ride down the bay was very pleasant & cheering. I enjoyed it very much. I came down in the *Adelaide*. Will leave at noon for City Point.

*Wednesday, June 22, 1864*

I arrived at City Point last night at 6 p.m. on the *Jno A. Warner*. Gen. Grant's Hd Qrs are on the bluffs just above the river in a pleasant grove of trees. Was introduced to Gen. Grant. He is a very pleasant man, smokes a great deal. All is quiet on the front.

The Prest. came to the Army yesterday. He is up to Adml. Lee's[122] fleet today on a visit. He went to Gen. Meade's Hd Qrs yesterday. Everything is quiet today.

*Friday, June 24, 1864*

The heat today is very intense. I have very little to do but find it difficult to keep cool. I go to Genl. Butler's Hd Qrs today to see my friends there.

*Saturday, June 25, 1864*

Came to Gen. Butler's Hd Qrs today. They are on the Appomattox about a mile from Point of Rocks. Found O'Brien & Nichols[123] there well & glad to see me. Went in swimming last evening in the Appomattox.

*Sunday, June 26, 1864*

Returned last evening from Pt. of Rocks. I came on horseback to Bermuda Hundred & thence by tug to City Pt. Gen. Ransom[124] is here on a visit to Gen. Grant. He is a young man & fine looking with a beautiful bearing.

*Monday, June 27, 1864*

The weather is shocking hot here. The poor soldiers must suffer severely. There is little firing & no excitement.

*Tuesday, June 28, 1864*

Our line is completed & working well from City Pt. to Ft. Monroe. The guerrillas troubled it a little from Fort Powhatan to Swan's Pt. opposite Jamestown Island, but Genl. Butler sent some colored Cavy out and dispersed them.

*Thursday, June 30, 1864*

Maj. Eckert teleghs today from Washn that he will leave today on a visit to the Army. He will be here tomorrow night. Weather is somewhat cooler.

## Notes

[1]Union Brigadier General George Crook, Commander, 2nd Infantry Division, Department of West Virginia.

[2]Union Major General Franz Sigel, Commander, Department of West Virginia.

[3]The Beardslee telegraph used an alphabet dial and indicator for both sending and receiving, therefore no knowledge of Morse code was required. The indicator would simply be moved to the letter to be sent and then the telegraph activated. The Beardslee sets, their hand turned generators, five miles of gutta-percha insulated wire, and various reels and poles were transported on what came to be known as "Flying Trains." The trains would move as close as possible to a Union force and then unload the equipment and set up for communications. About 30 of the "Flying Trains" were organized by Colonel Albert J. Myer. The USMTC never used the Beardslee equipment. (Plum, William, *The Military Telegraph During the Civil War in the United States,* Volume II, Pp. 38-39.)

[4]The wigwag flag system was created by Colonel Albert J. Myer prior to the Civil War. It consisted of a large flag suspended on a flagpole of approximately six feet in length. Each letter was represented by right and left flag movements. The code for flag use consisted of "1" and "2" representations for each letter. To send the representation, flag right would be a 1, flag left would be a 2, and flag center to the ground was the end of a letter. For example, an "A" might be 1-2-1. (Flag movements would be right, left, right, and center to the ground.) At night flares were used in place of flags to send a signal.

[5]The Wade-Davis Bill was in opposition to Lincoln's more lenient reconstruction plans. The bill proposed the following: (a) provisional governments for liberated Union territories until the end of the war, (b) the establishment of civilian governments only after one half of the white male population in a state signed loyalty oaths to the Federal Government, (c) no amnesty for

Confederate civil officers above the rank of minister or Confederate military above the rank of colonel.

[6]Union Major General John C. Frémont held no command having refused to serve under Major General John Pope.

[7]The Grand Strategy was built on General Winfield Scott's Anaconda Plan of 1861. General Grant's and President Lincoln's plan set out to accomplish the following: first, use the Army of the Potomac in Virginia to keep Lee's forces occupied and not allow any troops to be shifted to other areas; second, send Union troops into the Shenandoah Valley, known as the Bread Basket of the Confederacy, to destroy all the crops possible; third, contain Johnston's army; and fourth, threaten Richmond by approaching via the James River.

[8]Confederate General Joseph E. Johnston, Commander, Army of Tennessee and Department of Tennessee.

[9]Union Major General David Hunter assumed Command of the Department of West Virginia after serving in various positions in the War Department.

[10]Confederate Lieutenant General Richard Taylor, Commander, District of West Louisiana, Trans-Mississippi Department.

[11]George Low was a USMTC telegraph operator.

[12]P. J. Murray was a member of the USMTC.

[13]Union Major General Ambrose E. Burnside assumed Command of the 9th Corps, Army of the Potomac.

[14]Fort Pillow was located near Fulton, Tennessee, on the Mississippi River. It was the scene of the massacre of black Union troops and their white officers by the forces of General Nathan Bedford Forrest on April 12, 1864.

[15]Columbus, Kentucky, is located on the upper Mississippi River.

[16]Mrs. William Chandler of Randolph, Vermont, was the mother of Albert B. Chandler, the cipher clerk in the Telegraph Office.

[17]Confederate General Edmund Kirby Smith, Commander, Trans-Mississippi Department.

[18]The Battle of Sabine Cross Roads, Louisiana, occurred April 8, 1864. The Battle of Pleasant Hill, Louisiana, occurred April 9, 1864. These battles were part of the Red River Campaign.

[19]Salmon P. Chase, Union Secretary of the Treasury in the Lincoln Cabinet.

[20]The USS Miami was a 730 ton double-ender gunboat. On April 19, 1864, the Miami was rammed by the Confederate vessel Albemarle, and its commander, Lieutenant Commander W. W. Flusser, killed. The USS Southfield had been lashed together with the Miami. It was sunk when rammed by the Albemarle.

[21]The Red River Campaign in Louisiana continued from March 10 to May 19, 1864.

[22]Union Major General Joseph G. Totten, Chief, Corps of Engineers. His death was caused by pneumonia.

[23]Union Major General Frederick Steele, Commander, Department of Arkansas and 7th Corps, Department of Arkansas.

[24]Referring to the Beardslee telegraphic equipment. (See Note 3 above.)

[25]There was considerable rivalry between the Telegraph Corps and the personnel assigned to Colonel Albert J. Myer regarding telegraph authority. With the removal of the Beardslee equipment, the USMTC became the sole provider of telegraphic communications for the Union Army.

[26]The battery wagon was equipped with a portable battery of one hundred cells furnishing the electrical current. The wagon contained a desk and attached instruments for transmitting messages. The mobile capability allowed for rapid communications between the various deployed units. Lines could be constructed at a rate of two miles an hour to keep up with the troops.

[27]Catlett Station was located in Northern Virginia on the Orange and Alexandria Railroad, just north of Weaverville, Virginia.

[28]Union Major General Henry W. Halleck, Chief of Staff of the Union Army.

[29]William MacIntosh was a member of the USMTC.

[30]Union Major General Benjamin J. Butler, now Commander, Army of the James.

[31]There was action at Marks Mills, Arkansas, April 25, 1864.

[32]Union Brigadier General August V. Kautz, Commander, Cavalry Division, Army of the James.

[33]The Battle of the Wilderness in Virginia was fought May 5-7, 1864.

[34]Union Brigadier General Rufus Ingalls, Chief Quartermaster, Armies of the Potomac and the James.

[35]Union Brigadier General Alexander Hays, Commander, 3rd Division, 2th Corps, Army of the Potomac, died May 5, 1864. Union Brigadier General James S. Wadsworth, Commander, 4th Division, 5th Corps, Army of the Potomac, was mortally wounded May 6th and died in a Confederate hospital on May 8, 1864. Bates was incorrect about Union Brigadier General Alexander S. Webb, Commander, 1st Brigade, 2nd Division, 2nd Corps, Army of the Potomac, but Webb was severely wounded at the Bloody Angle at Spotsylvania on May 12, 1864. Confederate Lieutenant General James Longstreet, now Commander, 1st Corps, Army of Northern Virginia, was severely wounded by Confederate troops in the confusion of battle. Confederate Brigadier General John M. Jones, Brigade Commander, Trible-Johnson Division, 2nd Corps, Army of Northern Virginia, was killed May 5, 1864. Confederate Brigadier General Micah Jenkins, Brigade Commander, Fields's Division, 1st Corps, Army of Northern Virginia, was mistakenly killed by his own troops May 6, 1864. Confederate Brigadier General Leroy A. Stafford, Commander, 2nd Louisiana Brigade, Jackson's-Johnson's Division, 2nd Corps, Army of Northern Virginia, was mortally wounded May 5, 1864, and died May 8, 1864.

[36]Union Major General James B. McPherson, Commander, Department and Army of the Tennessee.

[37]Confederate General Pierre G. T. Beauregard, Commander, Department of North Carolina and Southern Virginia.

[38]Confederate Lieutenant General Ambrose P. Hill relinquished command of the 3rd Corps, Army of Northern Virginia after the Battle of the Wilderness. He retook command on May 22, 1864.

[39] The Battle of Spotsylvania, Virginia, was fought May 8-19, 1864.

[40] Union Brigadier General John H. H. Ward, Commander, 1st Brigade, 3rd Division, 2nd Corps, Army of the Potomac, was drunk at the Wilderness and ran from the fighting.

[41] The Battle of Rocky Face Ridge, Georgia, was fought May 7-9, 1864.

[42] The skirmishes at Beaver Dam Station, Virginia, occurred May 9, 1864.

[43] The action May 12, 1864, was part of the Battle of Spotsylvania, Virginia.

[44] Confederate Major General Edward Johnson, Commander, Division, 2nd Corps, Army of Northern Virginia, was captured along with many of his men May 12, 1864. He was exchanged the following summer. Confederate Major General Jubal A. Early, Commander, 3rd Corps, Army of Northern Virginia.

[45] Confederate Brigadier General George H. Steuart, Commander of a brigade in Johnson's Division, was captured with most of his unit.

[46] Union Major General Horatio G. Wright, Commander, 6th Corps, Army of the Potomac, succeeded Sedgwick in Corps command after Sedgwick's death at Spotsylvania.

[47] The Battle of Resaca, Georgia, was fought May 14-15, 1864.

[48] Fort Delaware was a Union prison on Pea Patch Island in the Delaware River.

[49] The railroad destroyed by General Sheridan's troops was the Virginia Central Railroad.

[50] Confederate Major General J. E. B. Stuart, Commander, Cavalry Corps, Army of Northern Virginia, was mortally wounded at the Battle of Yellow Tavern May 11, 1864, and died the next day.

[51] Union Brigadier General William F. Smith, Commander, 18th Corps, Army of the James.

[52] Union Major General Oliver O. Howard, Commander, 4th Corps, Army of the Cumberland.

[53] Union Brigadier General Kenner Garrard, Commander, 2nd Division, Cavalry Corps, Army of the Cumberland.

[54] Referring to the extension of the telegraph lines into Virginia.

[55] The railroad running through Resaca, Georgia, was the Western and Atlantic Railroad.

[56] The Final battle of Drewry's Bluff, Virginia, was fought May 16, 1864.

[57] Confederate Major General John C. Breckinridge, Commander, Department of Western Virginia.

[58] The railroad running through Appomattox Station, Virginia, was the Southside Railroad.

[59] An abatis is a fortification barrier of trees felled towards the enemy.

[60] Union Brigadier General Alfred T. A. Torbert, Commander, 1st Division, Cavalry Corps, Army of the Potomac.

[61] The railroad running through Allatoona, Georgia, was the Western and Atlantic Railroad.

[62] The Battle of Harris Farm, Virginia, was fought May 19, 1864.

[63] Union Major General David B. Birney, Commander, 3rd Division, 2nd Corps, Army of the Potomac.

[64]Union Brigadier General Robert O. Tyler, Commander, 4th Brigade, 4th Division, 2nd Corps, Army of the Potomac.

[65]Union Major General David Hunter was moved to the Command of Department of West Virginia.

[66]Union Major General Franz Sigel was moved to the command of Reserve Division, Department of West Virginia.

[67]Union Major General Edward R. S. Canby, Commander, Military Division of West Mississippi.

[68]The Independent Telegraph was a commercial telegraph company.

[69]Union Major General John A. Dix, Commander, Department of the East.

[70]Joseph Howard used the bogus proclamation as a means of driving up the price of gold.

[71]Confederate Brigadier General William S. Walker, Commander, 4th and 5th Military Districts of South Carolina, Department of South Carolina, Georgia, and Florida, was wounded and captured May 20, 1864.

[72]Union Brigadier General George Crook, Commander, 2nd Division, Department of West Virginia.

[73]Union Brigadier General William V. Averell, Commander, 2nd Cavalry Division, Department of West Virginia.

[74]The Battle of the North Anna River, Virginia, was fought May 23-May 26, 1864.

[75]Union Brigadier General Edward A. Wild, Commander, 1st Brigade, Hink's U.S. Colored Troops Division, Army of the James.

[76]Union Brigadier General John E. Smith, Commander, 3rd Division, 25th Corps, Army of the Tennessee.

[77]Confederate Brigadier General (Prince de) Camille A. J. M. Polignac, Commander, 2nd Division, District of Western Louisiana, was a French citizen with six years service in the French military.

[78]Confederate Brigadier General Joseph O. Shelby, Brigade Commander, Marmaduke's Cavalry Division, Department of Arkansas, Trans-Mississippi Department.

[79]The campaign of New Hope Church, Georgia, was fought May 25-June 4, 1864, and included fighting near Dallas, Georgia.

[80]Patrick Mullarkey was a member of the USMTC.

[81]Union Major General Francis Blair, Jr., Commander, 17th Corps, Army of the Tennessee.

[82]The Battle of Bethesda Church, Virginia, was fought May 31, 1864.

[83]Union Brigadier General Samuel W. Crawford, Commander, 3rd Division, 5th Corps, Army of the Potomac.

[84]Confederate Major General Simon B. Buckner, Second in Command, Trans-Mississippi Department.

[85]Union Brigadier General James H. Wilson, Commander, 3rd Division, Cavalry Corps, Army of the Potomac.

[86]The two railroads from Hanover Junction, Virginia, were the Virginia Central Railroad and the Richmond, Fredericksburg, and Potomac Railroad.

[87]Confederate Brigadier General Thomas L. Clingman, Brigade Commander, Hoke's Division, Department of North Carolina and Southern Virginia.

[88]The Battle of Cold Harbor, Virginia, was fought June 1-3, 1864.

[89]Confederate Brigadier General Pierce M. B. Young, Commander, Butler's (old) Brigade, Hampton's-Butler's Division, Cavalry Corps, Army of Northern Virginia.

[90]Union Brigadier General Charles Griffin, Commander, 1st Division, 5th Corps, Army of the Potomac.

[91]Union Brigadier General Henry H. Lockwood, Commander, 1st Division, 2nd Corps, Army of the Potomac.

[92]Bates was referring to the extension of the USMTC telegraph line to White House, Virginia, the major supply depot in support of General Grant.

[93]The Federal cavalry captured Allatoona Pass, Georgia, June 1, 1864.

[94]The final day of the Battle of Cold Harbor, Virginia, June 3, 1864.

[95]Union Brigadier General Francis C. Barlow, Commander, 1st Division, 2nd Corps, Army of the Potomac.

[96]Union Brigadier General John Gibbon, Commander, 2nd Division, 2nd Corps, Army of the Potomac.

[97]Colonel Peter A. Porter, 8th Regiment, New York Heavy Artillery, was killed June 1, 1864; Colonel Frank A. Haskell, 36th Wisconsin Infantry, was killed June 1, 1864; Colonel Orlando W. Morris, 66th New York, was killed June 3, 1864; Brigadier General Robert O. Tyler, Commander, 4th Brigade, 2nd Division, 2nd Corps, Army of the Potomac, was wounded June 3, 1864; Colonel James McMahon, 1st New York Regiment, was killed June 3, 1864; Colonel John R. Brooke, 53rd Pennsylvania Infantry, was wounded but not mortally; Colonel Richard Byrne, 28th Massachusetts Infantry, was mortally wounded June 3, 1864.

[98]Smith's Brigade was the 2nd Brigade, 2nd Division, 2nd Corps, Army of the Potomac. Colonel Orlando Smith commanded the Brigade until February 1864, when he resigned.

[99]Confederate Major General Henry Heth, Commander, Cavalry Division, 3rd Corps, Army of Northern Virginia.

[100]Confederate Brigadier General James B. Gordon had, prior to his death May 12, 1864, commanded a Cavalry Brigade in General Fitzhugh Lee's Cavalry Division of the Army of Northern Virginia.

[101]Union Colonel James D. Preston, 1st Vermont Infantry, was killed June 5, 1864; Union Colonel Samuel W. Benjamin, 8th New York Cavalry, was killed June 5, 1864; Union Brigadier General George J. Stannard, Commander, 1st Brigade, 2nd Division, 18th Corps, Army of the James, received his second wound of the war.

[102]Colonel Cesnola is not further identified.

[103]Union Rear Admiral David D. Porter, Commander, Naval Forces, Red River Campaign, Louisiana.

[104]Confederate Brigadier General John H. Morgan, Commander, Cavalry Brigade, Department of Southwestern Virginia.

[105] Confederate Brigadier General William E. Jones, Commander, Cavalry Brigade, Department of Western Virginia, was killed June 5, 1864.

[106] The Battle of Piedmont, Virginia, was fought June 5, 1864.

[107] Union Brigadier General Edward H. Hobson, Commander, 1st Brigade, 1st Division, District of Kentucky, 23rd Corps, Department of the Ohio.

[108] Union Brigadier General Stephen G. Burbridge, Commander, District of Kentucky, 23rd Corps, Department of the Ohio.

[109] Confederate Major General George E. Pickett, Commander, Division, 1st Corps, Army of Northern Virginia.

[110] Union Brigadier General Samuel D. Sturgis, Commander, Expeditionary Force, District of West Tennessee, Department of the Tennessee.

[111] The Battle of Brice's Cross Roads, Mississippi, was fought June 10, 1864.

[112] Union Major General Cadwaller C. Washburn, Commander, District of West Tennessee, Army of the Tennessee.

[113] Telegraphic communications with Washington, DC, existed from Cairo, Illinois, located on the upper Mississippi River. As the Union troops moved south, Cairo served as the connection for communicating with the authorities in Washington until new telegraphic lines could be established.

[114] Confederate Brigadier General John S. Marmaduke, Commander, Cavalry Division, District of Arkansas, Trans-Mississippi Department.

[115] The Confederate codes recovered by the U.S. Signal Corps were those used by the Confederates in their wigwag communications and not those employed on the telegraph.

[116] Confederate Lieutenant General Leonidas Polk was killed June 14, 1864.

[117] The assault on Petersburg, Virginia, lasted from June 15 to June 18, 1864.

[118] The telegraph line was extended by the USMTC linemen to provide General Grant's headquarters with a direct telegraphic communications link to Washington, DC.

[119] Confederate Lieutenant General Ambrose P. Hill, Commander, 3rd Corps, Army of Northern Virginia.

[120] The railroad line between Petersburg, Virginia, and Richmond, Virginia, was the Richmond and Potomac Railroad.

[121] To ensure privacy, Charles A. Dana, the Assistant Secretary of War, had his own series of the Union cipher system. It is possible that Bates was sent to the Army of the Potomac to translate Confederate cipher messages if intercepted or to teach fellow operators how to decipher the Confederate system.

[122] Union Rear Admiral Samuel P. Lee, Commander, North Atlantic Blockading Squadron.

[123] Richard O'Brien was the USMTC operator assigned as the Chief Operator at General Butler's Army of the James headquarters. J. Hervey Nichols was also a USMTC operator.

[124]Union Brigadier General Thomas E. G. Ransom was recovering from a wound received during the Battle of Sabine Crossroads, Louisiana.

# July, August, September 1864

The entries in the Bates diary throughout July, August, and September of 1864 continue to indicate high activity levels of telegraphic communications among Washington, General Grant, and the various prongs of the coordinated Union attacks. In most cases the reports appear to be timely, arriving within a matter of hours of the original transmission time. However in the case of the Union forces in the Mobile Bay area, the Bates diary shows that their telegraphic reports arrived seven to nine days after the date of transmission. At the time of the Mobile Bay action, there were no Union telegraph lines in the area. The messages had to be couriered to the closest Union telegraph office for electrical forwarding. That took time. As a consequence Bates frequently quoted news regarding the Mobile Bay endeavor that had been extracted from Richmond newspapers.

The July entries in the diary reflect great excitement in the Union regarding two specific military movements. First, General Early with his Confederate force threatened the city of Washington, causing both excitement and consternation. Early's actions during this raid clearly showed the vulnerability of the Union telegraph lines as described in Bates's entry of July 10th which stated, "The rebels today, under Gen. Early, broke the Balto road near Laurel, tore down all telegraph lines. We are thus completely isolated from the rest of mankind." (All of the major telegraph lines heading north out of Washington ran through Baltimore.) Second, the excitement and anticipation of the taking of Atlanta by Sherman began to turn to frustration as the city stayed in Confederate hands until September.

The extension of the telegraph lines in support of the Union's advancing forces continued to be reflected in the diary. On the 30th of August Bates reported that, "Today had Ft. Monroe contact City Pt. & we communicated direct from Washn to City Pt. The distance is 430 miles & there are 11 cables, the one at Ft. Monroe (25 miles) being the longest." And again on the 2nd of September when he reported, "Capt. Van Duzer Supt. mil Teleg telegraphs from Marietta, Ga. as follows— 3 p.m. our forces entered Atlanta 2 hours since. Will have line there before we sleep." The telegraph moved south with Sherman as he approached Atlanta and became essential to the commanders in the field. Throughout this period telegraphic communications were functioning efficiently. General Sherman's messages to Grant and Washington were arriving normally the same day as transmitted. Timely reporting was in fact becoming a reality.

Knowing that the Army was on the move on many fronts gave much of the Union populace a feeling of euphoria in the belief that defeat of the Confederate forces was imminent. This led to increased interest in both peace terms and reconstruction. The controversy over the "how and what" of reconstruction came to a head early in this period when on the 4th of July President Lincoln received the Wade-Davis Bill which he pocket-vetoed. He wanted more lenient policies such as those he was currently encouraging in the new governments in Louisiana (where a pro-Union constitution was later ratified on the 5th of September) and in Arkansas. On the 5th of August, still believing that Congress should set the criteria for the reconstruction period, Senator Benjamin Wade and Representative H. W. Davis issued their Wade-Davis Manifesto in direct opposition to the reconstruction plans of President Lincoln. This controversy continued to smolder for the remainder of the war years.[1]

In both the Confederacy and the Union, there was a rising interest in the possibility of peace negotiations. However, both governments knew that the other side's terms made negotiations impossible; the Confederacy's demand for recognition was absolutely counter to the Union's demand for an unconditional surrender. But the hope for peace continued to be expressed in the press and by politicians.

Presidential politics were rapidly coming to the forefront of public interest as the Democratic National Convention began the nominating process in Chicago on the 29th of August. The Democrat's opposition to the unconditional surrender requirement of President Lincoln was readily apparent as their lead-off speaker was the well-known Copperhead leader, Clement Vallandingham.[2] General George B. McClellan was nominated as their presidential candidate on a platform that called for "immediate efforts [to] be made for a cessation of hostilities." In his acceptance letter of September 8th, McClellan, in contrast to the President's unconditional surrender stand, spoke only in terms of reunion and maintained that when "any one State is willing to return to the Union, it should be received at once, with a full guarantee of all its constitutional rights."

On the 17th of September the Presidential candidate of the Radical Republicans, John C. Frémont, withdrew as a candidate. He feared that his candidacy would result in a Democratic victory which would lead to recognition of the Confederacy as well as the continuation of slavery. He pledged his support to President Lincoln. By late August

Lincoln felt that his chances for reelection were slim. However, with the fall of Atlanta and Sheridan's victories in the Shenandoah Valley in September, the general mood of the country and the Republican party was on the upswing. The Confederacy hoped that the Union Presidential elections would result in a new President with more liberal terms for peace.

However, General Grant's strategy of constant pressure on the Confederate armies continued. The Union military engaged in the Battle of Atlanta, the Battle of Mobile Bay, the Siege of Petersburg, battles around Richmond, and the clearing of the Confederates from the Shenandoah Valley. The Confederates were so totally occupied countering the Union thrusts that their only offensive actions consisted of General Early's raid on Washington and General Forrest's activities against Sherman's supply lines.

Early's raid on Washington early in July was followed by his raid on the town of Chambersburg, Pennsylvania, on July 30th in retaliation for Union actions in the Shenandoah. His actions led to General Grant's order on August 8th to General Sheridan to rid the Shenandoah Valley of all Confederate presence. The final battles of the Shenandoah were fought on the 19th and 22nd of September at Winchester and Fisher's Hill respectively, resulting in the expulsion of the Confederates from their "bread basket."

In the meantime further south Sherman continued his push with battles at Peachtree Creek, Bald (or Leggett's) Hill, Ezra Church (in late July), Utoy Creek; the raid on Lovejoy's Station and the battle of Jonesborough in August; and the fall of Atlanta on the 2nd of September. The combined efforts of the Army and Navy from the 5th to the 23rd of August resulted in the fall of the Mobile Bay defenses, leaving Wilmington, North Carolina, as the only port remaining open for Confederate ship traffic.

The Army of the Potomac was pressing the cities of Petersburg and Richmond throughout this period. On the 30th of July, the Battle of the Crater started with the detonation of a massive bomb in a tunnel dug by Union soldiers under the Petersburg defenses. Other battles around Petersburg soon followed: the Battles at Globe Tavern and Reams' Station in August. There was sporadic action at Deep Bottom in July; Chaffin's Bluff in August; and Fort Harrison, Fort Gilmer, and New Market Heights in September. Neither Petersburg nor Richmond fell to the Union during this period.          *Donald E. Markle*

*Friday, July 1, 1864*

Rumors come to us of an advance of the rebels down the Shenandoah Valley. Gen. Sigel is at Martinsburg [WV] with a small force & is very much alarmed. The force of the rebels is said to consist of Early's & Breckenridge's Divisions with McCausland's[3] Mtd Infy.

*Saturday, July 2, 1864*

Maj. Eckert reached here yesterday eve'g. He tells me that Secy. Chase has resigned & that the position has been tendered to Gov. Tod of Ohio.[4]

*Sunday, July 3, 1864*

Today I am twenty-one years old. How quickly does time fly & how ought we to improve each moment.

It seems but a short time ago that I was a schoolboy & in bib & tuckers. (Wonder where I'll be a year from now & if the war will be ended.)

Maj. Eckert went to Hd Qrs 5 a.m. today. I will go there tomorrow.

*Monday, July 4, 1864*

I left City Pt. at 5 a.m. & came by horseback to Gen. Meade's HdQrs just west of Petersburg. There is very little excitement here today for the 4th. No firing of consequence.

*Tuesday, July 5, 1864*

Left the front of Petersburg at 5 a.m. today & City Pt. at 11 a.m. for Washn. The ride down the James is very pleasant. Weather is not very warm. We passed the *Atlanta*[5] off Ft. Powhattan & the *Roanoke*[6] in Hampton Roads.

*Wednesday, July 6, 1864*

Arrived in Wash. 10 a.m. today. Found all well & glad to see me. I was pleased to get back to my post once more. The trip did me great good. I feel in excellent condition.

Senator Fessenden[7] has been appointed & confirmed Secy. of the Treasury. It gives universal satisfaction.

*Thursday, July 7, 1864*

The rebels have driven Gen. Sigel out of Martinsburg. Crossed the Potomac at Williamsport [MD] & are advancing into Md. said to be 30,000 strong. Our lines are cut between here and Pt. of Rocks.[8] It is said they intend to advance on Balto. & Washn. Great excitement prevails!

*Friday, July 8, 1864*

Tonight Gen. Lew Wallace[9] telegraphs that he encountered the forces of the Enemy at Monocacy Junction [MD] today & fought them from 9 till 4 when they overpowered him with numbers & he was compelled to fall back. He is retreating now on Balto. His troops very much disorganized & demoralized, the enemy pursuing.[10]

*Saturday, July 9, 1864*

Genl. Wallace has reached Ellicott's Mills on his way to Balto. The enemy today broke the Wilmington Railroad at Gunpowder Bridge, captured two trains of passrs cars. Gen. Franklin[11] & staff were on one of them. A train was set on fire & run on the bridge & the draw and part of the bridge were destroyed.

*Sunday, July 10, 1864*

The rebels today, under Gen. Early, broke the Balto road near Laurel,[12] tore down all telegraph lines. We are thus completely isolated from the rest of mankind. It is reported the enemy are approaching on the Rockville road.

Genl. Augur[13] has recd a despatch from a party of Cavalry stating that they were driven out of Rockville [MD] by the rebs at 1 p.m. today. We have not heard from Dwight[14] since noon. He was then at Darnestown on his way to Rockville. We are afraid he is captured.

*Monday, July 11, 1864*

Dwight came in circuit at Tenallytown[15] last night, having gone to the South of Rockville, eluding the rebels. The enemy are approaching Ft. Reno on the Rockville road & Ft. Stevens on the Brookville road. They are in sight at both Stevens & Reno.[16] Great excitement prevails throughout the City. Quartermaster employees are being armed & sent to the trenches & the clerks do guard duty.

*Tuesday, July 12, 1864*

An attack was fully expected to be made last night. The 6th Corps & one Div of the 9th are arriving by water from New Orleans. The Capital is felt to be safe.

*Wednesday, July 13, 1864*

This morning it is found the rebs have left our front. They are reported to have left in direction of Rockville. They have large trains & are full of plunder. The B & O RR was examined today & found to be uninjured. The teleg line was repaired & we are once more in communication with the North.

Genl. Wright has been put in command of the force operating against this force of the rebels. He moves out immediately toward Rockville.

*Thursday, July 14, 1864*

It is ascertained that Genl. Franklin escaped from rebels & is now in Balto. He was very fortunate. The rebels are said to be crossing the Potomac at Edward's Ferry.[17] Gen. Wright is following them closely. He is at Darnestown today. Genl. Ord[18] has been ordered here by rail to follow Genl. Wright. Ord is directed to report to Gen. Grant for assignment to the 10th Corps, Genl. Brooks[19] having resigned.

*Friday, July 15, 1864*

Railroad opened to Harper's Ferry today.[20] Gen. Howe[21] was then at Frederick. Gen. Hunter at Harper's Ferry. Hunter has started Crook with 8,000 men towards Aldie [VA] via Purcellville [VA] & cooperating with Genl. Wright may be able to hurt the rebels very much.

*Saturday, July 16, 1864*

Gen. McCook was today relieved from duty in this Dept & ordered to report to the Adj. Gen. at the expiration of a ten-day leave of absence. His brother Col. Dan McCook is lying very ill at Steubenville [OH] not expected to live.[22]

All of the 19th Corps has by this time arrived & what did not land here went to City Pt. The troops of the 6th Corps & all others that could be spared will be sent to Genl. Grant at once and a bold stroke will be made for Petersburg. We are expecting every day to hear of the taking of Atlanta by Sherman.

*Sunday, July 17, 1864*

Genl. Wright was ordered today to return to Wash with the 6th & 19th Corps leaving Gen. Hunter to pursue the Enemy. The 6th & the 19th will be sent immedy to City Pt.

We have rumors thro rebel sources that Gen. A. J. Smith[23] has been attacked by Gen. S. D. Lee[24] at Tupelo [MS] very near Okolona & after a 3 hour fight repulsed him.[25] Lee calls it a drawn battle, but it is presumed to be a Union victory.

*Monday, July 18, 1864*

Gen. Wright's troops & those of Crook have found a junction near Purcellville [VA] & attacked the Enemy's rear guard taking some wagons & horses & 60 prisoners.

Sherman's army is all across the Chattahoochee & on its way to Decatur [GA] & Stone Mountain [GA]. The railroad[26] will be broken at that point & destroyed as far East as possible. The railroad from Atlanta south[27] will then be broken & Atlanta invested.

Nothing new from Genl. Grant. I rode out to Mt. Pleasant Hospital[28] this morning to see [A. J.] Bosquet, opr from Arlington who is there sick.

*Tuesday, July 19, 1864*

Our lines to Harper's Ferry re-commenced working today. Weather pleasant. No news of importance.

*Wednesday, July 20, 1864*

A. J. Bosquet operator from Arlington died last evening at Mt. Pleasant Hospital. He will be buried tomorrow. He had no friends in this Country save a bro-in-law in Canada. It seems sad for one to die so far away from home & friends. He was a good boy.

*Thursday, July 21, 1864*

Gen. Sherman telegraphs from 3 miles from Atlanta that he has advanced up to within that distance of the City. Our forces occupy the Railroad from Decatur to near Atlanta[29] & have destroyed about five miles of it. We have had some fighting, rebels attacking and being repulsed each time with loss. Johnston has been relieved & Hood[30] put in his stead.

Wright & Crook formed a junction near Winchester & whipped the rebels under Early & captured 4 guns & 200 pris. besides a quantity of small arms.

*Friday, July 22, 1864*

Gen. Sherman telegraphs from near Atlanta, dated 7:30 p.m. 21st that the Enemy came out of his entrenchments the day before and attacked us with great fury.[31] Our men were protected by rail barricade & suffered little loss. They repulsed the rebels at all points after two hours fighting. He [the rebels] left 600 or 800 dead & a great number on the field of battle, of which we held undisputed possession. Our guns are now within easy range of the City and tomorrow (22nd) we will begin the bombardment.[32] It is thought by Gen. Sherman that Hood will evacuate the place. The rebel papers say that Rousseau[33] has struck the railroad between Montgomery [AL] & Opelika [AL].[34] This leaves the rebels but one railroad on which to retreat. Our Cavalry has gone east from Decatur [AL] to destroy the railroad & bridges over the Yellow River [AL] & Uleofanhatchee Creek [AL].

Gen. Hunter telegraphs that Gen. Averill has whipped the rebels at Winchester & they are retreating on all the roads to Strasburg [VA] & Front Royal [VA].

A call for 500,000 men was made by the Prest. on the 19th inst. to serve for one year. The draft will take place in 50 days from that date.[35]

*Saturday, July 23, 1864*

Gen. Sherman telegraphs dated 6:30 a.m. today that yesterday about 11 a.m. as we were arranging our troops the enemy fell suddenly upon the 17th Corps (Blair's) & forced them 500 yards, but these troops were reinforced by Dodge's Corps (16th)[36] & regained their grounds. The rebel Cavy got well into our rear and captured a few wagons at Decatur. About 4 p.m. the rebels sallied against Morgan L. Smith's Divsn[37] of 15th Corps & forced them back & got possession of two batteries, but the ground was soon recovered & the batteries retaken. The fight was pretty constant & severe, old p.m. darkness closed the contest. Our loss is estimated at 3,000 & as we fought on the defensive the loss of the enemy will be equally as large.

Our lines are now within a mile & a half of the heart of the City. Our front lines will be entrenched during today & hopes are entertained of a speedy victory.

Gen. Wright's troops have arrived within the entrenchments of Washn & will be refitted & equipped ready for transportation to City Point.

*Sunday, July 24, 1864*

All is quiet here today.

Gen. Hunter telegraphs that Crook has had a severe fight with the Enemy South of Winchester [VA][38] & that the Enemy is in very strong force in Crook's front & are pressing him. It is said that Longstreet is in the Valley with reinforcements from Richmond.

*Monday, July 25, 1864*

Gen. Sherman telegraphs dated 3 p.m. 24th that after examining the field he finds the rebel loss was far greater than was reported, 1,000 of their dead have been buried. Our loss cannot exceed 1,500.

Gen. Rousseau has arrived safely at Marietta [GA]. He destroyed the Depot of supplies at Opelika [AL] & the Railroad towards Montgomery for 30 miles, toward West Pt. [GA] for 5 miles & towards Columbus [GA] for 3 miles.[39] His loss all told was 30 men.

Gen. Garrard had also returned to Sherman having destroyed the bridge at Covington [GA] & Convers, 1 locomotive & train & a quantity of stores & destroyed the railroads for many miles.

As soon as Sherman's Cavalry rests he will swing rapidly around by their right flank and strike the railroad below Atlanta on the Macon road, the only remaining line of communication they have.

Grant is preparing to make an important movement about Wednesday looking to the capture of Petersburg.

*Tuesday, July 26, 1864*

Gen. Crook yesterday evacuated Martinsburg [WV], crossing the Potomac at Williamsport [MD] & marching for South Mountain [MD]. The pursuing Column of the Enemy is said to be quite large. Early having been reinforced by troops from Richmond, Gen. Wright with the 6th & part of the 19th Corps (19,000 in all), moved out today on the Rockville road to report to Gen. Hunter for orders. Hunter's troops will come this way to effect a junction with Wright.

*Wednesday, July 27, 1864*

No news of the Enemy today. Wright & Crook are rapidly approaching each other near the Monocacy [River].

Gen. Sherman moved the entire Army of the Tenn. round by the right this morning. He will strike the Macon road South of Atlanta. A cavalry force of 3,500 men under Genl. McCook will move to the RR striking farther South & a force under Stoneman will move by the left towards Griffin. After destroying the RR, Stoneman will march for Macon and attempt to liberate our officers confined there as prisoners. From there he will try to reach Anderson[ville][40] where 20,000 of our prisoners are now confined. Stoneman will not be able to do all this, but he will make a desperate effort.

Gen. Grant began a movement this morning which he expects will compel the rebels to withdraw their raiding force from Md.[41] It is to be hoped he may succeed. Weather very pleasant & a trifle warm.

*Thursday, July 28, 1864*

Gen. Sherman telegraphs dated 10 p.m. 27th that his movement to the right of the Army of Tennessee is being accomplished quietly, the Enemy making little opposition. The two Cavalry Expeditions got well off early yesterday morning.

Gen. Howard has been assigned to the Command of the Army of the Tenn,[42] Slocum[43] to the Command of the 20th Corps vice Howard, & Gen. D. S. Stanley[44] to command the 4th Corps vice Hooker [who was] relieved at his own request. Hooker asked to be relieved because Howard his junior was placed in Command of the Army of the Tenn.

Gen. Grant telegraphs that the 2d Corps & Sheridan & Cavy moved day before yesterday to the north bank. They surprised a small force of rebels & captured them with four 20 pd Parrott guns. The rebels attempted to drive us from our position near New Market on the Charles City road & were repulsed with losses.[45] Gen. Grant left City Pt. at 3:30 p.m. today for scene of action.

No news of the Enemy in Shenandoah Valley of importance. It is said they are running all the threshing machines & gathering all the crops.

The balance of the 19th Corps is arriving this p.m. They will be pushed out towards Wright who is near the Monocacy.

*Friday, July 29, 1864*

Gen. Couch[46] at Chambersburg [PA] reports that the Enemy is crossing in heavy force at Williamsport. Our force was moving to meet them.

The Enemy assaulted our right at Atlanta again yesterday, the 15th Corps bearing the blow & were handsomely repulsed.[47] Our men were under cover, the enemy were exposed. Our right is well swung around towards the Macon road but does not yet touch it.

The weather is extremely hot. Therm. 97 [degrees] in the shade.

*Saturday, July 30, 1864*

Nothing of importance from the Armies today. Gen. Sherman reports that Maj. Gen. W. H. T. Walker[48] killed on the 22nd inst. at Atlanta & it is reported by prisoners that Wheeler & Loring[49] were wounded.

Chambersburg[50] was occupied by the rebels at 3 o'clk this a.m. Gen. Couch's old Hd Qrs and Mr. McClives house together with other buildings were burned. Moseby [Mosby][51] crossed the Potomac near Pt. of Rocks this morning with 400 men & was at Adamstown [MD]

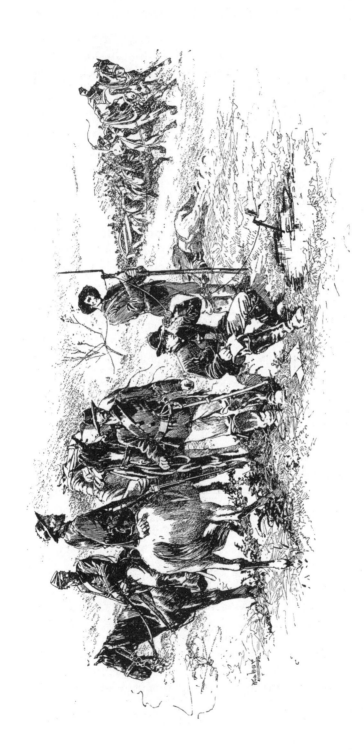

A Field Expedient

*(From Century Magazine, 38, 1889, p. 786)*

on the B & O road at 2 p.m. He cut the telegh lines. Maj. Thompson moved out from Poolesville [MD] and attacked him, results unknown.

Genl. Grant meets the Prest. at Ft. Monroe at 10 a.m. tomorrow (Sunday).

*Sunday, July 31, 1864*

Weather intensely hot today. No sign of rain. Gen. Grant telegraphs that finding his movement of the 2d Corps & Sheridan's Army to Deep Bottom drew all of the enemy's forces towards that point from Petersburg except 3 Divisions, he concluded to make an assault on the works of the latter place. Accordingly at 5 a.m. yesterday, the mine in front of Burnside which has been under way for sometime was exploded throwing 4 rebel guns into the air & burying almost an entire fourth of the Carolina Regt.[52] Our men immedy took possession of the crater & the parapet to the right & still held it up to last night.[53] An attempt to take a very strong work beyond failed & was compelled to fall back to our old lines.

Gen. Hunter reached Frederick [MD] today. It is not known where the Enemy is. Gen. Averill drove McCausland out of Chambersburg yesterday & McConnellsburg [PA] at 8 this morning toward Hancock. The rebels burned most of Chambersburg & nearly all the houses on the road. They were making arrangements to burn McConnellsburg when Averill came up & prevented it. Moseby recrossed the Potomac yesterday p.m. pursued by Col. Clendenin,[54] but with small prospect of being caught.

*Monday, August 1, 1864*

Information from Gen. Grant shows that the loss on our side in withdrawing from the position we took on 30th was full 4,000. The attempt failed because after the explosion 2 hours were allowed to elapse before any advance was made by Gen. Meade. Time was thus given to the Enemy to bring up reinforcements.

*Tuesday, August 2, 1864*

A Division of Cavalry is arriving here from City Point. Gen. Sheridan[55] comes up to command it together with all the cavalry of Hunter's & Augur's Dept.

The Enemy pursued by Averill went towards Cumberland where he was met by Kelly [Kelley][56] who fought them for two hours & compelled them to again retreat with the loss of all their dead & wounded, two caissons & 1 gun carriage & a large number of wagons, horses, etc.

Gen. Sherman telegraphs that Col. Brownlow[57] was just arrived at Marietta with a portion of his Regt. He was with McCook[58] who destroyed the Macon road for 12 miles & as well as a large bridge over the White Waters & 500 wagons including Gen. Hood's Hd Qrs train. Instead of keeping on however according to orders, McCook took the backtrack & began destroying the West Pt. Road & was surrounded by an overwhelming force of rebel Infy & Cavalry & most of the command were killed or captured. A portion cut their way out & 500 have reached Marietta & others are straggling. The loss to us in Cavalry is very severe, but the damage to the rebels is very great. It is said the road cannot be repaired for 15 days.

Schofield moved from left to right last night and today the Army of the Tenn. moves to East Pt [GA]. Hood will then be compelled to come out of his works & attack Sherman.

*Wednesday, August 3, 1864*

Nothing new of military importance. Gen. Hunter is at Monocacy [MD]. Sheridan arrived today with part of one Division of his Cavalry.

Gen. Sherman's Army was got into position yesterday ready to advance on East Pt.

Weather warm but pleasant.

*Thursday, August 4, 1864*

Today is the day appointed by the Prest. for fasting, humiliation & prayer. The Depts are all closed.

Richmond papers of yesterday claim that Genl. Stoneman was attacked by rebel Gen. Iverson[59] at Clinton [GA] 15 miles north of Macon on the 31st & was routed. 75 officers including Stoneman,[60] with 500 prisoners surrendered themselves & had arrived in Macon. The remnant was lying towards Eatonton [GA]. This report is supposed to be much exaggerated. Genl. McCook has turned up with 1,200 of his command at Dallas [GA] having cut his way through the Enemy. This leaves but 1,000 not yet accounted for and who may come in. They are under Col. Croxton.[61]

Genl. Hunter reports the Enemy advancing on H. Ferry in two columns, one by way of Charlestown & one by Sheperdstown [WV]. At 4:30 p.m. we were driven at Antietam Ford [MD] & the Enemy commenced crossing in heavy force with Cavalry and Infantry. The 9th Corps has been sent to the relief of H. Ferry.

*Friday, August 5, 1864*

Genl. Grant arrived here this morning from City Point on his way to Genl. Hunter's Hd Qrs. He goes up to organize against the Enemy in the Valley.

Gen. Sheridan telegraphs that Col. Adams[62] has arrived with 900 men. He was in Stoneman's command. Sherman's lines are being drawn closer to the Railroad.

The Enemy did not make the contemplated attack on H. Ferry. All reports now agree that no considerable force of rebels is in Md., nothing but a cavalry force & a large wagon train with which to carry grain & wheat collected in Maryland. One brigade of cavalry left today for Harper's Ferry. Another tomorrow. Gen. Wilson's Div of Cavy will begin leaving City Pt. today for Washn. With this large Cavalry force it is expected we will be able to drive the Enemy out of the valley & down as far as Gordonsville.

*Saturday, August 6, 1864*

Raining today quite hard. The ground needed rain badly.

Gen. Sheridan has been assigned to command all the troops in the field in the Depts of Washn, Md., West Va. & Penna. He left this morning for H. Ferry where all troops will be concentrated.

Gen. Grant returned here today from Gen. Hunter's Army. He leaves for City Pt. tomorrow.

*Sunday, August 7, 1864*

We have information dated New Orleans 30th, that Adml. Farragut[63] has begun an attack on Mobile.[64] Our troops under Granger made a landing on Dauphin's Island near Mobile.

Sherman reports that Palmer[65] has resigned & Jeff Davis[66] is recommended by Sherman & Thomas for promotion to the rank of Maj. Gen. & to take command of 14th Corps in Palmer's stead. Gen. Hunter has asked to be relieved from command of the Dept of West Va. because the Prest. found fault with him ordering south some rebel citizens in his Dept. who act as spies & send information & supplies to the rebels & point out Union men when the rebels enter into the town. I presume he will be relieved & Kelly [Kelley] put in his place. Kelly has been made a Maj. Gen. by brevet.

*Monday, August 8, 1864*

Genl. Custer's Brigade of Cavalry left here at dawn this morning for Harper's Ferry. Gen. Sheridan is making arrangements to march upon the enemy at once. His troops are all at H. Ferry now & he will commence moving them today in direction of Winchester [VA].

Gen. Kelly telegraphs that Averell yesterday defeated the Enemy at Moorefield [WV], capturing all his arty & 500 prisoners.[67]

Gen. Butler teleghs that the *Richmond Sentinel* of today contains the following details of the movements on Mobile.

*Mobile, Aug. 5th to Hon. J. A. Seddon,*[68] *Sec of War:*
17 vessels, 14 ships & 3 ironclads passed Ft. Morgan this morning. The *Tecumseh*, a monitor,[69] was sunk. The *Tennessee* the rebel flag ship surrendered after a desperate engagement with the Federal fleet. The *Galina* was captured. The *Gaines* was beached near the hospital. Adml. Buchanan[70] lost a leg & is a prisoner. The *Morgan* is safe & will try to run up tonight. A Monitor has been shelling Ft. Powell all day. The fleet has approached Mobile.

Signed D. H. Maury, Mj. Gen.[71]

A telegram from Cairo says news from below confirms death of rebel Gen. Forrest.[72]

*Tuesday, August 9, 1864*
No news. Very warm today. Stewart is away on furlough. When he returns Baldwin goes & then Tinker.[73]

*Wednesday, August 10, 1864*
*Richmond Examiner* of 9th has news from Mobile up to 7th, says no material change to situation. The *Morgan* the only rebel gunboat that was not sunk, beached on Island [and] had succeeded in passing the bars & reaching the City.

Gen. Grant telegraphs that an ordnance boat exploded at City Pt. yesterday noon killing two men & wounding several others, and throwing fragments of the explosion all over his Hd Qrs. Some consternation was created at first till it was found what the trouble was.[74]

*Thursday, August 11, 1864*
Genl. Butler forwards following from *Richmond Enquirer* of 10th.

*Mobile, Aug. 8*
On Friday night last, Lt. Col. Williams[75] evacuated & blew up Ft. Powell at the northern entrance of Grant's pass. Second despatch, Mobile, 8th. Fort Gaines was surrendered this

morning at half-past 9 o'clock by Col. Anderson[76] of 21st Ala. Regt. It had 50 guns, 600 men & was provisioned for 6 mos.

Ft. Gaines is on Dauphin Island [AL] opposite Ft. Morgan which is on the mainland. The *Morgan*, the only rebel gunboat that was not either sunk, beached or captured on the 5th, had succeeded in getting over the breach & reached the city.

Gen. Sheridan's march reached Berryville [VA] 20 miles from Harper's Ferry at 3 p.m. yesterday.

*Friday, August 12, 1864*

Gen. Sheridan telegraphs that he forced the Enemy to abandon his position at Winchester & to fall back in direction of Strasburg on the 11th. Sheridan was yesterday 8 miles south of Winchester & in pursuit of Enemy.

Gen. Grant telegraphs that it is certain 2 divisions of troops have left the vicinity of Petersburg for Early. They commenced leaving last Saturday. This will make Early's force about 40,000 now too strong for Sheridan to attack, but he [Sheridan] can act on the defensive until movements at Petersburg force the rebels to detach & send troops to that point.

*Saturday, August 13, 1864*

Gen. Canby teleghs that all his information leads to the conclusion that Kirby Smith is collecting his forces to move eastward to assist the forces operating against Sherman. Canby has made dispositions accordingly.

It rained considerably this eve'g. The air is much cooler in consequence.

*Sunday, August 14, 1864*

All quiet today. More rain has fallen. Tinker has been unwell. I have been unable therefore to go to Church today.

*Monday, August 15, 1864*

Gen. Sheridan telegraphs dated 11 a.m. 14th that he recd. Gen. Grant's telegram of the 12th on 13th which stated that two Divisions of Infantry had left front of Petersburg to join Early & directed him (Sheridan) to act on the defensive until Gen. G. by his movements there caused the rebels to detach troops from Early to reinforce Richmond. Sheridan was on Cedar Creek but said that he would fall back to the line of Winchester where he could be easily supplied. He was sorry that he had recd the orders & wants to push forward after the rebels.

Gen. Grant telegraphs dated from Deep Bottom 11:30 a.m. of the 14th stating that he had the night before moved the 2d Corps, 9,000 men of the 10th Corps & Gregg's Cavy to North side of the James to threaten Richmond from the North. He does not state any result of the movement.

Sherman telegraphs that he proposes to leave a Corps at the Chattahoochee to guard bridges, trains, stores, etc. & with the balance of his army, 60,000 men in fighting trim, to move to the south & S.E. of Atlanta & make "a devastating circle of ruin around the city." He will compel Hood to come out & attack us. Weather cool & pleasant. It rained a little more today.

Genl. Grant at this time has 75,000 men fit for service, 50,000 are absent, sick & wounded, 5,000 of these officers. He had 160,000 men when he reached the James River including Butler's force.

Surgeons & inspectors are examining all the northern Hospls & will send forward every man able to do duty.

*Tuesday, August 16, 1864*

Genl. Canby teleghs from New Orleans dated 9th that Ft. Gaines [on Dauphin Island in Mobile Bay] surrendered unconditionally on the 8th, 56 comd officers, 818 men & 26 Guns. Ft. Powell [in Mobile Bay] was abandoned the night before, its garrison escaping to Cedar Pt. 19 guns were left in our hands. Gen. Granger reinforced by 2,000 men was to proceed immediately to the investment of Ft. Morgan [in Mobile Bay]. Canby says he thinks Kirby Smith is trying to make a movement East of the Mississippi to aid the forces against Sherman.

A force of rebels have entered Illinois crossing the Ohio at Shawnee-town [IL] at which place they captured 3 Govt boats, laden with cattle. Troops and militia are being moved against them.

Genl. Grant teleghs that he has captured 6 guns & 400 pris. in his movement across the James. The rebels he says will be compelled to retain Longstreet's Corps at Richmond.

Sheridan has moved his forces back to Winchester in accordance with Gen. Grant's orders.

*Wednesday, August 17, 1864*

Capt. Van Duzer[77] teleghs from Kingston [GA] dated 3 p.m. today that telegh communications with Chattanooga had been broken since Sunday morning. Wheeler attacked Dalton [GA] but was repulsed by

Grant, Sheridan, Meade, Rawlins and a Telegraph Operator

*(From Century Magazine, 38, 1889, p. 792)*

Genls. Steedman[78] & Jno E. Smith[79] and retreated towards Spring Place [GA] pursued by our forces.

Nothing new at Atlanta except that the left is retired to prepare for the flank movement which will begin in a few days. Nothing new from Mobile. Sheridan reports that the stories of vast amounts of grain & plunder being taken off by Early are all humbug. His army is in & around Winchester. Nothing more from Gen. Grant's late movement.

*Thursday, August 18, 1864*

Gen. Warren telegraphs that the movement of the 2d & 10th Corps to the north of the James River is a success. There has been some fighting. The Enemy has been somewhat driven from their positions & have lost heavily.[80] We captured 400 pris, besides about 100 of their dead and wounded. Two of their Brig. Genls. were killed, Chambliss & Gherarde [Girardey].[81]

Gen. Warren's Corps has been relieved from the trenches & is held ready to be moved to the south of Petersburg as soon as the Enemy moves enough of his forces north of the James to oppose our progress there to warrant it. This movement will have the effect of preventing reinforcements going to Atlanta & of drawing back some that are in the valley. Grant says he will keep them busy.

Gen. Sheridan is at Charlestown [West] Va. He says Early has been considerably reinforced, that troops are still arriving. Torbert was driven out of Winchester yesterday. He had part of Wilson's & his own Divn.

Weather is considerably cooler. Great deal of rain has fallen lately.

*Friday, August 19, 1864*

Gen. Sherman telegraphs that Wheeler has gone up into East Tenn. & that he is going to take advantage of the opportunity this offered to break the Macon road again. Kilpatrick with 5 Brigade of Cavy, was to leave last night for that purpose. At the same time Sherman will demonstrate along his whole line.

Genl. Grant telegraphs that Warren's Corps was moved yesterday coming to & across the Weldon Railroad about one mile South of the Lead Works. From there he advanced towards Petersburg meeting the enemy. He had considerable fighting during the day. No report of the losses or of the results of the day's work. Some rebel wounded fell into our hands & some other prisoners.

*Saturday, August 20, 1864*

Sherman telegraphs that he had heavy demonstrations along his whole line yesterday to enable Kilpatrick to tear up the Macon road well. He thinks great things will result from this breaking of that Road. Gen. Dodge[82] was slightly wounded.

Sheridan reports that the Enemy has shown considerable force in his front & all his information still goes to show that Early has rec'd large reinforcements.

Fitz Lee's Cavalry is said to be on our right flank. Sheridan can bring into action 23,000 Infy & 3,000 Cavry.

Nothing new from Mobile after p.m.

Genl. Grant teleghs dated last night that the Enemy came out yesterday evening & attacked Warren's right but were repulsed with considerable loss in killed, wounded & prisoners. The prisoners captured say that Lee is running his men to death shifting them around from one place to another.

Our troops are firmly fixed in the Weldon road. Gen. Birney[83] Cmdg the 10th Corps reports that the Enemy attacked him in heavy force on the evening of the 18th. They attacked in column & driven strong but were handsomely met & repulsed. The rebel's loss is at least 1,000. The colored troops behaved excellently.

Gen. Grant's report says the Enemy have lost this week, not less than 4,000 perhaps more. It has rained considerable at Petersburg this week & a grateful change in the atmosphere has taken place.

*Sunday, August 21, 1864*

Weather cloudy, but cool & pleasant. Tinker is sick with jaundice & not at the office. Business very heavy.

The rebels attacked Sheridan's skirmish & picket lines near Charlestown [WV] today & followed it up with a movement of two Infy Divisions. The fighting lasted all p.m. but was not very brisk. He failed to penetrate our lines.

*Monday, August 22, 1864*

Gen. Grant telegraphs that the Enemy came out & attacked Warren in heavy force yesterday. They were easily repulsed & with heavy losses. We took some 500 prisoners. The 2d Corps has been withdrawn from the north bank of the James River & is now within supporting distance of Warren. Wheeler attacked Maryville, Tenn. last night with Artly. Result not known.

Morgan with 3,000 men is said to be approaching Cumberland Gap.

*Tuesday, August 23, 1864*

Sherman teleghs that Kilpatrick is back having broken the roads about Jonesboro. He had some pretty severe fighting but whipped the enemy every turn & brought in 1 gun & 70 prisoners & 3 battle flags. He spiked several guns which he could not bring off. It will take the rebels 10 days to repair this break & before that time Sherman will swing around the City and cut it again.

*Wednesday, August 24, 1864*

Maj. Eckert & I went to the Soldier's Home[84] last night to experiment with an instrument for telegraphing by means of a calcium light.[85] A key is arranged so as to show the light at pleasure & by this means dots & dashes can be made quite successfully. We communicated with Chandler who was at Smithsonian Institution, very readily. The Prest., Adml. Davis of the Navy, Col. Nicodemus of the Signal Corps, Col. Dimick[86] were in a tower at Soldier's Home witnessing the experiments.

Genl. Grant teleghs that the Enemy are furious over our possession of the Weldon Road. They attack us there every day but each time have been repulsed with heavy loss to them & small loss to us. Scouts report that Gen. W. H. F. Lee son of Robert E. Lee is mortally wounded.[87]

Gen. Burbridge reports from Ky. that Gen. Hobson has defeated the rebel Col. Johnson[88] in Webster Co. & is now pursuing him.

Weather cool & pleasant.

*Thursday, August 25, 1864*

The lines of cable arrived at Ft. Monroe yesterday. Will be put down in a few days. Gen. Sherman moved this morning to the south & east of Atlanta leaving the 4th Corps entrenched at Chattahoochee [River] Bridge.

Genl. Grant telegraphs that the rebels still continue to attack Warren on the railroad and are repulsed with heavy loss each time.

*Friday, August 26, 1864*

Gen. Grant telegraphs that Hancock who is south of Reams' Stn on the Weldon R.R. has had some severe fighting. The enemy attacked him yesterday & were repulsed. Sheridan says it is certain Early has recd re-enforcements & has advanced his line somewhat & shows indications of crossing the River at Sheperdstown [WV]. If he does cross Sheridan will attack his divided force.

We have not recd our June money yet.

*Saturday, August 27, 1864*

Genl. Grant reports that Hancock who was south of & near Reams' Stn was attacked by the rebels day before yesterday.[89] They fell on him in heavy force & with great fierceness & all afternoon the battle lasted with great fury. Gen. Hancock was at first pushed back but rallied his troops & repulsed the enemy with great slaughter. He says that the fighting was desperate resembling somewhat that of Spotslyvania but the numbers engaged made it less important. The enemy captured 3 guns from him but lost very heavily in killed & wounded. They retired at dark being unable to force our lines, leaving their dead & wounded on the field.

Gen. Meade says he thinks the Enemy will remain quiet now for some time. Gen. Sheridan reports that Early has fallen back to Leetown [WV] & Smithfield [WV]. He captured 200 prisoners yesterday. Since Kershaw's[90] div entered the melee Sheridan has taken 500 prisoners from that Divn.

Tinker left yesterday for Halifax on special service. He has a cipher with him. He will watch the movements of A. Keith, Jr. of Halifax, the rebel agent there.

*Sunday, August 28, 1864*

Richmond papers give the rumors that Ft. Morgan [AL] is in our possession. No particulars yet.

*Monday, August 29, 1864*

Sherman's army is in the vicinity of Fairburn [GA] & Red Oak [GA] on the West Pt. Road & from that point well out towards the Macon Road. He reports all going well. Gen. Sheridan reports that Early has fallen back some distance towards Winchester. He is following him closely.

It is thought troops have gone from the valley to Richmond & to Atlanta. The rebels say Hood is killed & Longstreet is in command at Atlanta.[91] It is believed that some of Longstreet's troops have gone to that point, but his whereabouts are not known.

The rumor from Mobile that Ft. Morgan is in our possession is confirmed through rebel sources.

*Tuesday, August 30, 1864*

Our new cable across the Chesapeake at Ft. Monroe was laid Sunday & began to work at midnight of that day. It works very well. Today had Ft. Monroe contact City Pt. & we communicated direct from

Washn to City Pt. The distance is 430 miles & there are 11 cables, the one at Ft. Monroe (25 Miles) being the longest.

Genl. Grant reports all quiet yesterday. Chicago [Democratic] convention is in session now. Gen. McClellan will probably be the candidate for Prest. It will be a great pity if he is elected.

*Wednesday, August 31, 1864*

Maj. Eckert went to Ft. Monroe today to see about laying a cable from Jamestown Island to Ft. Powhattan. The landlines between those points cannot be well guarded.

McClellan was today nominated for Prest. by the Dem. Convention at Chicago. He rec'd on the first ballot 200 votes. Seymour[92] of N.Y., 23. Pendleton[93] of O[hio] will likely be nominated for Vice Prest.

Richmond papers of the 26th confirm the capture of Ft. Morgan. It surrendered to the Federal force on Tuesday the 23rd.

Gen. Page[94] with 531 men was sent to New Orleans. Granger has landed 4,000 men on the Mainland at Grant's Pass & will probably invest Mobile at once.

*Thursday, September 1, 1864*

No news of importance from any source. Weather pleasant and cool.

*Friday, September 2, 1864*

Capt. Van Duzer Supt. mil. Telg. telegraphs from Marietta, Ga. as follows—"3 p.m. our forces entered Atlanta 2 hours since. Will have line there before we sleep." This is glorious news & will do us a world of good at this time. Nothing new from any other quarter.

*Saturday, September 3, 1864*

Later news from Atlanta shows that Sherman fought Hood near East Pt. & defeated him. Stewart's Corps[95] of Hood's Army was left in Atlanta & Slocum drove him out & now occupies the city.

Averell whipped Vaughn's Cavy[96] in the Valley yesterday & captured 25 wagons, a herd of cattle & some pris. Sheridan reports that Early is at last retreating. Gen. S. is in pursuit.

*Monday, September 19, 1864*

On Sunday Sept 4, I was taken ill with inflammation of bowels, was confined to my bed until Sept 12. The attack was quite severe but I had medical attention in time and soon got over it.

I came to the Office on the 13th but stayed but a short time being really weak.

Genl. Sherman after whipping part of Hood's army under Hardee at Jonesboro on the Macon road, capturing some 3,000 pris. followed him to Lovejoy's Station 26 miles South of Atlanta where the rebels made a stand in an entrenched position.[97] In the meantime, Hood with the balance of his army in Atlanta finding Sherman on his only RR line,[98] blew up his magazines, burned 80 cans of ordnance, 5 tons of ammunition etc., destroyed several locomotives & evacuated the place on the night of the 1st. Gen. Slocum with the 20th Corps occupied the town next morning. He found large quantities of stores, 3,000 stands of small arms & a number of cannons some of which were spiked.

Gen. Sherman withdrew his army to the vicinity of Atlanta after remaining above Lovejoy's several days. He issued a congratulatory order to his troops in which he stated that since May 5, his troops had been in one constant battle or skirmish and they needed rest. He accordingly brought them to Atlanta for this purpose & to organize a new campaign.

Nothing new from Mobile. The rebels in Arkansas have concentrated to West, seriously threatening Genl. Steele's lines of communication & Missouri.

Gen. A. Smith's Division[99] has been ordered to Ark., & will enable Steele to fight the enemy successfully.

Gen. Gillem surprised John Morgan the noted rebel raider near Greenville [in] East Tenn. about ten days since & in the fight Morgan was killed. His remains were sent to Abingdon, Va. where they were buried. Thus ends the career of the most celebrated chieftain.[100]

On the 17 inst the rebels made a raid on a cattle herd near Coggins Pt. [VA], on the James River & succeeded in driving off 2,500 beef cattle.[101]

In the Shenandoah Valley all has been quiet till today when Gen. Stevenson[102] at Harper's Ferry reports that our Cavalry drove a force of the rebels on the Opequon [Creek] a distance of 2 miles capturing 200 of them. He also reports that heavy cannonading has been heard all day in the direction of Berryville [VA] & Winchester.

### Tuesday, September 20, 1864

The draft proceeded in the deficient districts throughout the country yesterday & the day before. All seems to have passed off quietly.[103]

Gen. Sheridan reports that he fought Early all day yesterday near the Berryville Pike at the crossing of the Opequon Creek. He completely defeated the Enemy driving him through Winchester captur-

Tapping a Wire

*(From Century Magazine, 38, 1889, p. 788)*

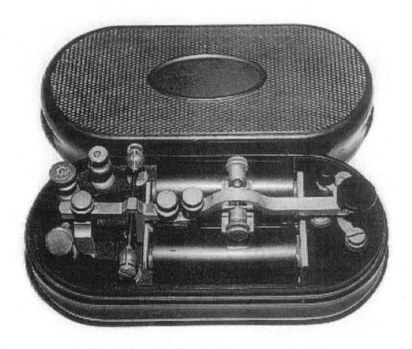

Wiretapping Equipment—Tillotson Lineman Pocket Test Set
*(Courtesy of W1TP Telegraph and Scientific Instrument Museum)*

ing 5,000 prisoners which includes 2,000 of his wounded left in Winchester, 15 battle flags & 5 pieces of artillery.[104] Genl. D. A. Russell[105] comdg a Div in 6th Corps, was killed. Gen. McIntosh[106] lost a leg. Gens. Upton[107] & Chapman[108] were slightly wounded. The rebels cost in killed: Genls. Rhodes [Rodes],[109] Gordon[110] & Terry[111] & severely wounded Genls. Ramseur,[112] Fitz Lee & York.[113] The enemy's loss cannot fall short of 7,000, ours is severe probably 4,000. Medical supplies have gone forward from H. Ferry.

The news of the glorious victory was sent to all the Govs. as soon as possible & 100 guns were ordered to be fired at the different arsenals.

*Wednesday, September 21, 1864*

Sheridan reports that he followed the retreating enemy as far as Strasburg. He occupies that place. The rebels hold a strong position called Fishers Hill. Our Cavalry are out on the enemy's flanks.

*Thursday, September 22, 1864*

Gen. Sherman reports that Hood has moved from Lovejoy's Stn to near Palmetto Station [GA] on the West Pt. road where his men are entrenching. Gen. Sherman does not understand what this movement means but will watch him closely.

Gen. Sheridan reports dated Strasburg 9 p.m. 21st that Gen. Wilson's Cavly Divn had a fight with Enemy at Front Royal yesterday, driving them out, & up the Luray Valley about six miles. Towards evening 2d Division & part of the 3rd Div 6th Corps had a sharp fight with the enemy resulting in our gaining & holding a strong position on the crest of a hill.

Everything else quiet. Gen. Sheridan has been appointed a Brig. Gen. in the regular Army for his gallant service.

*Friday, September 23, 1864*

Gen. Sheridan telegraphs that he achieved another victory over Early at Fisher's Hill[114] yesterday. Early's army occupied a very strong position & Sheridan maneuvered until 4 p.m. when Crook's Corps was shifted to the extreme right. He attacked the Enemy furiously & drove everything before him. At the same time the 6th & 9th Corps advanced on the front & the whole rebel army seemed to be broken up. Nothing saved them from total destruction but the darkness of the night. They fled up the valley in the greatest confusion. 16 pieces of cannon were captured & a great many pris. Genl. Sheridan has not the time to get the number. Besides there are great caissons, artillery, horses etc. & 2,000 prisoners of those taken yesterday have reached Winchester. This good news was quickly sent to the North. It brought gold down to [$]209 from [$]215. It was [$]220 at the first board.

*Saturday, September 24, 1864*

Nothing new of importance from Genl. Sheridan. He is pursuing the Enemy up the valley. He reports the 20 pcs [pieces] of artly were taken & large amounts of ammn, entrenching tools, etc. etc. Gold closed at [$]199 this evening.

*Sunday, September 25, 1864*

Gen. Sheridan's advance was at Mt. Jackson yesterday evening. He says the houses in the valley are many of them filled with rebel wounded.

The Prest. on Friday requested Montgomery Blair, PostMrGenl. to resign. The Prest. in his letter to Blair says: "As you have repeatedly assured me that you were willing & ready to resign any time that it would be relief to me, I have now to state that I think the time has come." Ex. Gov. Wm. Dennison[115] of Ohio has been proffered the position. He is absent in the country now & can't be reached by telegh.

*Monday, September 26, 1864*

Sheridan's advance is near New Market. He drove the rebels from Mt. Jackson but they traveled so fast he could not bring on an engagement with them. Torbert had a little fight with Wickham's Cavy[116] at Luray capturing a hundred prisoners.

The rumor that Mobile had surrendered unconditionally to our forces was recd today. Said to have come thro rebel sources. This report is discredited however. It sent gold down to [$]180 but it rallied the rumor being contradicted & went to [$]194.

*Thursday, September 29, 1864*

No news of importance yesterday & the day before.

Charlie Tinker had orders today to come home from Halifax. Genl. Sheridan's forces entered Staunton Monday according to rebel papers. Early recrossed the Shenandoah & went towards Pt. Republic. Sheridan pursued him but could not bring on an engagement.

Genl. Grant telegraphs that the 18th Corps advanced early this morning & captured the very strong fortifications below Chaffin's Farm[117] to the south & west of Drewry's Bluff. At the same time Gen. Birney with 10th Corps advanced on the New Market road & [has]

taken some very strong earthworks & a few prisoners & scattered the enemy before him.

Genl. Grant left Birney about 6 miles from Richmond. At 4 p.m. he telegphs that at last accounts Kautz was in sight of Richmond on the Darby road. A Div of Infy has been sent to his support. Gen. Ord's 18th Corps took 15 guns & several hundred prisoners. Genl. Grant's object was not to carry Richmond but to cause the Enemy to so weaken the Petersburg garrison as to enable us to take that place. The main object however [is] to prevent Lee sending troops to reinforce Early.

*Friday, September 30, 1864*

Genl. Grant reports that Genl. Warren attacked & carried the Enemy's line today on their extreme left. He immediately prepared to follow up his success. He captured a few prisoners.[118]

## Notes

[1]Radical Republicans, Representative Henry W. Davis of Maryland and Senator Benjamin Wade of Ohio, issued a response in the *New York Tribune* to Lincoln's pocket veto of their Wade-Davis Bill. This statement became known as the Wade-Davis Manifesto.

[2]The leader of the Copperheads or Peace Democrats was Clement Vallandingham, a former Ohio politician. The name Copperhead may have been associated with the Peace Democrats because many of the them wore the cut-out portion of a penny depicting the goddess of liberty in their coat lapels.

[3]Confederate Brigadier General John McCausland, Commander, Ransom's-Lomax's Cavalry Division, Valley District, Department of Northern Virginia.

[4]Governor David Tod of Ohio declined, for health reasons, Lincoln's request to make him the Secretary of the Treasury.

[5]The *Atlanta* was a captured Confederate Navy side-wheel steamer weighing 623 tons.

[6]The *Roanoke* was a Union Naval steam frigate rebuilt as an ironclad in 1862.

[7]William P. Fessenden, Senator from Maine, filled the post of Secretary of the Treasury from July 1, 1864, until he reentered the Senate on March 4, 1865.

[8]Point of Rocks, Maryland, on the Potomac River, west of Frederick, Maryland.

[9]Union Major General Lewis Wallace, Commander, 8th Corps, Middle Department.

[10]At the Battle of Monocacy July 9, 1864, Wallace's defensive actions delayed Early's march to Washington, allowing time for more defensive measures around the capital.

[11]Union Major General William B. Franklin, Commander, 19th Corps, Department of the Gulf, was captured by Major Harry W. Gilmor's raiders in a train raid as he traveled North, but escaped the same night.

[12]Laurel, Maryland, a small town midway between Baltimore and Washington was on the Baltimore and Ohio Railroad.

[13]Union Major General Christopher C. Augur, Commander, 22nd Corps and Department of Washington.

[14]J. H. Dwight was a member of the USMTC assigned to a telegraph station in rural Maryland.

[15]Tenallytown, Maryland, was located in the proximity of the Maryland/District of Columbia line, in the vicinity of present day Chevy Chase, Maryland.

[16]Forts Reno and Stevens were constructed to protect the city of Washington. Fort Reno was located in the Northwest quadrant of the city near the Maryland state line. Fort Stevens was also in the Northwest quadrant near the present day site of Walter Reed Army Hospital. Skirmishing with Early's forces at Fort Stevens occurred on July 11, 1864.

[17]Edward's Ferry was located on the upper Potomac River, southwest of Poolesville, Maryland.

[18]Union Major General Edward O. C. Ord, Commander, 18th Corps, Army of the Potomac, was later wounded during the storming of Ft. Harrison near Richmond, thereby negating his opportunity to command the 10th Corps as desired by General Grant.

[19]Union Brigadier General William T. H. Brooks, Commander, 10th Corps, Army of the James, resigned his commission on July 18, 1864, due to ill health.

[20]The railroad built to Harper's Ferry was a branch of the Baltimore and Ohio Railroad.

[21]Union Brigadier General Albion P. Howe, Commander, Reserve Division, Department of West Virginia.

[22]Union Brigadier General Alexander D. McCook was assigned to the Army of the Cumberland in a non-command position. His brother, Union Brigadier General Daniel McCook, Jr., was mortally wounded at the Battle of Kennesaw Mountain and was taken back to Ohio where he died July 17, 1864.

[23]Union Major General Andrew Jackson Smith, Commander, Detachment Army of the Tennessee, Department of the Cumberland.

[24]Confederate Lieutenant General Stephen D. Lee, Commander, Department of Alabama, Mississippi and East Louisiana.

[25]The Battle of Tupelo, Mississippi, occurred July 14, 1864.

[26]The railroad along the Chattahoochee north of Atlanta was the Western and Atlantic Railroad and to the south was the Atlanta and West Point Railroad.

[27]The railroad south of Atlanta was the Macon and Western Central Railroad.

[28]Mt. Pleasant Army General Hospital, located in an area of Washington known as Mt. Pleasant, was built in 1862 after the government had been pressured by the Sanitary Commission.

[29]The railroad at Decatur, Georgia, was the West Point or the Montgomery and Atlanta Railroad.

[30]Confederate General Joseph E. Johnston was relieved as Commander, Army of Tennessee, and replaced by General John B. Hood, effective July 18, 1864.

[31]The Battle of Peachtree Creek, Georgia, was fought July 20, 1864.

[32]The Battle of Atlanta commenced July 22, 1864.

[33]Union Major General Lovell H. Rousseau, Commander, 4th Division, 20th Corps, Department of the Cumberland, as well as the District of Nashville.

[34]The railroad between Montgomery and Opelika, Alabama, was the West Point or Montgomery and Atlanta Railroad.

[35]President Lincoln issued a draft proclamation for 500,000 volunteers to enter the Union Army for a period of one year. He felt the draft necessary to refill the ranks after the losses from the severe fighting in Virginia.

[36]Union Major General Grenville M. Dodge, Commander, Left Wing, 16th Corps, Army of the Tennessee.

[37]Union Brigadier General Morgan L. Smith, Commander, 15th Corps, Army of the Tennessee.

[38]The second Battle of Kernstown, Virginia, was fought July 24, 1864. After the battle Union forces retreated to Bunker Hill, West Virginia.

[39]The railroad at Opelika, Alabama, toward West Point was the Atlanta and West Point Railroad; toward Columbus it was the Columbus Railroad.

[40]Andersonville, Georgia, was the location of a large Confederate prisoner of war camp known for gross mistreatment of Union prisoners.

[41]Confederate forces of General Jubal A. Early.

[42]Union Major General Oliver O. Howard was picked by Sherman to command the Army of the Tennessee after the death of Major General James McPherson on July 22, 1864.

[43]Union Major General Henry Slocum was named Commander, 20th Corps, Army of the Cumberland.

[44]Union Major General David S. Stanley was named Commander, 4th Corps, Army of the Cumberland.

[45]There was skirmishing at Deep Bottom, Virginia, July 27-29, 1864.

[46]Union Major General Darius N. Couch, Commander, Department of the Susquehanna.

[47]The Battle of Ezra Church, Georgia, was fought July 28, 1864.

[48]Confederate Major General William H. T. Walker, Commander, Division of Hardee's Corps, Army of Tennessee, was killed during the Battle of Atlanta on July 22, 1864.

[49]Confederate Major General Joseph Wheeler, Commander, Cavalry Corps, Army of Tennessee, was not wounded as reported. Confederate Major General William W. Loring, Commander, Division, Polk's-Stewart's Corps, Army of Tennessee, was wounded during the Battle at Ezra Church, Georgia.

[50]Chambersburg, Pennsylvania, is located approximately 24 miles northwest of Gettysburg. Confederate Brigadier General John McCausland, the

Confederate Cavalry commander, threatened to burn the town unless $500,000 in currency or $100,000 in gold were paid to him in reparation for Hunter's destruction in the Shenandoah Valley. The money could not be raised so the town was set ablaze July 30, 1864.

[51]Confederate Lieutenant Colonel John S. Mosby, Commander, 43rd Virginia Cavalry Battalion.

[52]The 18th and the 22nd South Carolina Regiments of Brigadier General S. Elliott's Brigade were defending a salient known as Pegram's Salient when the bomb exploded directly underneath them. Five companies of the 22nd South Carolina were blown up with the left of Pegram's battery, and four companies of the 18th were thrown into the air. The loss for the 22nd was 179, and for the 18th 43 dead, 43 wounded, and 86 missing, buried, or captured. (Bushrod Johnson's Report, *The War of the Rebellion: A Compliation of the Official Records of the Union and Confederate Armies*, Series I, Volume 40, Part 1, p. 787.)

[53]The explosion of the Petersburg, Virginia, mine and the Battle of the Crater occurred July 30, 1864.

[54]Union Lieutenant Colonel David R. Clendenin, 8th Illinois Cavalry, was later brevetted a Brigadier General after he assisted in the defense of Washington.

[55]Union Major General Philip H. Sheridan was given command of the Army of the Shenandoah and the Middle Military Division, effective August 6, 1864.

[56]Union Brigadier General Benjamin F. Kelley, Commander, Forces West of Sleepy Creek, Department of West Virginia.

[57]Union Colonel James R. Brownlow, Commander, 1st Regiment, Tennessee Cavalry.

[58]Union Brigadier General Edward M. McCook, Commander, 1st Division, Cavalry Corps, Department of the Mississippi.

[59]Confederate Brigadier General Alfred Iverson, Jr., Commander, Brigade, Martin's Division, Wheeler's Cavalry Corps.

[60]Union Major General George Stoneman, Commander, Cavalry Division, 23rd Corps, Army of the Ohio, was captured in the abortive raid to free the prisoners at Andersonville, but was later exchanged in October of 1864.

[61]Union Colonel John T. Croxton, Commander, 2nd Brigade, 3rd Division, 14th Corps, Army of the Cumberland.

[62]Union Colonel Charles F. Adams, Jr., Commander, 5th Massachusetts Cavalry.

[63]Union Rear Admiral David G. Farragut, Commander of the Naval Forces in the Battle of Mobile Bay.

[64]The Battle of Mobile Bay, Alabama, commenced August 5, 1864.

[65]Union Major General John M. Palmer, Commander, 14th Corps, Army of the Cumberland, was relieved on August 7, 1864, at his own request.

[66]Union Brigadier General Jefferson C. Davis, Commander, 2nd Division, 14th Corps, Army of the Cumberland, effective August 22, 1864.

[67]A skirmish near Moorefield, West Virginia, was fought August 7, 1864.

[68]James A. Seddon, was the Confederate Secretary of War from November 1862 until February 1865.

[69]Monitor was a generic term for an ironclad.

[70]Confederate Admiral Franklin Buchanan, Commander of the Mobile Bay Defenses, suffered a broken leg and was captured.

[71]Confederate Major General Dabney H. Maury, Commander, Mobile Defense Force.

[72]Rumors of Forrest's death were unfounded.

[73]Frank Stewart, George Baldwin, and Charles Tinker were fellow operators in the War Department Telegraph Office.

[74]The explosion was the result of a time-clock bomb planted by a Confederate team led by Captain John Maxwell.

[75]Not further identified.

[76]Confederate Colonel Charles D. Anderson, Commander, 21st Alabama and Post Commander of Fort Gaines, Alabama.

[77]Union Captain J. C. Van Duzer was assigned as a superintendent to the USMTC Construction Corps to direct the installation of new telegraph lines.

[78]Union Major General James B. Steedman had been Commander of the Post of Chattanooga from October 1863 to May 1864.

[79]Union Brigadier General John E. Smith, Commander, 3rd Division, 15th Corps, Army of the Tennessee.

[80]The Battle of Globe Tavern or Weldon Railroad, Virginia, was fought August 18-21, 1864.

[81]Confederate Brigadier General John R. Chambliss, Jr., Commander, Brigade, W. H. F. Lee's Division, Cavalry Corps, Army of Northern Virginia, and Confederate Brigadier General Victor J. B. Girardey, Commander, Wright's Brigade, Mahone's Division, 3rd Corps, Army of Northern Virginia, were killed August 16, 1864.

[82]Union Major General Grenville M. Dodge, Commander, Left Wing, 17th Corps, Army of the Tennessee, was severely wounded in the head on August 19, 1864, but survived and later returned to duty.

[83]Union Major General David B. Birney, Commander, 10th Corps, Army of the James.

[84]The Soldier's Home was located on a hill in Southeast Washington. It was also the place that President Lincoln used as a summer residence to avoid the hot, humid weather of Washington.

[85]The Calcium Limelight had been invented in 1816 by Thomas Drummond. It consisted of a block of calcium heated to incandescence in jets of burning oxygen and hydrogen. It provided a bright light used initially for spotlighting (hence the expression "being in the limelight"). The disadvantage of the light was that each light required the almost constant attention of an individual operator, who had to keep adjusting the block of calcium as it burned and to tend the two cylinders of gas. The signaling experiment was an attempt to use the light source for the transmission of signals. The intensity of the light provided a strong potential for the transmission of signals over considerable distance as long as line of sight could be maintained. Although

Bates considered the test a success, the obvious maintenance problems did not allow for its use by the USMTC.

[86]Probably Charles Henry Davis, USN. Union Colonel William J. L. Nicodemus, Chief Signal Officer; and Colonel Justin Dimick, retired Artillery Officer.

[87]Confederate Major General William H. F. ("Rooney") Lee (Robert E. Lee's eldest son), Commander, Division, Cavalry Corps, Army of Northern Virginia. The report was unfounded.

[88]Probably Colonel Adam R. Johnson, 10th Kentucky Partisan Rangers.

[89]The Battle of Reams' Station, Virginia, was fought August 25, 1864.

[90]Confederate Major General Joseph B. Kershaw, Commander, Division, 1st Corps, Army of Northern Virginia.

[91]The report of the death of General Hood was unfounded, as was the rumor of General Longstreet taking over the command.

[92]Horatio Seymour, an anti-war Democrat, opposed Lincoln's policies on emancipation, *habeas corpus*, and conscription. He served as Governor of New York State from 1853-55 and again from 1863-65, and ran against Grant for the presidency in 1868 as the nominee of the Democratic party.

[93]George H. Pendleton, member of the House of Representatives and a Copperhead, actively campaigned against the policies of President Lincoln and the conduct of the war. He was chosen as McClellan's running mate.

[94]Confederate Brigadier General Richard L. Page, Commander, Page's Brigade, District of the Gulf, Department of Alabama, Mississippi and East Louisiana, was captured by Union forces in the surrender of Fort Morgan in Mobile Bay.

[95]Confederate General Alexander P. Stewart, Commander, Polk's Corps, Army of Tennessee.

[96]Confederate Brigadier General John C. Vaughn, Commander, Cavalry Brigade, Valley District, Army of Northern Virginia.

[97]Skirmishing around Lovejoy's Station, Georgia, occurred September 2-5, 1864.

[98]The railroad lines out of Atlanta (southward) were the Atlanta and West Point Railroad and its branch the Macon and Western Railroad.

[99]Union Brigadier General Andrew J. Smith, Commander, 3rd Division, 17th Corps, Army of the Tennessee.

[100]Union Brigadier General Alvan C. Gillem, Commander, 4th Division, Cavalry Corps, Army of the Cumberland. General John Hunt Morgan had been placed in command of East Tennessee and Southwestern Virginia on June 22, 1864. He was killed in a surprise raid on Greenville, Tennessee, on September 4, 1864.

[101]A Confederate wiretap on the Union telegraph line between City Point, Virginia, and Washington produced an unenciphered message from Washington regarding the movement of the beef. The information was used by Wade Hampton for his successful raid and diversion of the beef to Petersburg.

[102]Union Brigadier General John D. Stevenson, Commander, Reserve Division, Department of West Virginia.

[103]The implementation of the latest draft call from President Lincoln. Rioting had accompanied some of the earlier draft calls.

[104]The Third Battle of Winchester, Virginia, was fought September 19, 1864.

[105]Union Brigadier General David A. Russell, Commander, 1st Division, 6th Corps, Army of the Shenandoah, was killed September 19, 1864.

[106]Union Brigadier General John B. McIntosh, Commander, 1st Brigade, 3rd Division, 6th Corps, Army of the Shenandoah, was severely wounded September 19, 1864, and lost a leg.

[107]Union Brigadier General Emory Upton, Commander, 2nd Brigade, 1st Division, 6th Corps, Army of the Shenandoah, was wounded September 19, 1864.

[108]Union Brigadier General George H. Chapman, Commander, 2nd Brigade, 3rd Division, Cavalry Corps, Army of the Shenandoah, was wounded September 19, 1864.

[109]Confederate Major General Robert E. Rodes, Commander, Division, Valley District, Department of Northern Virginia, was killed September 19, 1864.

[110]Confederate Major General John B. Gordon, Commander, Johnson's Division, Valley District, Department of Northern Virginia. The rumor of his death was incorrect.

[111]Confederate Brigadier General William Terry, Commander, Brigade, Gordon's Division, Valley District, Department of Northern Virginia, was not killed but was wounded September 19, 1864.

[112]Confederate Major General Stephen D. Ramseur, Commander, Early's (old) Division, 2nd Corps, Army of Northern Virginia, was not wounded at Third Winchester.

[113]Fitzhugh Lee was severely wounded and out of action until nearly the end of the war. Confederate Brigadier General Zebulon York, Commander, Consolidated Louisiana Brigade, Gordon's Division, Valley District, Department of Northern Virginia, lost his left arm in battle September 19, 1864, never again holding field command.

[114]The Battle of Fisher's Hill was fought September 22, 1864.

[115]Secretary Blair was forced from office to gain Radical Republican support in the upcoming election. William Dennison (ex-Governor of Ohio) accepted the Cabinet position of Postmaster General and served until his resignation in 1866 due to personal conflicts with President Johnson.

[116]Confederate Brigadier General William C. Wickham, Commander, Brigade, F. Lee's Cavalry Division, Valley District, Department of Northern Virginia.

[117]The Battle of Fort Harrison or Chaffin's Farm, Virginia, was fought September 29-30, 1864.

[118]The Battle of Peeble's Farm, Virginia, was fought September 29-October 2, 1864.

# October, November, December 1864

Military communications were not only used to report the military events of the day, but also the logistic requirements of the armies. For example on the 9th of October, General Sherman telegraphed that he was in need of forage, and the very same day General Thomas advised him that supplies were on the way to the front.

This last quarter of 1864 was one of rapid movement of the various armies with the USMTC, in conjunction with the Signal Corps, providing the necessary communications between the field commanders and General Grant. It became normal practice to employ the wigwag flag system to relay messages from an area without a telegraphic capability to a telegraph outpost station, where they were then transmitted using telegraph wires. The USMTC and the Signal Corps had by this time achieved a compatible working relationship that ensured that critical information could be transmitted from very remote areas.

Bates's diary entries for the last period of 1864, excluding the period in November when he was home on leave, were reported in a very matter of fact manner even though they included accounts of the destructive actions of both Sherman and Sheridan and reports of battle casualties. He did not comment on the magnitude of battle losses, merely the outcome and the names of any officers killed or wounded. Of particular interest in this portion of the diary are references to intercepted cipher communications between the Confederates in Canada and Richmond and carried by Richard Montgomery.[1]

The Union was able to track the advance of General Sherman on his March to the Sea through the print media in the South. The system of acquiring the Confederate papers was effective as the newspapers were normally received at the War Department office the day after printing. Communications were not established with Sherman until the 12th of December when his forces communicated via the Signal Corps from Ft. McAllister to the Union Naval vessels offshore at Savannah. General Foster communicated via the telegraph with Washington on the 12th of December and General Sherman on the 14th, although Sherman's message did not arrive in the War Department until the 18th due to the circuitous route required for transmission.

The presidential election was of the highest importance in the final months of 1864. Lincoln was more optimistic about reelection as Sherman's taking of Atlanta and Sheridan's victories in the Shenandoah Valley had greatly boosted morale in the Union. The election, held on the 8th of November, resulted in Lincoln's reelection. He received over 55 percent of the popular vote and 212 out of 233 Electoral College votes. The absentee military vote in 12 states was 78 percent in favor of Lincoln—119,754 out of 154,045 votes cast; the military remained committed to the President.

Other political actions during this period included Lincoln's formal establishment of Thanksgiving as a National Holiday; Nevada's entrance into the Union as the 36th State (prior to the presidential election); a call on December 19th for an additional draft of 300,000 men; and the initiation of correspondence between Francis P. Blair, Sr.,[2] a prominent Maryland politician, and Jefferson Davis to explore avenues for possible peace talks. This initiative led ultimately to the Hampton Roads Peace Conference—a failed effort.[3]

There were several notable Confederate activities in the Union. First, on the 19th of October Confederates in Canada crossed the border and raided three banks in St. Albans, Vermont, escaping with over $200,000 in cash. Second, on the 6th of November over 100 Copperhead leaders and Confederate agents were arrested in Chicago, charged with plotting against the U.S. And finally, on the 25th of November Confederate agents acting under orders from Jacob Thompson, the Confederate leader in Canada, set fires in the major hotels and Barnum's Museum in New York City. The fires in the hotels were unsuccessful as the New York Police had been warned in advance. However the Confederates did succeed in burning down the Barnum Museum.

Military actions in the fall of 1864 centered on several geographic fronts, including Missouri, Georgia, Tennessee, Virginia, and the Carolinas—all basically continuations of General Grant's overall strategy. In Missouri the raids of Confederate General Sterling Price came to an end on the 25th of October when his troops were defeated at the crossing of the Marais des Cygnes River. The raids had caused over a million dollars worth of damage to government and private property. In late November, there were Union actions in Nebraska—skirmishes at Plum Creek Station and Spring Creek on the 26th. In Colorado the Sand Creek Massacre of the Arapaho and Cheyenne Indians took place on the 29th.

In October Sherman's forces in Georgia skirmished with the forces of Hood at Allatoona, Rome, Dallas, Resaca, La Fayette, and Round

Mountain. On the 16th of November, Sherman's forces left Atlanta and began their March to the Sea where they met the Navy under Admiral Dahlgren. This was accomplished on December 13th at Fort McAllister near Savannah, Georgia, where the Union fleet was waiting with fresh supplies. The year of 1864 closed with the occupation of Savannah on December 21st.

As Sherman moved east, Confederate General Hood moved west and north in an attempt to recapture the state of Tennessee and hamper Sherman's supply lines—a futile attempt with Sherman's army living off the land. After skirmishes along the way, Hood's forces entered Tennessee on the 22nd of November and met Union forces in hard fighting at Franklin in the Nashville area on the 30th of November. Hood's army lost badly at the Battle of Franklin, and after frequent skirmishes the two armies met again in the Battle of Nashville on the 15th and 16th of December. These two battles succeeded in destroying the effectiveness of Hood's army for the remainder of the war. On the 24th of December Admiral Porter bombarded Fort Fisher in North Carolina prior to Butler's bungled attack on the Fort.

Union pressure on Richmond and Petersburg continued throughout the period with the Battle of Peeble's Farm from the 29th of September to the 2nd of October; and skirmishes at Darbyville, New Market, and Four Mile Creek on the 7th of October, Hatcher's Run on the 8th and 9th of December, and Fort Holly on the 10th of December. The Army of the Potomac's actions succeeded in keeping the Army of Northern Virginia so occupied that General Lee could not send troops to other fronts to alleviate manpower shortages.

Early in the fall of 1864, military activity intensified in the Shenandoah Valley. Sheridan was determined to drive Confederate forces out of the Valley. Union and Confederate forces met in skirmishes at Mount Crawford and Bridgewater on the 2nd of October, Mount Jackson on the 3rd, and Tom's Brook on the 8th. On the 19th of October, the Battle of Cedar Creek effectively ended Confederate actions in the Shenandoah Valley. General Sheridan's troops now turned their attention to destroying the crops and stores of the Valley.

The fall of 1864 was a critical period for the Union. Lincoln was reelected, and the Union military continued to tighten its hold on the Confederacy.                    *Donald E. Markle*

*Saturday, October 1, 1864*
I am suffering from a severe cold in my throat. Can hardly speak above my breath. Otherwise I am feeling well.

Genl. Grant teleghs that the Enemy made 3 assaults in heavy force on his line at Chaffin's Farm yesterday afternoon & were repulsed each time. Late in the evening the Enemy in superior force attacked Potter's Div.[4] of the 9th Corps whilst it was moving to get to the Dept. of Warren. Potter was driven back until reinforced by Griffin's Divn when the Enemy were checked with heavy loss. Potter lost considerably in killed, wounded and captured. Our troops entrenched during the night. We have report from Sheridan up to the 29th at Harrisonburg. Early was still demoralized & routed & had retreated through Brown's Gap. Our Cavy entered Staunton on the 26th & destroyed the Govt repair shops & a large amount of rebel Govt supplies. From there they went to Waynesboro & destroyed the Govt tannery & large amounts of leather & stores of all kinds.

Gen. Sheridan has burned all the grain & hay that he could not use on his march. This will be bad for the rebels as they depended principally on the Shenandoah Valley for grain. Gen. Sheridan will soon retire to Front Royal & bring up supplies & be ready to make an advance at any time.

*Sunday, October 2, 1864*

Nothing of importance today albeit Chandler left last evening for Vt. He will return in about 3 weeks & will bring a wife with him.

*Monday, October 3, 1864*

Genl. Sheridan telegraphs that he cannot make an advance on Charlottesville owing to the great distance from his base & he suggests that the 6th & 19th Corps be sent to the Army of the Potomac. Gen. Grant has approved of this & directed the movement to be made at once. The troops will come by rail from Front Royal to Alex[andria][5] and then by water to City Point.

Genl. Schofield reports that Genl. Gillem had quite a severe fight in East Tenn. one day last week lasting from 3 p.m. of one day till noon of the next when the rebels retreated to Zollicoffer [TN]. No details given.[6]

*Tuesday, October 4, 1864*

No further movement in the Army of the Potomac. Gen. Wilson has been relieved from duty with Sheridan and ordered to report to Sherman as his Chief of Cavalry. He will be brevetted a Major General.

*Wednesday, October 5, 1864*

Genl. Thomas Comdg Army of the Cumberland who has been sent from Atlanta by Genl. Sherman to drive Forrest out of Tennessee reports that he has made such dispositions of troops as will either destroy Forrest or compel him to go south at once. Washburne[7] with 3,000 Cavy is at Clifton on the Tenn. [River] & will move at once to the enemy's rear.

The rebels have captured Big Shanty [GA] near Dalton & are moving northward. They have burnt bridges & tore up RR track & telegraph wire for ten miles in vicinity of Big Shanty.[8] Genl. Sherman has ample supplies of all kinds in Atlanta & will not be inconvenienced by the present state of the railroad.[9]

Nothing new from Gen. Grant & nothing whatever from Gen. Sheridan.

*Thursday, October 6, 1864*

Gen. Grant left City Pt. this morning for Washington on a short visit.

Genl. Thomas reports from Nashville that our forces were fighting most of yesterday at Allatoona. Details not known but the rebels have been driven from the [rail]road.

*Friday, October 7, 1864*

Gen. Thomas reports that in the fight at Allatoona the Enemy under Genl. French[10] had 7,000 men. The fight lasted nearly all day & resulted in the enemy's being driven off with great loss. Estimated at 1,000. We lost 100 killed & 200 wounded. The enemy's dead & wounded were left in our hands. Telegraph O.K. to Allatoona. Nothing heard from Sherman.

The rebels under Moseby [Mosby] made an attack yesterday upon the force guarding the Construction train on Manassas Gap RR at Salem [VA]. We fell back to White Plains [VA] but advanced again this a.m. Very little damage done.

Genl. Butler reports that the Enemy came out early this morning on the Darby road & drove Gen. Kautz with some loss. He also attacked Birney but was repulsed with great slaughter. We captured some few prisoners.

*Saturday, October 8, 1864*

Genl. Grant returned to City Pt. today.

Butler reports that rebel Genl. Gregg[11] Cmd'g Field's Div[12] was killed yesterday. Gen. Bratton[13] was wounded.

Gen. Sheridan has reached Woodstock [VA] with his army. He has burned 2,000 barns filled with grain & flour & 70 mills filled with flour & wheat. He has killed & transferred to his troops 3,000 sheep & has brought off a large quantity of cattle, horses, etc. He has destroyed all farming implements & has made the Shenandoah Valley untenable for a rebel army.

400 wagonloads of refugees[14] from the vicinity Harrisonburg [VA] came with Gen. Sheridan & have been sent to Harper's Ferry.

*Sunday, October 9, 1864*

Today opened blustery & cold & has continued so all the day. Fires are very comfortable & overcoats are necessary.

Genl. Thomas at Nashville telegraphs that he has had nothing direct from Sherman, but that Gen. Corse[15] at Allatoona reports that he (Sherman) was on the Railroad between Kennesaw & Atlanta[16] repairing it.

Line is open to Allatoona & will be open to Atlanta today or tomorrow. The Railroad will require some days yet. Gen. Sherman has enough supplies for the present but urges forward the shipment of forage. His wants have been anticipated by Genl. Thomas & large quantities have been sent as far to the front as possible. Rousseau reports that Forrest has escaped him by crossing the Tennessee in flat boats above and below Florence [AL] while he was detained by high water in the Shoal Creek & Elk River.

Major Gen. Burbridge arrived at Garrettsburg, Ky. two days since with his command from an expedition to the Salt Works at Abingdon, Va. He encountered a large force of rebels there posted behind entrenchments and immediately attacked them driving them from their works, but ammunition giving out they were forced to retire, having accomplished but little of what was intended. The 6th Corps & one Div of Cavalry only will be moved from Sheridan's Army to the James.

*Monday, October 10, 1864*

Gen. Sherman telegraphs from Allatoona that Hood crossed the Chattachoochee & before he (Sherman) was aware of it had got a Corps to Powder Springs. Genl. Sherman instantly resolved to leave Slocum with 20th Corps in Atlanta & move to Marietta with the balance of his army. This he did & reached Kennesaw Oct 8 just in time to witness at a distance the battle at Allatoona. Gen. Corse had been ordered from Chattanooga with reinforcements & met the Enemy & handsomely repulsed him, he [the enemy] leaving his dead & wounded on the field.

As soon as Hood discovered Sherman's appearance he moved to Dallas & Van Wert [GA] & is today crossing the Coosa [River] 12 miles below Rome [GA] bound west. Sherman suggests if he passes over to the Mobile & Ohio road that he (Sherman) destroy the railroad to Chattanooga & move with wagons to Milledgeville, Millen & Savannah. He says it is impossible to protect that long line of [rail]road & he can leave Thomas with what troops he has & the reinforcements ordered to Nashville, to defend the state. Sherman says he can make the march & can make Georgia *home*.[17]

*Tuesday, October 11, 1864*

Gen. Sheridan reports that his Cavalry had a sharp fight near Fisher's Hill on the 9th[18] with all of rebel Cavy of the Valley under Rosser.[19] The enemy was routed & 11 pieces of Artillery captured & 330 prisoners. We took 47 wagons & ambulances including the Hd Qrs wagons of Rosser, Lomax,[20] Wickham & Pollard.[21]

Our forces pursued the retreating rebels 26 miles. Sheridan proposes to send the 6th Corps to Alexa. across the country. He has been directed to do this.

*Wednesday, October 12, 1864*

Yesterday was election day in Pa., Ohio, Ind. & today in Md. Penna. will give a union majority of about 3,000 on the home vote. Ohio about 25,000 & Indiana about 20,000. Cox[22] & Pugh[23] of Ohio defeated, Voorhees of Ind. doubtful.[24] The vote of the Soldiers will increase these majorities some considerable.[25]

Genl. Grant has given Genl. Sherman permission to make his proposed movement to the Atlantic coast, breaking up the road from Atlanta to Chattanooga.

*Thursday, October 13, 1864*

Genl. Thomas telegraphs that Hood is at Dalton & that no communication has been had with Gen. Sherman. All quiet in other quarters.

*Friday, October 14, 1864*

Gold was up to [$]218 today, closing [$]213. There is nothing to cause this immense ride, but the actions of the gold speculators.

*Saturday, October 15, 1864*

Last heard from Gen. Sherman was that he was south of Resaca on way to attack Hood. Hood had taken Dalton with a small garrison. Gold closed [$]220 today.

*Sunday, October 16, 1864*

A rebel cipher was brought to our office today from Jake [Jacob] Thompson[26] in Canada to Jeff Davis. It was translated by Baldwin & myself. Thompson informs Davis that Washington is sufficiently garrisoned to resist any attack until assistance could arrive. He advises that no movement be made in this direction. He says that the reelection of Lincoln is almost certain & urges upon Davis the immense necessity for the South gaining advantages over the Northern Armies.

*Monday, October 17, 1864*

Gen. Sherman telegraphs from Ship's Gap, Ga. dated 5 p.m. 16th that Hood has retreated to the South west. The RR is all right from Atlanta to Resaca,[27] from Resaca to Dalton 20 miles are destroyed. Ten days will suffice to finish it.

Slocum is all right in Atlanta, has plenty of provisions and forage. Troops in good spirits. Hood has yet failed to accomplish any military results. If he fails to invade Tenn. as he has promised his men to do he will lose more by desertion than he has captured. Thus far in losses the result has been in our favor.

*Tuesday, October 18, 1864*

Gen. Schofield telegraphs from Chattanooga that the rear of Hood's Army left Lafayette [GA] yesterday morning going south. Gen. Sherman is west of the RR at the Gaps of Taylor's Ridge.[28]

*Wednesday, October 19, 1864*

Heavy firing has been heard all day in the direction of Strasburg & Front Royal.[29] It is reported the enemy attacked Gen. Sheridan in heavy force.[30] Nothing official.

*Thursday, October 20, 1864*

Charlie Tinker & Chandler returned to the City last evening. They are both very much improved in health. Baldwin goes to Balto today to remain for a week. When he returns I will go home for three or four weeks.

Gen. Sheridan telegraphs from Cedar Creek dated 10 p.m. 19th that the enemy attacked his army yesterday with great vigor & broke our lines in some confusion, capturing twenty pieces of artillery & some prisoners. Genl. S. arrived on the ground himself at 1 p.m. having just returned from Washington. He quickly reformed the lines & drove the enemy at all points routing him completely, capturing 43 pieces of artly, 2,000 prisoners, 100 wagons & ambulances, etc. Genl. Ramseur is severely wounded & a prisoner.[31]

On our side Gen. Bidwell is killed.[32] Genls. Wright[33] Grover[34] & Ricketts[35] wounded.

This makes 59 pieces of artillery he has taken in one month. His first battle was fought on the same day of the month—19th Sept.[36]

### Friday, October 21, 1864

Nothing further from Sheridan except that the number of cannons captured will be 50 instead of 43. This of course includes the 20 taken from us in the morning. Among our casualties are Genls. Bidwell killed, Col. C. R. Lowell[37] & Col. Thoburn killed,[38] Col. Kitching[39] & McKensie [Mackenzie][40] wounded. The enemy were pursued beyond Fisher's Hill.

Gen. Sherman telegraphs from Summerville, Ga. dated yesterday that Hood retreated south. Sherman moved to pursue him on that line as far as Galesville. He will then send the 4th Corps to Thomas & with the rest of the Army march into the heart of Ga. destroying all the roads & coming out at Savannah or Charleston.

### Saturday, October 22, 1864

Genl. Sheridan reports that he followed the Enemy with Cavy to near Mt. Jackson [VA]. From our men who were captured & escaped he learns that the enemy's rout was complete, many of the rebels threw away their arms in the flight.

### Sunday, October 23, 1864

The cipher which was intercepted on the 15th has been to Richmond & the reply dated Oct 19th returned.[41]

Jeff Davis says that Longstreet will soon attack Sheridan then move north as far as practicable towards unprotected points. (This was done last Wednesday but instead of moving north he is compelled to go south.) Davis says a blow will soon be stricken near Richmond on Grant's Army, that it is not quite time.

Sherman has reached Galesville, Ga. & will now go to Atlanta & get ready for his grand movement to Savannah, destroying all the railroads as he goes & taking all the horses & Negroes & living off the country. He will start about Nov. 1st.

Nothing new from any other quarter except Mo. Curtis[42] fought Price[43] yesterday near West Pt., Mo. compelling him to retreat southward.[44]

No one here knows where Rosecrans is or what he is doing. Grant has directed him to be relieved.[45]

*Tuesday, October 25, 1864*

No news from any quarter. I am anxiously awaiting return of Baldwin so that I can leave for home.

*Friday, October 28, 1864*

Baldwin left Balto today & I leave Wshn at 3 p.m. for home.

*Monday, October 31, 1864*

I find Pittsburgh as black & dark as ever,[46] if anything more so. Houses built within a year or two are fast assuming the prevailing color. It keeps me polishing my face & hands continually.

*Friday, November 18, 1864*

Information from blockading fleet off Wilmington shows that the rebel ram *Albemarle* was blown up by a torpedo in charge of Lt. Cushing[47] and eleven men. All but Lt. C. and one man were drowned or taken prisoners. It was a daring feat & great credit is due Cushing for his gallant act. The affair happened near Goldsboro, N.C.

The torch light procession last night was a very grand affair. The display of fire works was brilliant.[48] Today it drizzles rain & is dull & unpleasant.

*Saturday, November 26, 1864*

I neglected to state previously that Abraham Lincoln was reelected Prest, by an increased majority. He carried all the states but New Jersey, Del., & Ky. Gov. Seymour of N.Y. was defeated by Hon. R. E. Fenton.[49] All loyal hearts are gratified at this.

*Sunday, November 27, 1864*

Geo & I arrived at Washn safely and well last night. Found everything about as we left it.

On the 15th of this month Gen. Sherman marched from Atlanta with 60,000 picked men for Savannah. He destroyed the R.R. from

Chattanooga south[50] & burnt all of military importance in Atlanta.
Up to this time we learn from rebel papers he has captured
Milledgeville & Gordon & probably Macon.[51]

Hood's army is south of the Tenn. [River] threatening Chattanooga
& Nashville but Gen. G. H. Thomas with a large force is on the alert
& can counteract any movement Hood may make.

No apprehension is felt for the safety of either Nashville or Chattanooga.

About the 12th of this month Gen. Gillem was defeated near Bull's
Gap in East Tenn. & all his artillery captured by Breckenridge who
now occupies Bull's Gap. Our forces under Burbridge are now advancing & will assume the offensive at once.

In the Army before Richmond & Petersburg nothing new has
transpired of importance.

*Monday, November 28, 1864*

Gold is up to [$]233 today.

A rebel Cavy force under Rosser & McCausland attacked & captured our garrison at New Creek [VA] today. Genl. Sheridan[52] sent a
cavalry force to intercept the rebs, on their return.

*Tuesday, November 29, 1864*

A. J. Smith's Div. has all reached Nashville & gone to the front. The
6th Corps is ordered from Sheridan's Army to City Point.

*Wednesday, November 30, 1864*

Weather mild & beautiful. Nothing of importance from the armies.

Richmond papers state that Gen. Breckenridge is about starting on
a campaign that will carry dismay into Ky. He was at Bristol [TN] on
the 25th. Rebel papers state that Bragg has gone to Augusta [GA] from
Wilmington [NC] with 10,000 men. They do not state exactly where
Sherman is but it is inferred that about the 24th he was in the vicinity
of Macon & Gordon & was marching towards Millen, going rather to
the south of Augusta. All Govt. property, machinery, etc. have already
been removed from Augusta to a place of safety.

*Thursday, December 1, 1864*

Genl. Thomas telegraphs that Gen. Schofield was attacked yesterday at 4 p.m. by one or two Corps of the Enemy near Franklin [TN].
The fight lasted till dark resulting in the complete repulse of the
rebels, with a loss to them of fully 5,000 including 1,000 prisoners, a

Brig. Genl. being among the captured.[53] Our loss very light, probably less than a thousand.

Friday, December 2, 1864

Genl. Thomas telegraphs that owing to the superior force of the Enemy's Cavalry he thinks best to withdraw to the defenses around Nashville until Genl. Wilson's Cavy is all equipped. Gen. Grant has teleghed him to attack Hood & not let him stay where he is. Gen. Burbridge has started on an Expedition from Cumberland Gap having for its object the recapture of Bull's Gap & the forcing of Breckenridge out of East Tenn. Burbridge was to be at Bean's Station today.

Genl. Grant telegphs that Gen. Gregg[54] made a reconnaissance yesterday down the Weldon R.R. He captured Stony Creek Station with 2 cannon 200 pris. destroyed the Depot with 3,000 sacks of corn & an amount of other supplies.

Last night I received a letter from A. Carnegie Supt Pittsburgh Divn Penna R.R. asking me if I would accept the position of Supt, Telegh P.R.R. if offered me. Salary [$]125 pr mo.

I learn today that Col. Thos. A. Scott[55] told Maj. Eckert some time ago that the situation would probably be open soon & asked him to name a man for the place. He at once spoke of me (as he says) & Col. S. told him that he too had thought of me but did not want to deprive the Maj. of me. I replied to Mr. Carnegie today stating that I would accept if offered provided the salary were increased.

The position is a very fine one & included the line on the Sunbury & Erie Railroad. I feel very highly honored by such an offer & am sorry I am not more capable of filling it.

Saturday, December 3, 1864

Gen. Sheridan telegraphs that Gen. Merritt[56] has returned from his Expedition East of the Blue Ridge. He reports it as a success. He says from 5 to 6,000 head of cattle including from 3 to 4,000 head of sheep & nearly 1,000 head of fatted hogs for the rebel Govt were driven off or destroyed. From 5 to 700 horses including mares & colts were brought away. From 30 to 40 guerrillas were killed or captured. A forage depot of the guerrillas was destroyed where several hundred tons of hay were stored.

Great preparations are going on at Ft. Monroe & in the Armies before Richmond indicating early movements there. As soon as the water is let in through Dutch Gap Canal[57] a movement will be made by our fleet having for its object the destruction of the rebel fleet in

James River. At the same time a movement of the Army will take place.

Richmond papers admit that Sherman is South of Augusta across the Oconee [River].

*Sunday, December 4, 1864*

Stmr. *Genl. Lyon* with prisoners from Savannah arrived this evening at Ft. Monroe with Savannah papers of the 30th inst. Gen. Sherman was reported beyond Millen but a rumor was circulated just as the *Lyon* left that his Cavalry were within 6 miles of Savannah. A force of 1,000 Infy with Artly had landed at Boyd's Landing on the Broad River from Beaufort with the intention of breaking the R.R. between Savannah & Charleston.[58] The same paper contains a communication from the Mayor of Milledgeville to the Mayor of Macon dated Nov. 25th asking the latter person to send them bread & meat, or there would be great suffering among the people.

This would indicate that Gen. Sherman had cleaned them out pretty successfully. The same communication stated that the Railroad Bridge[59] & the Bridge over the Oconee were both destroyed.

*Monday, December 5, 1864*

The Hilton Head correspondent of the *N.Y. Herald* reports that Dahlgren[60] & Foster[61] are in communication with Sherman.

From rebel sources we learn that Foster has destroyed the R.R. bridge over the Pocotaligo River[62] in S.C.

Gen. Thomas at Nashville reports that the Enemy planted a battery on the night of Dec 3rd on the river at Bell's Landing & succeeded capturing two boats on their way down. Comdr. Fitch[63] in command of the fleet there went down with an ironclad & two gunboats and soon drove the Battery away & recaptured the two Stmrs.

Hood is in about the same position not having touched the R.R. yet, but is entrenching himself where he is.

*Tuesday, December 6, 1864*

Congress met yesterday. The President's message was not received and read until today—it is very good.[64]

*Wednesday, December 7, 1864*

Gen. Grant telegraphs that this morning Gen. Warren with 27,000 men moved from his position near Reams' Station down the Weldon Railroad towards Hicksford. The object is to break the Weldon road thoroughly. Gen. Butler this morning sent some troops across the James about Dutch Gap & captured the rebel pickets & now holds the opposite side of the River. This will be of advantage to us in opening the Dutch Gap Canal.

6,500 Infy & two batteries will be sent this evening by Gen. Butler to cooperate with the Navy in the capture of Wilmington, or at least the mouth of Cape Fear River. They embarked on Steamers at Bermuda Hundred.

Gen. Palmer in N. C. is ordered to make a movement up the Roanoke River to cut if possible the Railroad below Weldon. This will create a diversion in favor of both Warren and the attack on Wilmington.

### Thursday, December 8, 1864

Genl. Grant ordered Gen. Thomas day before yesterday to attack Hood at once but we rec'd telegrams today from Thomas dated 4 & 10 p.m. [on the] 7th in which he says nothing of having made an attack. Gen. Grant has suggested that if he has not struck yet that he be ordered to hand over his command to Schofield & assume himself a subordinate position. Grant has also suggested the propriety of calling on Ohio, Indiana & Illinois to furnish 60,000 men for 30 days.

### Friday, December 9, 1864

Gen. Grant recommended yesterday that if Thomas had not attacked Hood to order him to turn over his command to Schofield. Gen. Halleck answered that no one here wanted to see Thomas relieved & added that Grant should give a positive order to that effect. Genl. Grant today telegraphed to suspend the order until it was seen whether Thomas would to do anything. Nothing new from Sherman or Warren.

Thomas telegraphs dated 2 p.m. today that he had made every preparation to attack Hood tomorrow morning but that a freezing rain storm had come on, which would prevent our soldiers from fighting to any advantage. He would make the attack however as soon as possible.

### Saturday, December 10, 1864

There was a heavy snowstorm last night throughout the entire North & west. Lines nearly down.

### Sunday, December 11, 1864

Snow rapidly disappearing making sidewalks & streets very slushy and muddy.

Nothing at all from Sherman or Warren. Genl. Thomas will in all probability attack Hood tomorrow or Tuesday. The storm has rendered it impossible before.

*Monday, December 12, 1864*

Genl. Grant telegraphs that Warren destroyed completely the Railroad from the Nottoway to Hicksford[65] & had returned to Sussex C.H.

By the arrival of a vessel from Pt. Royal we learn that Genl. Foster has destroyed the R.R. bridge at Pocotaligo [SC] on the Road between Charleston & Savannah & had communicated with Sherman.[66].

*Tuesday, December 13, 1864*

Richmond papers of yesterday and today state that Sherman is within five miles of Savannah & his troops were drawn up in line of battle. Communication with Savannah had been broke[n].

*Wednesday, December 14, 1864*

Richmond papers of today give no further news from Sherman. The weather has moderated very much. Genl. Sheridan is going to send some of Crook's Army to Gen. Grant. They will start very soon.

We rec'd a telegram this evening from Genl. Foster at Hilton Head [SC] dated Dec. 12th 10 a.m. stating that he had just recd despatch from Genl. Howard commanding right wing of Gen. Sherman's Army. Howard was near the Savannah Canal & his despatch says that the Army has met with perfect success thus far & men are in best spirits possible & in excellent condition. They had accumulated a considerable number of cattle, horses & were well supplied.

Sherman's Army were then advancing on Savannah & it is thought the works were attacked on the 11th as heavy firing was heard in that direction.

Genl. Foster had taken a good position between the Coosawhatchie & Tullifinney Rivers 1,200 yards from the Railroad & but one train had succeeded in stealing past since he had held that position.

*Thursday, December 15, 1864*

Genl. Thomas telegraphed that he would attack the enemy this morning. No report has come from him yet.

Genl. Grant left City Point last evening for Washington. It was a short visit.

From rebel papers we learn that Burbridge has entered Bristol, East Tenn. capturing three trains of cars & some prisoners. No further particulars.

It is rumored today that Sherman has captured Savannah.[67]

*Friday, December 16, 1864*

Genl. Thomas telegraphs from Nashville that he attacked Hood yesterday & drove him on the right seven miles & on the centre 4 miles, driving him from all his works, & capturing 17 pieces of artly & 1,500 prisoners. The attack will be renewed today.[68]

From rebel papers we learn that Genl. Sherman has captured the very strong Fort McAllister in Ossabaw Sound at the mouth of the Ogeechee River.

*Saturday, December 17, 1864*

News this morning from Thomas says that the report of Thursday's captures is greatly exceeded by the actual figures. Yesterday the fighting was renewed & Gen. Thomas telegraphs that our forces were completely successful, capturing five or six thousand prisoners & some 40 guns. The retreating rebels threw away their arms as they fled. Genl. Thomas is still pursuing. Gen. Stoneman telegraphs via Cumberland Gap that on the 10th he moved towards the Holston [River in TN]. He attacked & routed Basil Duke's[69] command, capturing Col. Morgan, brother of John [Hunt Morgan] & a whole wagon train. We since learn by rebel papers that Stoneman has advanced up the railroad to & beyond Marion destroying the R.R. as he goes.[70] He has no doubt destroyed the Salt works near Abingdon [VA].

*Sunday, December 18, 1864*

Attended Wesley Chapel this morning. Heard Dr. Bowman, Chaplain of the Senate[71] preach from John 3:8. Hon S. P. Chase[72] the newly appointed Chief Justice was there.

From Genl. Thomas we learn that yesterday our Cavalry attacked Stevenson's rebel Divn[73] of Infantry six miles beyond Franklin & routed them, dispersing them in all directions, capturing three guns.[74] The pursuit was to be continued today. Genl. Thomas's Hd Qrs yesterday were at Franklin.

Sherman closely invests Savannah. We rec'd a telegram yesterday morning from Genl. Foster dated Wednesday 14th. He says that he met Sherman at Ft. McAllister which was taken by assault on the 13th by Hazen's Division of the 15th Corps.[75] The garrison of 1,200 men & armament of 21 guns fell into our hands. This important capture opens up to us the great Ogeechee River & enables us to supply Sherman directly. A Division of Infy held Argyle Island, above Savannah & the troops were so disposed as to prevent any escape from the city.[76]

During Sherman's March his men lived on the turkeys, chickens, sweet potatoes & other good things of the richest part of Georgia. Their march was but feebly resisted. The men are all in excellent condition & fine spirits.

Last Tuesday Admiral Porter's fleet left Hampton Roads for the mouth of Cape Fear River. It consisted of over 60 ships of different kinds including five iron clads. Wilmington is to be attacked today. 7,000 troops accompany the expedition, under command of Maj. Gen. Butler.

We learn from Genl. Canby that his expedition sent out from Vicksburg & Baton Rouge to cut the Railroad communications of Hood have been completely successful. The one from Vicksburg has returned, having destroyed the Mobile & Ohio RR for 30 miles above Jackson including several important depots & several cars & engines. The bridge over the Big Black [River] was also destroyed.

*Monday, December 19, 1864*
The following is Secy. Stanton's bulletin of last night. [The following newspaper articles were pasted in the diary.]

*Headquarters Department Cumberland near Franklin, Tenn. Dec. 16.*
Report just received from Major General Wilson states that at 8 p.m. to-day he attacked and dispersed Stevenson's division of rebel infantry, and a brigade of cavalry, capturing three guns.

The 4th United States Cavalry, and Hatch's division of cavalry,[77] did the work, making several beautiful charges, breaking the rebel infantry in all directions. Had it only been light the rebel rearguard would have been entirely destroyed. As it is, it has been severely punished. The whole army will continue vigorous pursuit in the morning. This attack was made six miles beyond Franklin.

George H. Thomas, Major General

*Headquarters Department Cumberland near Franklin, 8 p.m. Dec. 17*
We have pressed the enemy today beyond Franklin, capturing his hospital containing over fifteen hundred wounded, and about one hundred and fifty of our wounded, in addition to the above. General Knipe,[78] commanding a division of cavalry

drove the enemy's rearguard through Franklin to-day, capturing about two hundred and fifty prisoners and five battle flags, with a very little loss on our side. Citizens of Franklin represent Hood's army as completely demoralized. In addition to the captures of yesterday, reported in my despatch of last night I have the honor to report the capture of General Rucker[79] and about two hundred and fifty prisoners of the enemy's cavalry, in a fight that occurred about 8 o'clock last night between General Rucker and General Hatch of our cavalry. The enemy has been pressed together both in front and on both flanks. Brigadier General Johnson[80] succeeded in striking him on the flank, just beyond Franklin, capturing quite a number of Prisoners, the number not yet reported, my cavalry is pressing him closely though, and I am very much in hopes of getting many more prisoners tomorrow.

George H. Thomas, Major General

Other despatches (unofficial) from Nashville state that one thousand prisoners were captured by Wilson and that General Rousseau, commanding at Murfreesboro, reports Forrest killed [unfounded, see December 25, 1864] and fifteen hundred of his men captured.

The superintendent at Nashville reports that the railroad from Nashville will be open to Franklin tonight, and will rapidly follow Thomas thus furnishing him supplies and enable him to rush on after Hood.

*War Department, Dec. 18*

Major General John A. Dix, New York

An official despatch from General Sherman was received to-day, dated near midnight, Dec. 13, 1864, on the gunboat *Dandelion*, Ossabaw Sound. It was written before General Foster had reached him. He reports, besides some military details of future operations, which are omitted, the following particulars of his operation.

*On Board Dandelion*

Ossabaw Sound, 11:50 p.m. Dec. 13

Today at 5 p.m. General Hazen's division of the 15th Corps carried Fort McAllister by assault, capturing its entire garrison and stores.

This opened to me Ossabaw Sound, and I pulled down to this gunboat to communicate with the fleet. Before opening communications, we had completely destroyed all the railroads leading into Savannah, and invested the city. The left is on Savannah River, three miles above the city, and the right on the Ogeechee at Kingsbridge.

The Army is in splendid order, and equal to anything. The weather has been fine, and supplies abundant. Our march was most agreeable and we were not at all molested by guerillas. We reached Savannah three days ago, but owing to Fort McAllister, we could not communicate. But now we have Fort McAllister, we can go ahead. We have already captured two boats in the Savannah River, and prevented their gunboats from coming down. I estimate the population of Savannah at 25,000 and the garrison at 15,000. General Hardee commands. We have not lost a wagon on the trip, but have gathered in a large supply of Negroes, mules, horses, etc., and our teams are in better conditions than when we started. My first duty will be to clear the army of surplus Negroes, mules and horses. We have utterly destroyed over two hundred miles of railroad and consumed stores and provisions that were essential to Lee's and Hood's armies. The quick work made with Fort McAllister, and the opening of communications with our fleet and consequent independence for supplies, dissipates all the boasted threats to head us off and starve the army. I regard Savannah already gained.

Yours truly

W. T. Sherman, Major General

On last Friday gold was [$]231. Today it was as low as [$]213 & is now [$]217.

The glorious news of our victories has electrified all hearts with joy. Everyone is pleased. Today the weather is damp & rainy. Walking is very unpleasant. Streets flowing with mud.

*Tuesday, December 20, 1864*

No further news from Sherman.[81] From Thomas we learn that he is pursuing Hood with energy. Every hour prisoners are captured, some 2 or 300 were taken yesterday. The Prest. made a call last night for 300,000 men.[82]

Sherman Communicates from Fort McAllister

The ship located in the bay receives a wigwag message and relays
it by flag, ship-to-ship, up the Atlantic coast to Union controlled
offshore islands of the Carolinas. From there the message is telegraphed
to General Grant at City Point, Virginia.

*(Courtesy of the Library of Congress)*

*Wednesday, December 21, 1864*

Genl. Thomas telegraphs that our forces came up with the rear guard of the enemy yesterday at Duck River & captured 5 guns & about 100 prisoners. HdQrs of Gen. Thomas were at Columbia [TN]. A strong force has been sent via Stevenson [AL] to Decatur from which place we will threaten Florence & prevent Hood from crossing the Tennessee.

To cooperate with this movement Adml. Lee[83] has sent gunboats up the Tenn. to Florence. Genl. Thomas is confident of capturing the greater part of the rebel Army.

Nothing yet from Wilmington N.C. It has no doubt fallen into our hands ere this. Adml. Porter & Gen. Butler were to have attacked it Monday the 19th & we should hear first through rebel sources.

Last night considerable snow & sleet fell & today there is a cold drizzling rain, rendering the streets very dirty & muddy.

*Thursday, December 22, 1864*

Gen. Grant telegraphs that news from the Richmond papers of today states that 30 vessels of the Federal fleet have arrived off Wilmington but the severe state of the weather has thus far prevented an attack. Gen. Bragg in an official report says he is fully able to hold Wilmington.

Genl. Thomas telegraphs that the rebel Gen. Lyon[84] who had crossed the Cumberland & gone into Ky. has been defeated. Lyon being compelled to burn most of his baggage etc. & losing a considerable portion of his men.

Nothing further from Gen. Sherman.

*Friday, December 23, 1864*

Genl. Grant telegraphs that a rebel telegraph operator has come into Gen. Ord's lines who states that he left Richmond this morning, that news had been rec'd there from Beauregard announcing the fall of Savannah, it having surrendered unconditionally to our forces on the 20th.[85] Also that Gen. Whiting[86] telegraphed to Jeff Davis that Fort Fisher at the mouth of Cape Fear now had been captured.[87]

This is glorious news indeed & we wait anxiously to hear of its confirmation.

*Saturday, December 24, 1864*

Nothing yet from Sherman or Foster. We are all very anxious.

*Sunday, December 25, 1864*

Genl. Thomas teleghs from 8 miles beyond Columbia, Tenn. that last evening, Genl. Wilson had two short skirmishes with Forrest 6 miles from Pulaski, driving him precipitably & capturing a few prisoners.[88]

Gen. Granger was at Huntsville [AL] with 1,250 men on the 22d & was waiting for Steedman daily expected, when he would push for Decatur & try to prevent Hood crossing the Tennessee. It is rumored that Hood is superseded by Forrest.

At 7 p.m. we received a telegram from Gen. Sherman dated Savannah, Ga. Dec. 22 via Ft. Monroe stating that Hardee had escaped from him the day before with the main force of his army & his light artillery.[89] Sherman captured in Savannah 150 heavy guns, 32,000 bales of cotton worth $20,000,000, 13 locomotives, 190 cars, 3 steamers & lots of ammunition etc. There are 20,000 citizens in the City quiet & well disposed. The rebels blew up their ironclads & burned their navy yard. Gen. Foster opened communications with the City on the 22d taking up what torpedoes could be seen & passing the rest. Arrangements are made to remove all the obstructions.[90]

*Monday, December 26, 1864*

This morning was ushered in with a booming of cannon, 300 having been fired in honor of the capture of Savannah. Fireworks have been going off all day. Every other person you meet has a pistol in his hand with which he occasionally fires a salute.

We are barren of news today except a drop from Thomas. He was about 6 miles north of Pulaski last night & Genl. Wilson had driven Forrest through Pulaski the evening before on the keen jump, the rebels running as fast as they could, making no stand whatever. Wilson says the rebel army is making its way to Lamb's Ferry [AL] & Florence, fearing to go towards Decatur, lest our forces should get in their rear. Thomas is very confident of being able to capture or destroy most of the remnant of Hood's Army.

*Tuesday, December 27, 1864*

We learn from Richmond papers that our fleet attacked Ft. Fisher at the mouth of Cape Fear River on Saturday the 24th. The powder boat that was to be floated against Ft. Fisher, blew up when within 300 yards of it doing no material damage.

*Wednesday, December 28, 1864*

Last night Gen. Butler arrived at Ft. Monroe having left Wilmington on Monday.

On Sunday at noon our vessels opened upon Ft. Fisher & continued a vigorous fire until night. Under cover of this fire we landed troops to the northwest of the fort & gallantly assaulted the outworks. We captured an entire battalion of 350 men in one of the outworks & at another place a battery with 65 men. Finding that an assault on the fort itself was impracticable owing to the fact that the beach was so narrow to allow of but 1,000 men moving at a time & that 17 guns commanded the approach, the troops were withdrawn. Adm. Porter however continues the bombardment & has strong hopes of success.

Genl. Thomas telegraphs that the main body of Hood's army has crossed the Tennessee & that the rear guard will probably be captured. No further news from Gen. Sherman. It is presumed that he will organize a new campaign to begin about Jany 1st & will strike for Raleigh, N.C. thus cutting the principal means of communication of the rebels & in all probability compelling Beauregard to evacuate Charleston.

Genl. Stoneman telegraphs from Knoxville that he has returned to that place from his recent expedition. He reports it completely successful at every point. He destroyed all of the RR bridges west of the New River in S. W. Va., burnt depots, destroyed track, 13 trains with Engines attached, besides a great many separate cars, 50,000 bushels of salt, destroyed the salt & lead works, breaking the kettles & filling the wells & shafts with shells, railroad iron etc., brought off 2,000 horses & many mules & inflicted very great damage on the Enemy with but comparatively small loss to us.

Gen. Stoneman deserves great credit for this work. In his former military career he has been uniformly unsuccessful.

*Thursday, December 29, 1864*

Adml. Lee telegraphs from near Florence, Ala. that he has destroyed a new fort that was built there, destroyed 2 guns & all the visible means of crossing. The Tennessee River is very high and he will be able to prevent the rebels from crossing below that point. Transports with supplies for Gen. Thomas have arrived there.

*Friday, December 30, 1864*

All of the troops under Gen. Butler in the attack on Fort Fisher have returned to City Point.[91]

*Saturday, December 31, 1864*

Snow has been falling lightly all day & melts as it falls. This evening it is colder.

Genl. Grant sends 8,000 men from Ft. Monroe Monday p.m. with orders for them to go to the mouth of Cape Fear River. They will make an attack on Ft. Fisher & endeavor to capture it.

Genl. Dana[92] at Memphis reports that his cavalry when last heard from had struck the Mobile & Ohio RR 5 miles south of Corinth [MS] & had already destroyed 5 miles of road & were proceeding further south.

Genl. Canby reports that Gen. Granger when last heard from was 12 miles from East Pascagoula on the road to Mobile. A force from Pensacola [FL] had captured Pollard [AL] & destroyed the bridge over the Escambia River.

Nothing from Gen. Sherman or Gen. Grant. Gen. Thomas reports that he has sent A. J. Smith with a force to Eastport [TN] to cross the Tennessee & try to cut the Mobile & Ohio R.R.

## Notes

[1]Richard Montgomery continued to serve as a courier throughout the war and was never discovered. He later testified at the Lincoln assassination trial regarding the Confederate ciphers.

[2]Francis Preston Blair, Sr. from Maryland had been a leading force in the founding of the Republican Party. He served Lincoln in various unofficial roles during the Civil War period. Reputedly it was Blair who offered the Command of the Union Army to Robert E. Lee at the onset of the war. Blair wrote to Jefferson Davis about the possibility of a reconciliation between the North and the South. After receiving President Lincoln's permission, he visited Richmond and discussed his thoughts with the Confederates.

[3]The Hampton Roads Peace Conference was held February 3, 1865.

[4]Union Brigadier General Robert B. Potter, 2nd Division, 9th Corps, Army of the Potomac.

[5]The railroad between Front Royal and Alexandria, Virginia, was the Manassas Gap Railroad.

[6]A skirmish at Pulaski, Tennessee, occurred September 26, 1864.

[7]Union Major General Cadwallader C. Washburn, Commander, District of West Tennessee, Army of the Tennessee.

[8]The railroad at Big Shanty, Georgia, was the Western and Atlantic Railroad.

[9]This refers to Hood's operations against Sherman's communications and supply lines which were conducted October 1-22, 1864.

[10]Confederate Major General Samuel G. French, Commander, Polk's-Stewart's Corps, Army of Tennessee.

[11]Confederate Brigadier General John Gregg, 1st Corps, Army of Northern Virginia, was killed in action on the Darbytown Road October 7, 1864, while Commander of Hood's old Division.

[12]Confederate Brigadier General Charles W. Field, Commander, Hood's Division, 1st Corps, Army of Northern Virginia.

[13]Confederate Brigadier General John Bratton, Commander, Jenkin's old Brigade, Field's Division, 1st Corps, Army of Northern Virginia.

[14]The refugees consisted of families from the Shenandoah Valley whose farms and crops had been destroyed by the Union Army. They could not subsist any longer in the Valley.

[15]Union Brigadier General John M. Corse, Commander, 4th Division, 15th Corps, Army of the Tennessee.

[16]The railroad between Kennesaw and Atlanta was the Western and Atlantic Railroad.

[17]General Sherman was indicating that his troops would be well-fed along the route to the Sea, thanks to the Georgia farms along the way.

[18]The Battle of Tom's Brook, Virginia, was fought October 9, 1864.

[19]Confederate Brigadier General Thomas L. Rosser, Commander (temporary), F. Lee's Division, Army of the Valley District.

[20]Confederate Major General Lunsford Lomax, Commander, Ransom's old Cavalry Division, Valley District, Department of Northern Virginia.

[21]Confederate Major James Pollard, assigned to the 9th Virginia Cavalry.

[22]Democrat Samuel S. Cox, editor-publisher of the *Columbus Statesman* in Columbus, Ohio, was defeated for reelection to the U.S. House of Representatives.

[23]Democrat George E. Pugh, former Senator from Ohio, was defeated in his bid to reenter the U.S. Congress on the peace platform.

[24]Senator Daniel Voorhees, a Republican of Indiana, was reelected.

[25]Republicans made gains in congressional races in Pennsylvania, Ohio, and Indiana. On October 13, 1864, a state constitution abolishing slavery was ratified by Maryland voters.

[26]Jacob Thompson, ex-U. S. Senator from Mississippi and Secretary of the Interior in the Buchanan Cabinet, was recruited by President Davis to head the covert operations in Canada and was sent to Toronto. He worked closely with the Copperhead movement and organized the burning of New York as well as the St. Albans bank raid.

[27]The railroad between Atlanta and Resaca was the Western and Atlantic Railroad.

[28]The railroad at Taylor's Ridge was the Western and Atlantic Railroad.

[29]Information of this nature may well have been passed by telegraph operator chatter and not as part of an official message.

[30]The Battle of Cedar Creek, Virginia, was fought October 19, 1864.

[31]Confederate Major General Stephen D. Ramseur, Commander, Rode's old Division, Valley District, Department of Northern Virginia, was mortally wounded on October 19, 1864, at Cedar Creek and died the next day.

[32]Union Brigadier General Daniel D. Bidwell, Commander, 2nd Brigade, 2nd Division, 6th Corps, Army of the Shenandoah, was killed October 19, 1864, during the Battle of Cedar Creek.

[33]Union Major General Horatio G. Wright, Commander, 6th Corps, Army of the Shenandoah, was slightly wounded at Cedar Creek.

[34]Union Brigadier General Cuvier Grover, Commander, 2nd Division, 19th Corps, Army of the Shenandoah, was wounded at the Battle of Cedar Creek.

[35]Union Major General James B. Ricketts, Commander, 6th Corps, Army of the Shenandoah, was severely wounded in the Battle of Cedar Creek.

[36]The reference to September 19, 1864, is to the Third Battle of Winchester.

[37]Union Colonel Charles R. Lowell, Commander, Reserve Brigade, 1st Division, Cavalry Corps, Army of the Shenandoah, was mortally wounded October 19, 1864, at Cedar Creek and died the next day.

[38]Union Colonel Joseph Thoburn, Commander, 1st Infantry Division, Department of West Virginia, was killed at Cedar Creek.

[39]Union Brigadier General John H. Kitching, Commander, Army of the Shenandoah, was mortally wounded October 19, 1864, at Cedar Creek and died January 10, 1865.

[40]Union Colonel Ranald S. Mackenzie, 2nd Connecticut Artillery, was wounded October 19, 1864, at Cedar Creek.

[41]The reply was being returned from Richmond to Toronto (via Washington) by Union Agent Richard Montgomery.

[42]Union Major General Samuel R. Curtis, Commander, Department of Kansas.

[43]Confederate Major General Sterling Price, Commander, Army of Missouri, Trans-Mississippi Department.

[44]Action occurred at Byram's Ford, Missouri, October 22, 1864.

[45]General Rosecrans, as Commander of the Department of Missouri, was having difficulties with various political factions in Missouri and proved to be inept in the administration of his command. He was finally relieved of command on December 2, 1864, and replaced by Major General Grenville Dodge.

[46]Pittsburgh, Pennsylvania, had become an early industrial center with heavy coal dust air pollution.

[47]On October 28, 1864, Union Naval Lieutenant William B. Cushing led 15 men up the Roanoke River in a steam craft and succeeded in blowing up the CSS ram *Albemarle*. For his action Cushing was promoted and received a vote of thanks from Congress.

[48]The fireworks display was to celebrate the reelection of Lincoln.

[49]Horatio Seymour was defeated by Reuben E. Fenton, a Congressman and strong supporter of President Lincoln, for governor of New York. Fenton served two terms and was then elected to the U.S. Senate.

[50]The railroads south of Chattanooga were the Memphis and Charleston Railroad, the Western and Atlantic Railroad, and the East Tennessee and Georgia Railroad.

[51]Reports of Sherman's movements through Georgia had to be derived from non-telegraphic sources. USMTC linemen traveled with Sherman's army, but considered it too dangerous to string the telegraph lines during the Army's rapid March to the Sea. The wigwag system was used for communications within the Army.

[52]Union Brigadier General Philip H. Sheridan had been made a Brigadier General of the regular Army September 20, 1864, and was promoted to Major General November 8, 1864.

[53]The Battle of Franklin, Tennessee, was fought November 30, 1864. Confederate Brigadier General George W. Gordon was captured. Five Confederate Generals were killed in the battle: Major General Patrick R. Cleburne, Commander, Buckner's Division, Hardee's-Cheatham's Corps, Army of Tennessee; Brigadier General States R. Gist, Commander, Brigade, Hardee's-Cheatham's Corps, Army of Tennessee; Brigadier General Hiram B. Granbury, Commander, Brigade, Cleburne's Division, Hardee's-Cheatham's Corps, Army of Tennessee; Brigadier General John Adams, Commander, Brigade, Loring's Division, Polk's-Stewart's Corps, Army of Tennessee; and Brigadier General Otho F. Strahl, Commander, Brigade, Cheatham's-Brown's Division, Hardee's-Cheatham's Corps, Army of Tennessee. Brigadier General John C. Carter, Commander, Maney's Brigade, Brown's Division, Cheatham's Corps, Army of Tennessee, was mortally wounded in the battle and died December 10, 1864.

[54]Union Brigadier General David M. Gregg, Commander, 2nd Division, Cavalry Corps, Army of the Potomac.

[55]Union Colonel Thomas A. Scott was the Assistant Secretary of War for Transportation. In late 1864, he returned to his pre-war position as Vice-President of the Pennsylvania Railroad.

[56]Union Brigadier General Wesley Merritt, Commander, 1st Division, Cavalry Corps, Army of the Shenandoah.

[57]Gen. Butler ordered a canal to be built, cutting a bypass around a large bend in the Dutch Gap River, Virginia. On the first day of the year, the project was to be completed with a powder blast for the final excavation. When the blast occurred, the dirt fell back into the ditch, and the project was then dropped.

[58]The railroad between Savannah and Charleston was the Charleston and Savannah Railroad.

[59]The railroad at the Oconee River was the Georgia Railroad.

[60]Union Rear Admiral John A. B. Dahlgren, Commander, South Atlantic Blockading Squadron.

[61]Union Brigadier General John G. Foster was in charge of operations against Charleston, South Carolina, in late 1864.

[62]The railroad bridge at the Pocotaligo River was for the Charleston and Savannah Railroad.

[63]Union Commander LeRoy Fitch was in Command of a division of gunboats to patrol the Ohio, Tennessee, and Cumberland Rivers.

[64]The President's annual address opened with the state of foreign affairs. He then stated that the financial status of the government was satisfactory despite the war although he did call for increased taxation. The new Agriculture Department was developing on schedule, and he called for reconsideration of the Thirteenth Amendment abolishing slavery. He ended by speaking of peace and stating that peace will only come on the terms of the North.

[65]The railroad between Nottoway and Hicksford was the Richmond and Danville Railroad.

[66]The initial communication from General Sherman after he reached the sea was to General Foster and Admiral Dahlgren, both aboard Union ships near Fort McAllister. Communications, made by signal flagmen, were relayed to a shore island in Union hands and thence to General Grant by telegraph.

[67]The rumored capture of Savannah was incorrect.

[68]The Battle of Nashville, Tennessee, was fought December 15-16, 1864.

[69]Confederate Brigadier General Basil W. Duke, Commander, Morgan's Brigade, Department of West Virginia and East Tennessee.

[70]The railroad at Marion, Virginia, was the Virginia and Tennessee Railroad.

[71]Dr. Thomas Bowman, a Methodist, became Chaplain of the Senate in 1864, serving until 1865. Prior to coming to the Senate, he had been the President of Indiana Asbury College (now DePauw University).

[72]Salmon P. Chase, ex-Secretary of the Treasury in the Lincoln Cabinet, was named Chief Justice of the Supreme Court December 6, 1864. The vacancy arose with the death of Chief Justice Roger B. Taney.

[73]Confederate Major General Carter L. Stevenson, Commander, Infantry Division, Hood's-Lee's Corps.

[74]There was a skirmish at Hollow Tree Gap, Tennessee, December 17, 1864.

[75]Union Brigadier General William B. Hazen, Commander, 2nd Division, 15th Corps, Army of the Tennessee.

[76]This assured the fall of Savannah, Georgia.

[77]Union Brigadier General Edward Hatch, Commander, 5th Division, Cavalry Corps, Military Division of the Mississippi.

[78]Union Brigadier General Joseph F. Knipe, Commander, 7th Division, Cavalry Corps, Military Division of the Mississippi.

[79]Confederate Colonel Edmund W. Rucker, Commander, 1st Brigade, Chalmer's Division.

[80]Union Brigadier General Richard W. Johnson, Commander, 6th Division, Cavalry Corps, Military Division of the Mississippi.

[81]December 20, 1864, was the day the Confederates evacuated Savannah, Georgia.

[82]President Lincoln issued a further call for 300,000 more volunteer troops to put down the rebellion.

[83]Union Rear Admiral Samuel P. Lee, Commander, Mississippi Squadron.

[84]Confederate Brigadier General Hylan B. Lyon, Commander, Department of Western Kentucky.

[85]Federal forces occupied Savannah, Georgia, on December 21, 1864.

[86]Confederate Major General William H. C. Whiting, Commander, Department of North Carolina.

[87]The report of the fall of Ft. Fisher proved to be premature.

[88]There was skirmishing at Lynnville and Richland Creek, Tennessee, December 24, 1864.

[89]This telegram was written the same day as Sherman's famous one presenting Lincoln with the city of Savannah as a Christmas present. The messages were relayed to Fort Monroe for further transmission to Washington, DC.

[90]Referring to the U.S. Navy's ability to enter the harbor of Savannah.

[91]The Battle for Fort Fisher occurred December 24-25, 1864. Union troops landed on December 25 after a severe naval bombardment, that began on December 24, and were closing on the Fort just as darkness fell. Confederate troops approached from the north, and the Union troops were ordered to be withdrawn. General Butler was severely criticized for what was seen as a Union failure.

[92]Union Brigadier General Napoleon J. T. Dana, Commander, Department of Vicksburg, Department of the Mississippi.

# January, February, March 1865

The diary entries for the first quarter of 1865 give a clear indication of just how extensive a role the telegraph played in General Grant's grand strategy. Throughout the month of January there are frequent references regarding the movement of Union troops from one area to another, such as "troops sent east to aid Grant" and Generals Schofield, Sheridan, and Thomas being ordered to send troops east to Annapolis for further orders. As the various campaigns came to conclusion, the troops were being massed for the final thrust against the Army of Northern Virginia.

At the same time, there was an increase in the telegraphic communications between General Grant and President Lincoln. The telegraph line between Grant at City Point and Lincoln in Washington was being used extensively in both directions. The main thrust of these communications was not day-to-day military reporting but a more elevated discussion between the two men on strategic questions. A shift in the nature of the telegraphic communications was beginning to take place—a move from the strictly tactical to the strategic.

Bates initially referred to Richmond papers when reporting on the movements of General Sherman. Sherman first communicated with Grant in written correspondence and finally through routine telegraphic communications once they were established between the two armies. In addition Bates recorded that Sherman and Grant met at City Point on the 28th of March—the first face-to-face meeting between the two generals since prior to Sherman's March to the Sea. The entire Atlanta Campaign had been directed by the telegraph.

Bates noted in his diary that Jefferson Davis advocated the arming of slaves for the Confederate army in a speech on the 6th of February. However, according to Bates, that part of the speech was deleted from the printed text in the Richmond newspapers.

The year of 1865 opened with great optimism for the Union and deep pessimism for the Confederacy. From the events happening on all fronts, the Union knew that the war was at last in its final stages, while in the Confederacy, the die-hard Confederates refused to believe their cause lost even though the populace knew very well the end was near.

Among the main political issues/events of concern in 1865 were peace initiatives to end the hostilities; the inauguration of President Lincoln for a second term; and the postwar status of the black population, both in the Union and Confederacy. These issues held center stage in both Richmond and Washington.

On January 5th President Lincoln approved travel documents for James W. Singleton to enter the Confederacy for unofficial peace talks, fully aware that the Confederacy would probably not agree to the Union terms. His trip and that of Frances P. Blair, Sr., who met with President Davis on the 12th of January, resulted in a Confederate promise to meet with Union officials on the 3rd of February at Hampton Roads, Virginia, to discuss a peace initiative.

The two sides arrived at the Hampton Roads Conference with very different agendas. Davis sent his team "with a view to secure peace to the two countries"[1] while Lincoln arrived "with the view of securing peace to the peoples of our one common country."[2] Consequently the conference that was held on the 3rd of February failed to reach agreement. It did however press home to the Confederates the Union commitment to an unconditional surrender policy, which considered an armistice followed by negotiations to be unacceptable. Upon his return to Washington from Hampton Roads, President Lincoln proposed an initiative to his cabinet that would have paid the slave states $400,000,000 if they would lay down their arms by the 1st of April. The Cabinet was not in favor of the initiative, and nothing further was done on the proposal.

In early March Grant received a communiqué from Lee requesting that the two meet to try and bring an end to the war. Grant did not know what criteria to follow. Lincoln informed him that his only correspondence with Lee on the subject of peace must be limited to the "capitulation of Gen. Lee's army"; all else was to be handled at the national level.[3] General Grant in turn so informed General Lee.

On the 12th of February the Electoral College elected President Lincoln for his second term in the White House. His inauguration was held on the 4th of March and was enthusiastically attended. His now famous inaugural speech contained the essence of his reconstruction policy with the phrase, "with malice toward none."

Another difficult issue for both the Union and the Confederacy during the early part of 1865 was that of slavery. On the 6th of January, the House of Representatives began to debate the proposed 13th amendment to the Constitution abolishing slavery. The amendment had already passed the Senate. After much debate the amendment passed the House on the 31st of January and within two days it had been ratified by three states: Illinois, Michigan, and Rhode Island.

In January of 1865, the Confederacy abolished its practice of returning captured black soldiers who were escaped slaves to their previous owners. Instead, they agreed to treat them as prisoners of war and to exchange them in hopes that the Union would once again agree to the exchange of prisoners. Grant's prior refusal had been a very sensitive point throughout the Union because it was punitive to Union soldiers held in Southern prisons.

Dissatisfied with President Davis's meddling in military tactics, the Confederate Congress, passed a resolution challenging Davis's total control of the military. Congress advised Davis on the 16th of January to make General Lee the General-in-Chief of all the Confederate armies. President Davis bowed to the resolution and offered the position to General Lee who accepted on January 23rd. It was too late to have any impact on the outcome of the war. Military activity during this period continued to center on the strangulation tactics of General Grant and his various armies.

A major shift of Confederate policy occurred on the 18th of February when General Lee proposed that the Confederate army be allowed to arm slaves to alleviate the South's severe manpower shortage. He stated that in order to make them good soldiers they must be freed. The initiative was debated in the Confederate Congress, and the bill was signed into law by President Davis on the 13th of March. It allowed each state discretion in deciding whether to free slaves who went into the army. The legislative action was too late to help the Confederate cause.

The year of 1865 opened with the gathering of the largest Union fleet ever assembled for the Fort Fisher, North Carolina, campaign, which opened on the 13th of January. After an extensive naval bombardment the troops landed, and Fort Fisher fell on the 15th of January, followed by the fall of Wilmington, North Carolina, on the 22nd of February. This action closed the last seaport of the Confederacy, leaving blockade runners with no entry into the Confederacy for the delivery of vital supplies.

Simultaneous with the Fort Fisher campaign, there was sporadic Indian fighting in the far west. On the 7th of January, Union forces battled Indians in Colorado at Julesberg and Valley Station, and on March 7th fighting erupted at Fort Larned, Kansas. Many Indians were loyal to the Confederacy as Richmond had offered them an independent Indian State in exchange for their loyalty.[4]

Military actions included the movement of Sherman into the Carolinas, Sheridan's continuing efforts to clear the Shenandoah Valley of Confederates, the siege of Petersburg and the fighting around Richmond, and the opening of the Mobile Campaign late in the period.

Sherman opened his Carolina campaign on the 19th of January when he began his march into South Carolina. The march met little resistance in February as he moved first through Columbia on the 17th of February and Charleston on the 18th. His forces met their first major resistance at Kinston, North Carolina, March 8-10 and also at Monroe's Cross Roads and Solemn Grove, South Carolina, on March 9-10. On the 11th of March, Sherman's troops entered Fayetteville, North Carolina, and continued to move north. The Battle of Averasborough, North Carolina, followed on the 16th of March and the Battle of Bentonville, March 19-21st. By the end of March the troops of General Sherman were approaching the southern border of the state of Virginia.

In Virginia, Sheridan continued to cleanse the Shenandoah Valley of Confederate troops. On the 1st of March he skirmished with Confederates at Mount Crawford, Virginia, and the next day at Waynesboro, Virginia, conducted the final defeat of the rebel forces in the Valley. Sheridan's troops then moved south to assist General Grant with his efforts against Petersburg and Richmond.

The attempts to take Richmond and Petersburg continued throughout this period with associated battles in Virginia at Hatchers Run, February 5-7; at Fort Stedman, March 25; and at Dinwiddie Court House and White Oak Road, March 31. These actions led to Lee's decision to retreat from the Richmond area. Both sides continued to maneuver for position, but the Union was constantly tightening its hold on both cities.

On the 17th of March, General Canby led his troops ashore and opened the Mobile Campaign. His goal was to capture the city of Mobile, Alabama. The initial battle of the campaign occurred on the 26th of March when the Union arrived at Spanish Fort, Alabama, and commenced a siege.

Sensing that the end was near, President Lincoln accompanied by his wife and son departed for City Point, Virginia, on the 23rd of March. The President remained until the 8th of April—long enough for him to enter the city of Richmond after the it fell to the Union.

*Donald E. Markle*


*Sunday, January 1, 1865*
Did not get to Church today. Weather clear and cold. No news.

*Monday, January 2, 1865*

About 300 Officers of the Army called on the Prest. today at noon, after which citizens were received.

*Tuesday, January 3, 1865*

Commander Hull[5] of Phila Navy Yard reports that Stmr *Massachusetts*[6] has just arrived there. Capt. West[7] reports that our forces are preparing to move at Charleston.

Gen. Sheridan is directed to send another Division of troops to Balto as soon as transports are ready to convey them to Wilmington, N.C.

*Wednesday, January 4, 1865*

Two inches of snow fell last night. There is sleighing today. Weather is quite cold.

The troops to operate against Fort Fisher leave Ft. Monroe today & will reach Adml. Porter on Friday.

*Saturday, January 7, 1865*

Gen. Thomas teleghs that his cavalry captured & burned Hood's pontoon train and 180 wagons with supplies.

Gen. Dana's Cavy under Grierson[8] when last heard from had destroyed the Mobile & Ohio RR to Okolona [MS] & were still on their way. All the bridge culverts, engines, cars, etc. in their line of march were destroyed. The expedition thus far has proven a complete success.

Genl. Orders (Adj. O.) No. 1 were issued today relieving Major Gen. B. T. Butler from command of the Dept. of Va. & N.C. & ordering him to report from Lowell, Mass., by letter to Adj. Gen.[9]

*Sunday, January 8, 1865*

Lt. Gen. Grant has designated Maj. Gen. Ord to take temporary command of the Dept. of Va. & N.C. in Gen. Butler's place.[10]

Genl. Grant has ordered Thomas as soon as he is assured that Hood has gone south from Corinth [MS] to send Schofield's Corps by rail to Annapolis, Md. there to rendezvous for further orders. The Dept. of the Cumberland & the Dept. of the Ohio will then be united under Genl. Thomas.

*Monday, January 9, 1865*

Gen. Thomas today sends a report of Col. W. J. Palmer of the Anderson Cavalry who followed & destroyed Hood's pontoon Train of

70 boats & about 200 wagons containing supplies, also 3,000 stand of small arms & captured 200 prisoners. His force was but 600 men.

*Tuesday, January 10, 1865*
Jennie[11] & I attended the President's levee last night. It was crowded. We were much pleased with the visit.

Gen. Marcy[12] telegraphs from Vicksburg that Gen. Grierson has arrived there. His raid was very successful. He destroyed 40 miles of the Mobile & Ohio road & 30 miles of the Miss. Central, captured & destroyed 4 locomotives, 100 cars, 30 bridges, 300 wagons with supplies for Hood, 4,000 new carbines, water tanks, depots, etc., burnt a large woolen factory, together with a large quantity of leather & supplies of different kinds, brought off 600 horses & mules, 1,000 Negroes, 600 prisoners, whipped Forrest's corps of dismounted men & intercepted despatches stating that reinforcements were coming up from Mobile. These troops arrived on cars whilst the fight was going on & Grierson went to their rear & captured them. Hood will not be able to repair the road in 2 months.

*Wednesday, January, 11, 1865*
Missouri Legislature today passed the ordinance which makes them a free state.[13] Hail, free Missouri.

*Friday, January 13, 1865*
Adml. Porter was to sail from Beaufort, N.C. together with a land force on Wednesday. We will hear from the second attack on Ft. Fisher soon.

*Saturday, January 14, 1865*
Gen. Grant telegraphs that Richmond papers of today state that our fleet reappeared off Wilmington & it was rumored that the bombardment of Ft. Fisher had begun.

*Sunday, January 15, 1865*
Mr. Blair (F. P.) [Frank P., Sr.][14] arrived at City Pt. yesterday from Richmond on his way to Washn. He is accompanied by two commissioners from Alabama. They will arrive in Washn Monday.

Tennessee in Convention assembled last week passed the ordinance abolishing slavery. It will be voted on by the people Feby 22nd.[15]

Hon. Edwd Everett of Mass.[16] died at 4 1/2 a.m. today of Apoplexy. It is a singular coincidence that the Rev. Dr. Channing[17] in a sermon delivered at the Capitol this morning eulogized Mr. Everett for his efforts during the war to sustain our cause. He spoke of Mr. Everett in the very highest terms and that without knowing of his decease.

*Monday, January 16, 1865*

Genl. Terry[18] Comd'g the expedition before Wilmington reports that he arrived off Wilmington on Friday the 13th & had landed his Infantry & stores. He occupies 2 lines across the peninsula above Ft. Fisher & had 6 siege guns in position. He had captured & burned a boat on the river.[19]

4,500 troops of the 19th Corps from Gen. Sheridan's Army left Ft. Monroe yesterday & today reinforce Terry. From rebel papers we learn that the bombardment was kept up all day Saturday & Sunday but without any injury to the fort.

Genl. Schofield's Corps began yesterday at Eastport, Miss. to embark enroute for Washington, D.C.

*Tuesday, January 17, 1865*

Ft. Fisher is ours! Gen. Terry telegraphs from Ft. Fisher dated 2 a.m. [on the] 16th that it was decided to assault that place on the 15th & accordingly after a very heavy bombardment by the Navy at 3 p.m. a charge was made. The fight was desperate & lasted till 10 p.m. when the rebels surrendered. We have 2,000 prisoners including Gen. Whiting[20] & Col. Lamb[21] the Comdr of the Port, & 70 guns of different caliber.

The troops of the 19th Corps will have reached there by this time & Wilmington will no doubt speedily fall.

Great credit is due to the Army & Navy for their hearty cooperation. Adml. Porter says Terry is his *beau ideal* of a soldier & a General. It is said that today Gen. Butler gave his evidence before the Committee on the Conduct of the War & that as he was explaining why Ft. Fisher could not be taken by assault, the news of its capture was announced.

*Thursday, January 19, 1865*

Rebel papers of today state that Sherman has occupied Pocotaligo [SC] in very heavy force. One of the federal monitors has sunk near Fort Sumter, supposed to have been caused by a torpedo.[22] A rebel deserter came into our lines in Gen. Ord's front this p.m. & reports that it is stated that Wilmington has been captured by the federals with $33,000,000 worth of cotton which was set on fire by the rebels but was extinguished by our forces before being damaged.[23]

*Monday, January 23, 1865*

Latest news from Cape Fear river shows Adml. Porter 8 miles up the river moving cautiously for fear of torpedoes. Porter thinks the pirates *Tallahassee* & *Chickamauga*[24] were blown up at Ft. Caswell. Five blockade runners had been captured by Federal Fleet.

Schofield's troops have commenced arriving today. This week will bring them all here. They are ordered to be embarked & report by telegraph from Ft. Monroe for orders.

Gen. Meagher[25] with 7,000 troops, fragments of regts belonging to Sherman's army will arrive in City today, enroute for Savannah.

*Tuesday, January 24, 1865*

At 3 a.m. today three rebel rams passed the obstructions near the Howlett Battery & one was sunk. One, the *Drewry*, blown up by a shot from Battery Parsons, one the *Fredericksburg* was disabled having got aground & the 3rd, the *Virginia* was somewhat injured, but to what extent is not known.[26]

*Wednesday, January 25, 1865*

Adml. Farragut[27] leaves Annapolis today for the James River to take personal command there.

*Thursday, January 26, 1865*

Genl. Grant leaves City Pt today for Fort Fisher.

Genl. Thomas is ordered to send A. J. Smith's Division about 12,000 strong & a Div of Cavy 5,000 strong to Gen. Canby to operate from the Gulf on Montgomery & Selma. Canby will if possible capture Mobile.

Schofield's troops are arriving fast. Last news from Terry places him about 8 miles from Wilmington advancing slowly.

*Friday, January 27, 1865*

Weather still very cold. River is frozen up & skating splendid. No news of importance.

*Saturday, January 28, 1865*

News from Richmond is to effect that Breckenridge is rebel Secy. War in place of Seddon. Lee is Genl-in-Chief.[28] Johnston is in Command of the Army of Northern Va. Dick Taylor relieves Hood in Alabama.[29] No news from the north.

*Sunday, January 29, 1865*

Gen. Ord telegraphs that Alex. H. Stephens, R. M. Hunter & J. A. Campbell[30] have come to our lines in Gen. Wilcox's [Willcox][31] front (9th Corps A of P) desiring to be passed over on their way to Washn to confer with Prest. Lincoln with a view to end of war. They will not be admitted until the President's instructions are recd.

*Monday, January 30, 1865*

Maj. Eckert leaves tonight for City Point carrying instructions to Genl. Grant in regard to the peace commissioners.

*Tuesday, January 31, 1865*

Secretary Seward leaves tonight for Ft. Monroe where he will confer with Stevens, Hunter & Campbell.

*Wednesday, February 1, 1865*

The Prest. telegraphs Maj. Eckert to report to Mr. Seward at City Point.

Congress yesterday passed the Constitutional amendment forever abolishing slavery in the United States.[32] Illinois Legislature today ratified it by a large majority. There was an exciting scene yesterday in Congress at the passage of the act. The people rose as if an electric shock had struck them & cheer after cheer rent the air. A national salute was at once fired in the City in honor of the Memorable event. The president today signed the bill.

*Thursday, February 2, 1865*

Mr. Lincoln today went to Ft. Monroe to confer with Stevens, Hunter & Campbell, the peace commissioners.

*Friday, February 3, 1865*

7 p.m. The Prest. & party leave Ft. Monroe tonight for Washn. Stevens and his party leave for Richmond.[33]

Gen. Canby teleghs from New Orleans Jan. 26 that all his preparations are made for an expedition into the interior from the Gulf, that he will try to capture Mobile on his way—18,000 men from Thomas' army are enroute to Canby.

News from Sherman is that he is on his way to Branchville [SC].

*Saturday, February 4, 1865*

The Prest. & party returned this morning from Ft. Monroe having had an interview with Stevens & Hunter which has resulted in the peace commissioners returning to Richmond with no concessions from us. At this time the only way it seems is to fight it out.

From today's Richmond papers we learn that Sherman is half way between Pocotaligo & Branchville marching rapidly for that place.

*Sunday, February 5, 1865*

Gen. Grant has sent a cavalry force down the Weldon road to destroy rebel wagon train that conveys supplies from Bellefield to Petersburg. An Infy force goes as far as Stony Creek in support of the movement.[34]

*Monday, February 6, 1865*

Genl. Grant's cavalry force has returned having found but 18 wagons which they destroyed. They captured 100 prisoners.

Gen. Schofield left Ft. Monroe yesterday for mouth of Cape Fear. He commands now the Dept. of N.C.[35]

*Tuesday, February 7, 1865*

A telegram from Gen. Foster[36] dated Hilton Head, 2d places Sherman at River's Bridge [Salkehatchie River, SC] on the 2d & states that he will be halfway between Branchville & Augusta on the 3d.

Up to this time 10 states have ratified the Constitutional amendment abolishing slavery. They are in order as follows: Ills., R.I., Md., Mass., Pa., N.Y., Wva., Mich., Mo. & Me.

Today is a turning point in my life for the better I hope. I have made a decision in my mind in reference to a matter which has been troubling me very much for several months. May God help me to keep my resolution.[37]

*Wednesday, February 8, 1865*

Weather pretty cold. Snow fell to a depth of an inch & then turned to sleet.

Gen. Grant has extended his line to the left 4 miles. It puts him so near the Southside RR but assures him good crossings of Hatcher's Run when he does move. Gen. Lee in his report to the Rebel War Dept says Gen. Pegram was killed in the late action on the enemy's right.[38]

*Thursday, February 9, 1865*

Richmond papers of 8th say that flour has sold for $1,200 per bbl., Cabbage [$]20 per head & everything else in proportion. Our spies report that although the failure of the peace negotiations has been used by the [other] party to arouse the people it has had a very depressing effect.

Jeff Davis in a speech made on the evening of the 6th inst. said that every slave would be armed. This was excluded from the published accounts.

Ohio has ratified the [13th] amendment to the Constitution. Delaware has refused to ratify it.

*Friday, February 10, 1865*

Nothing new of great importance. From rebel papers we learn that Sherman has struck the Augusta RR[39] near Branchville, S.C.

*Saturday, February 11, 1865*

Gen. Schofield telegraphs from Federal Point, N.C. Feb 8 that he had arrived that morning with one Divn. & would immediately commence operations without waiting for the other troops of his command. He thinks he will be able to take Ft. Anderson and possibly Wilmington with the force he has.

Lt. Gen. Grant reached the city last night to appear before the Committee on the Conduct of the War.

*Monday, February 13, 1865*

Nothing of importance today. Gen. Grant returned to the Army Saturday p.m.

*Tuesday, February 14, 1865*

From rebel papers of today we learn that Sherman crossed the Edisto [River] above Branchville [SC] & advanced towards Columbia occupying as far up as Orangeburg 20 miles above Branchville.

A force of 3,000 men demonstrated the 10th on James Island against the enemy but found the rebels in force.[40] The rebels have fallen back from the Combahee [River] & our forces have occupied the R.R. to the Ashepoo [River].[41] Gen. Hardee[42] reports that 18 additional steamers have appeared off the bar.

On Saturday our forces below Wilmington made 3 assaults on the rebels near Ft. Anderson but were repulsed. The fleet also kept up a heavy fire without doing much injury. There is great terror in the South in reference to Sherman's movements. Everybody is alarmed.

*Wednesday, February 15, 1865*
Rained most all day. Freezes slightly as it falls. Col. Stager goes to N.Y. tomorrow.

*Thursday, February 16, 1865*
Weather very unpleasant. Raining.

*Friday, February 17, 1865*
Rebel papers report that Sherman's advance is skirmishing near Columbia.[43] The rebel Congress has at last declined to arm the slaves. In the Senate the vote was 116 to 10 against it.[44]

*Saturday, February 18, 1865*
From today's Richmond papers we learn that Sherman entered Columbia yesterday morning, that place being evacuated by Beauregard.[45] It is not known in which direction he will now move, but it is expected that he will go toward Florence, N.C.[SC] & thence to Wilmington.

*Sunday, February 19, 1865*
Attended St. John's Church this morning with a Miss Kenny[46] of Philada & from there went to Mr. Johnson's on 9th St. & took dinner. Had a very pleasant visit.

*Monday, February 20, 1865*
Genl. Grant telegraphs that the *Richmond Examiner* of today says that Charleston was evacuated by the rebels last Friday. We hope this news will soon be confirmed.

*Tuesday, February 21, 1865*
Gen. Gillmore telegraphs dated Charleston, S.C. 18th that the rebels evacuated that place on the night before & Mayor Macbeth surrendered the City to Gen. Schimmelfennig[47] that day at 9 a.m. We have captured 200 pieces of good artillery. The rebels burned all the cotton, warehouses, QM stores, RR bridges and two ironclads.[48] Gen. Gillem[49] has orders to send all his spare troops to the mouth of Cape Fear River.

*Wednesday, February 22, 1865*

The Secy. of War last night sent orders to all forts, arsenals & army HdQrs in the U.S. to fire a national salute at noon today in honor of the restoration of the flag of the Union upon Fort Sumter. The War Dept. was brilliantly illuminated tonight as was also the White House & other public buildings.

We today recd information that Gen. Schofield compelled the rebels to evacuate Ft. Anderson Saturday night. We occupied it on Sunday taking 10 heavy guns.

Admiral Porter kept up a heavy bombardment on Fort Anderson all day Saturday which was replied to briskly at first but afterwards slackened. The possession of this fort will probably give us Wilmington.

A few days since Gen. Crook & Gen. Kelly [Kelley] were surprised & captured at Cumberland by a party of sixty rebels.[50]

*Thursday, February 23, 1865*

We have information today that Sherman is in Charlotte, N.C.

*Friday, February 24, 1865*

Gen. Schofield has captured Wilmington. Our forces under General Terry entered the city at 9 a.m. 22d. A large amount of supplies were taken which the rebels could not destroy. The number of prisoners captured is not given. This is glorious news. Soon there will be nothing left to the Confederacy but Richmond & that too must fall.

*Saturday, February 25, 1865*

We have nothing of interest.

Gen. Canby has started a Cavalry expedition out from Vicksburg. Gen. Thomas has started one from Decatur, Ala. towards Selma & Montgomery & one from Knoxville, Tenn. into North Carolina in direction of Charlotte & Sheridan leaves Winchester Monday for Lynchburg, to go from there across to Grant or into N.C. as circumstances admit.

*Sunday, February 26, 1865*

Lines all worked well today. No news. Was at office all day.

*Monday, February 27, 1865*

I reran wires in Navy TE office[51] today. Weather clear & very pleasant.

*Tuesday, February 28, 1865*

Nothing of importance today. No further news from Sherman.

*Friday, March 3, 1865*

It has rained nearly all this week.

Citizens in Shenandoah Valley report that Genl. Sheridan entered Staunton yesterday having met but little opposition from the Enemy.

Tonight Gen. Grant telegraphs that he has just read a communication from Gen. Lee which was in substance as follows: Genl. Longstreet & Gen. Ord had an interview some days since in regard to exchange of prisoners & the conversation turned on the subject of the war, in the course of which Ord stated that if Genl. Lee desired to have an interview with Genl. Grant, the latter would not decline. Genl. Lee now says he wishes to leave no means untried to bring an end to the calamities of war & proposes to meet Grant at 11 a.m. Monday the 6th inst. & adds that he has power to carry out any agreement made at the interview.

A reply to Gen. Lee has been promised by Gen. Grant at noon tomorrow.

*Saturday, March 4, 1865*

The Prest. replied to Gen. Grant today that he should have no conference with Genl. Lee except in regard to capitulation of his army. Such questions rest solely with the Prest. & Genl. Grant has no right to decide on them. A great many people have reached Washn yesterday & today to witness the re-inauguration of Prest. Lincoln. It still continues to rain. The streets are covered with mud making it exceedingly unpleasant.

At about 11 a.m. the procession formed in front of & above the War Dept. & marched to the Capitol. At half past twelve the Prest. appeared on the platform. For some time before the Sun had been struggling thro the clouds & just as the Prest. came on the stage, the Sun shone forth in all its brightness. The omen was favorable, every man noticed it & it is hoped that it pictures the history of our country. We have been under dark clouds for 4 years & now the signs of peace brighten. At the same time, half past twelve, the moon was visible in the East & the star Venus in the West.

Since noon the weather has been very pleasant.

*Sunday, March 5, 1865*

Attended church this morning at the Capitol with Miss Kenny of Phila. Bishop Simpson preached from the text, "I, if I be lifted up, will draw all men unto me." The discourse was excellent. I noticed the Prest. & Mrs. Lincoln, Secy. Stanton & several other persons of distinction present.

### Monday, March 6, 1865

Deserters to Grant's army report that Genl. Sheridan has captured Charlottesville with Genl. Early & nearly his entire army of 2,000 men & that one portion of his force has moved towards Gordonsville & one towards Scottsville where the James River canal was cut.

Nothing new of Sherman.

### Friday, March 10, 1865

Our business is increasing very fast.

Gen. Sheridan's official report of his operations up to 2d show that he captured 1,400 men & 17 pcs artly & destroyed 400 wagons & ambulances, a large quantity of Govt. Saddles & stores of all kinds. He was on the 2d at Waynesboro. Gen. Early escaped to the Mountains.[52]

### Sunday, March 12, 1865

It is reported by the rebels that Gen. Bragg[53] had a fight with our forces near Kinston & drove us back capturing 1,500.[54]

Sheridan has crossed the James River cutting the canal near Hardwicksville. We are having dry, clear weather now & the mud is fast disappearing.

### Monday, March 13, 1865

Gen. Sheridan sends a despatch dated Columbia, Va. Mar. 10 stating that he had arrived at that place that morning. His forces had destroyed nearly all the bridges & all the track from Staunton to Gordonsville[55] & also towards Lynchburg.[56] The canal has been destroyed pretty thoroughly, the locks having been broken & the bank in many places cut away. He said he would continue his expedition to Goochland C.H. & from thence to the Fredericksburg road & to the White House.

Today we have the report that he is within five miles of Richmond.

Gen. Schofield telegraphs that the enemy attacked his force Mar 10th near Kinston & after a severe fight the enemy withdrew leaving his dead & badly wounded & several hundred prisoners in our hands. Genl. Schofield was going to the front in person.

*Tuesday, March 14, 1865*

Gen. Schofield telegraphs that he has recd a despatch from Sherman dated Laurel Hill on 8th. He stated that all was well & they had done finely. He would be in Fayetteville [NC] on the 11th. Had plenty of provisions. Schofield said that on the 10th Bragg was fairly beaten & retreated across the Neuse [River] that night. Bragg on the 11th held the north bank of the river at Kinston.

*Wednesday, March 15, 1865*

Secy. of War left for City Pt. at 11 a.m. today to see General Grant. Weather mild & pleasant.

*Thursday, March 16, 1865*

Gen. Grant telegraphs that he has recd letter from Sherman dated Fayetteville, N. C. Mar. 12 in which he says that everything is progressing finely, having met no serious opposition. Hardee keeps in his front at a respectful distance.[57] At Columbia he destroyed immense arsenals & RR establishments & 43 cannons; at Cheraw [SC] he found much machinery & war material including 25 cannon & 3,600 barrels powder. In Fayetteville he found 20 cannon & much other material. An officer who brought his letter says that before daylight on the 10th, Hampton[58] got in rear of Kilpatrick's HdQrs & surprised & captured all the staff but 2 officers. Kilpatrick escaped, formed his men & drove the enemy with great loss, re-capturing about all that he had lost. Hampton left 85 dead on the field.[59]

*Friday, March 17, 1865*

Gen. Sheridan telegraphs from RR bridge over the South Anna [River] dated 15th via Yorktown [on] 17th that he has reached that point safely. There is not a bridge on the RR between South Anna & Lynchburg.[60] He destroyed 15 miles of the Fredksburg RR & immense stores. Gold has fallen as low as [$]160 today.

*Saturday, March 18, 1865*

Lines between here & Phila are broken & also between Phila & Pittsbg by freshets.[61] A great many bridges are washed away. No news.

*Monday, March 20, 1865*

All our business is sent & recd via Havre de Grace [MD]. Cable being broken at that place. No news of importance.

*Saturday, March 25, 1865*

Gen. Schofield teleghs from Goldsboro, N.C. that he occupied that place on Tuesday 21st & Sherman reached there the day after. All is well. The railroad[62] is in good order except the bridges being burned. The depot facilities at Goldsboro are very fine. Gen. Terry from Wilmington was within a few miles of Goldsboro. He had captured 2 locomotives & 2 cars & was using them.

Gen. Grant telegraphs that at 4:30 this morning 3 divisions under the rebel Gen. Gordon[63] made a sudden attack on Fort Steadman [Stedman] & captured it. Several attempts to retake it were made by the 1st & 3d Brig of Hartranft's (1st) [3rd] Div 9th Corps,[64] but were only temporarily successful, until the arrival of the 2d Brig when a charge was made & the enemy driven from the fort with a loss of 2,800 rebel prisoners & ten battle flags. All the guns were retaken uninjured & all our lines reoccupied. The loss of the enemy is very heavy in killed & wounded. Ours sums up about 2,000 in killed, wounded & missing. Gen. McLaughlin of our Army was captured.[65]

*Tuesday, March 28, 1865*

Genl. Sherman reached City Pt. this morning on a visit to Gen. Grant.[66] He returns today & will move his forces at once north towards Weldon. No movement has taken place in the A of P since Saturday.

*Wednesday, March 29, 1865*

It is supposed that the Armies before Richmond will make an advance either today or tomorrow. Gen. Sheridan with about 20,000 Cavalry starts on a raid today towards Danville.[67]

## Notes

[1] Letter from Jefferson Davis to his Peace Commissioners, dated January 28, 1865.

[2] Letter from President Lincoln to F. P. Blair, Sr., dated January 18, 1865.

[3] Letter from President Lincoln to General Grant, dated March 3, 1865.

[4] In 1861 the Confederacy established the Department of the Indian Territory. They promised the Indians better treatment than under the Union and even promised them representation in the Confederate Congress after the war. (Botelho, Michael A., Albert Pike and the Confederate Indians. *Heredon, Transactions of the Scottish Rite Research Society,* 1993, Vol. 2., Pp. 41-56, 137-138.)

[5] Commander Joseph B. Hull, United States Navy.

[6] The *USS Massachusetts* was a 765 ton side-wheel steamer used against Confederate naval activity on inland waterways.

[7]Union Lieutenant Commander William C. West, Captain of the *USS Arietta*, North Atlantic Squadron, U.S. Navy.

[8]Union Brigadier General Benjamin H. Grierson, Commander, Cavalry Division, District of Tennessee, Army of the Tennessee.

[9]Union Major General Benjamin F. Butler was relieved of his command due to the failure of the first attack on Fort Fisher, near Wilmington, North Carolina.

[10]Union Major General Edward O. C. Ord returned to active duty with the Union Army in December of 1864 after recovering from a wound received in the storming of Fort Harrison on September 29th. He replaced General Butler as Commander, Army of the James.

[11]Jennie was the sister of David Homer Bates.

[12]Union Major General Alfred T. Marcy, Inspector General Department.

[13]The Missouri ordinance passed in January of 1865 led to a new constitution for the State of Missouri that outlawed slavery. It was very severe in punishment for Missouri residents who had been Confederates and was replaced by a new constitution in 1875. (*Encyclopedia Americana*, 1986, Vol. 19, p. 261.)

[14]Blair met with Davis on January 12, 1865.

[15]The Constitutional Convention to provide for the return of civil government to Tennessee met on January 9, 1865. It proposed amending the state constitution to do away with slavery. The proposition was approved by popular vote on February 22, 1865, and civil government replaced the military governor on April 6, 1865. (Kane, Joseph N., Anjonen, Steven, & Powell, Janet., (Eds.) *Facts About The States*, p. 483.)

[16]Edward Everett had served in the U.S. House of Representatives, in the Senate, as Secretary of State in the Fillmore Administration, and as Governor of Massachusetts. As a renowned orator his speech preceded President Lincoln's at the dedication of the Gettysburg National Cemetery.

[17]The Reverend Dr. William E. Channing was a Unitarian minister from Massachusetts.

[18]Union Brigadier General Alfred H. Terry was promoted to the rank of Major General, USV, January 16, 1865. He commanded Terry's Provisional Corps, Department of North Carolina, as of January 6, 1865.

[19]The second attack on Fort Fisher, North Carolina, began January 13, 1865.

[20]Confederate Major General William H. C. Whiting, Commander of the Department of North Carolina, was mortally wounded and captured during the battle at Fort Fisher January 15, 1865. He died in New York as a prisoner March 10, 1865.

[21]Confederate Colonel William Lamb, Commander of Fort Fisher, was captured January 15, 1865, and remained a prisoner for the remainder of the war.

[22]The monitor was the *USS Patapsco,* an 1875 ton ironclad. It was sunk January 15, 1865, when it struck a mine in Charleston Harbor, South Carolina.

[23]The rumor was false. Wilmington had not yet fallen.

[24]The *CSS Tallahassee,* a 500 ton Confederate raider, eluded capture at Fort Fisher; the *CSS Chickamauga,* a 586 ton raider, was sunk by her crew to avoid capture at Fort Fisher.

[25]Union Brigadier General Thomas F. Meagher held only minor commands in the Union Army after his resignation was rejected in December of 1863.

[26]The Howlett Battery was part of the Confederate defense line for Richmond. The Battery Parsons was a Union battery located on the James River. It was commanded by Lt. Charles A. Parsons. Two of the rebel rams, the *Drewry* and the *Virginia* became grounded as they attempted to come past Trent's Reach and disrupt the Union activities at City Point, a major supply depot for the Union. The *Fredericksburg* attempted to dislodge the two grounded vessels. Both the *Virginia* and the *Fredericksburg* were destroyed by their crews later in the war.

[27]Union Vice Admiral David Farragut was promoted to that rank on December 23, 1864. He was the first Vice Admiral in U. S. Naval History.

[28]James A. Seddon's resignation as Secretary of War was not accepted until February 6, 1865, when Confederate Major General John C. Breckenridge was named to that cabinet position. In January of 1865, Breckenridge commanded the Department of West Virginia and the Department of East Tennessee. President Davis, on January 23, 1865, signed into law a bill that created the position of General-in-Chief of the Confederate Army. By mutual consent of the Confederate Congress and President Davis, the position was given to General Robert E. Lee, who assumed command on February 6th.

[29]Confederate General Joseph E. Johnston was not given the command of the Army of Northern Virginia. He did not return to command status until February 25, 1865, when he was given command of the Army of Tennessee and the Department of Tennessee and Georgia; and the Department of South Carolina, Georgia and Florida. Later in March he was also given command of the Department of North Carolina. Confederate Lieutenant General Richard Taylor assumed command of the Army of Tennessee on January 23, 1865, in addition to his command of the Department of Alabama, Mississippi, and East Louisiana. General Hood relinquished both his command and his temporary commission in the Confederate Army.

[30]Alexander H. Stephens, Vice President of the Confederacy; Robert M. T. Hunter, the President *pro tem* of the Confederate Senate; and John A. Campbell, Confederate Assistant Secretary of War and an ex-U. S. Supreme Court Justice, comprised the Confederate Peace Commission that resulted from Blair's meeting with President Davis. The Commission was to meet with President Lincoln and Secretary of State Seward at Hampton Roads in early February.

[31]Union Major General Orlando B. Willcox, Commander, 1st Division, 9th Corps, Army of the Potomac.

[32]The Thirteenth Amendment to the Constitution passed the House of Representatives by a vote of 119 to 56.

[33]The Hampton Roads Peace Conference failed as the Confederate Commissioners wanted to negotiate while Lincoln insisted on surrender first, reunification second.

[34]The Battle of Hatcher's Run, Virginia, was fought February 5-7, 1865.

[35]Union Major General John M. Schofield, who as of February 9, 1865, commanded the 23rd Corps and the Department of North Carolina.

[36]Union Major General John G. Foster, Commander, Department of the South.

[37]Probably referring to his decision to move his entire family to Washington, DC, to live with him.

[38]Confederate Major General John Pegram, Commander, Division, 2nd Corps, Army of Northern Virginia, was killed at the Battle of Hatcher's Run February 6, 1865.

[39]The railroad at Augusta, Georgia, was the Georgia Railroad that became the South Central railroad east of Augusta.

[40]The skirmish on James Island, South Carolina, took place February 10, 1865.

[41]The railroad along the Ashepoo River was the Charleston and Savannah Railroad.

[42]Confederate Lieutenant General William J. Hardee, Commander, Department of South Carolina, Georgia, and Florida, was given command of Hardee's Corps, cooperating with General Johnston's forces, February 16, 1865.

[43]The burning of Columbia, South Carolina, took place February 17-19, 1865.

[44]The information was incorrect; the Confederate House of Representatives voted to use slaves as soldiers on February 20, 1865. The Confederate Senate had approved the measure on March 8th.

[45]Confederate General Pierre G. T. Beauregard, Commander of the Military Division of the West, a position with no troops under his immediate command.

[46]Miss Sallie J. Raphael Kenny became the wife of David Homer Bates on May 15, 1867.

[47]Union Brigadier General Alexander Schimmelfennig, Commander, 1st Separate Brigade, Department of the South.

[48]The Confederate vessels blown up to escape capture were the CSS *Chicora*, an ironclad, and her sister ship, the CSS *Palmetto State*, also an ironclad. Both were destroyed February 17, 1865.

[49]Union Brigadier General Alvan C. Gillem participated in General Stoneman's raid into North Carolina.

[50]Two Union Generals were captured the night of February 21/22, 1865, at Cumberland, Maryland: Major General George Crook, Commander, Department of West Virginia; and Major General Benjamin F. Kelley, Commander, Forces West of Sleepy Creek, Department of West Virginia. They were sent to Libby Prison in Richmond where they remained until exchanged in March of 1865, at which time they both returned to the U.S. Army.

[51]The Union Navy Telegraph Office was located at the Navy Yard in Southeast Washington on the Anacostia River.

[52]The Battle of Waynesborough, Virginia, was fought March 2, 1865.

[53]Confederate General Braxton Bragg, Commander, Department of North Carolina under General Joseph Johnston.

[54]The Battle of Kinston, North Carolina, was fought March 8-10, 1865.

[55]The railroad between Staunton and Gordonsville was the Virginia Central Railroad.

[56]The railroad from Staunton towards Lynchburg was the Orange and Alexandria Railroad.

[57]On the 16th of March, 1865, Sherman and Hardee met in battle at Averasborough, North Carolina.

[58]Confederate Major General Wade Hampton, Commander, Cavalry, Johnston's Command.

[59]The Battle of Monroe Crossroads and Solemn Grove, South Carolina, was fought March 9-10, 1865.

[60]The railroad between South Anna and Lynchburg was the Southside Railroad.

[61]Freshets are floods caused by torrential rains.

[62]The railroad at Goldsboro, North Carolina, was the Wilmington and Weldon Railroad.

[63]Confederate Major General John B. Gordon, Commander, 2nd Corps, Army of Northern Virginia.

[64]Union Brigadier General John F. Hartranft, Commander, 3rd Division, 9th Corps, Army of the Potomac.

[65]Union Brigadier General Napoleon Bonaparte McLaughlin, Commander, 3rd Brigade, 1st Division, 9th Corps, Army of the Potomac, was captured March 25, 1865, and confined to Libby Prison until Richmond fell.

[66]Generals Sherman and Grant and Admiral Porter met with President Lincoln aboard The *River Queen* to detail their future military plans. There were also general discussions regarding Lincoln's reconstruction plans.

[67]This movement was a precursor to the Battles of Dinwiddie Court House and White Oak Road, fought March 31, 1865.

# April, May, June 1865

The Bates diary for April, May, and June of 1865 has two contrasting themes: first, euphoria as the end of the war was clearly in sight, and second, great sadness caused by the assassination of President Lincoln. The euphoria is expressed on the 3rd of April when Bates enters his joy at the occupation of Richmond in his diary. The Confederate capital had come to be seen as the heart of the rebellion, and its falling denoted that the end was in sight.

Throughout these last months of the war, Bates continued to make reference to the extension of the telegraph lines. On the 6th of April he commented on the movement of the telegraph line with Grant to Jetersville near Amelia Court House, and in May he spoke of reestablishing the telegraph lines to Fredericksburg and Danville.

Many of the early April telegraphic communications focused on the pursuit of Lee's army and its impending surrender. The telegraph line between Grant and Lincoln was in daily use as Grant reported on his written communications with Lee. Lincoln in return advised him of his specific requirements for the surrender. Bates closely followed these events, and the diary contains pasted newspaper articles that chronicled the events as they unfolded. Many of the written letters between Grant and Lee were published in Union newspapers the same day as they were written.

After the surrender of General Lee, it did not take the U.S. Government long to begin reductions in its military forces. Bates's diary entry of April 14, 1865, commented on the changes that were taking place in the military.

The assassination of President Lincoln on the 15th of April was a cause for great sorrow and inflicted a heavy workload on the Telegraph Office. Bates was on duty in the cipher room on that night and remained on duty until early the next morning. In his book, *Lincoln in the Telegraph Office*, he wrote: "Although I was on duty in the cipher room that evening, I have no direct remembrance of anything that occurred prior to the moment when someone rushed into the office with blanched face saying, 'There is a rumor below that President Lincoln has been shot at Ford's Theater. . . .' A relay of mounted messengers in charge of John C. Hatter[1] was immediately established by Eckert, and all night long they carried bulletins in Stanton's handwriting addressed to General Dix, New York City, which were at once given to the Associated Press and flashed over the wires throughout the country."[2]

Bates and three other operators remained in the Telegraph Office the entire night of April 14 and 15, relaying and receiving messages. They provided support to various governmental officials and ensured that information was released to the general public. On the 20th of May Bates was subpoenaed to testify at the trial of the conspirators regarding the handwritten ciphers reportedly found on John Wilkes Booth's body, but in fact found in his room at the National Hotel. The cipher was the same as that which Bates and his two compatriots succeeded in breaking early in the war years, the Vicksburg Square.

In late May and June Bates was looking forward to the peaceful times ahead. He commented with pleasure on the reopening of mail routes, railroad lines, and telegraph communications to the southern areas, as well as the reductions in the military and the general feeling that peace had arrived. His only entry for the month of June 1865 was personal, speaking of going to Pittsburgh to bring his family to Washington where they were to live with him in Georgetown.

The spring of 1865 was a time of high hopes for the Union and utter desperation for the Confederacy. Military and political issues were intertwined as surrender approached. For example, April opened with the Battle of Five Forks near Petersburg that resulted in cutting General Lee's last lifeline for supplies, thereby forcing the Army of Northern Virginia to evacuate both Petersburg and Richmond and retreat toward Amelia Court House. The next day, April 2nd, an event took place of enormous political and military significance, as Davis and most of the Confederate Cabinet fled Richmond. Two days later President Lincoln made a symbolic visit to the ruined Confederate capital.

Lincoln returned from City Point, Virginia, on the 9th of April, but before he left, he advised General Grant to "let the thing be pressed,"[3] referring to the surrender of the Confederate armies. After arriving back in the capital, Lincoln on the 11th of April, in recognition of General Lee's surrender, gave his final speech in which he referred to his flexibility on the subject of reconstruction and alluded to suffrage for certain categories of black individuals. The speech was well received and reported widely by the Union and Southern press.

In anticipation of the complete end of hostilities, President Lincoln on the 13th of April ended the draft and curtailed the acquisition of supplies for the armies. He began to turn his attention to the post-war period. This was not to be—on the 14th of April while attending a play at Ford's Theater, Lincoln was shot by John Wilkes Booth, dying on the morning of the 15th. Andrew Johnson was sworn in as President of the United States, and while the transition of governmental powers was smooth, hysteria associated with the assassination was rampant throughout the Union.

Events moved rapidly during the early days of the Johnson Administration starting with the debate over the proposed terms that Sherman offered Johnston for the surrender of his army. It was felt in Washington that the terms exceeded the ground rules given to Grant and had strayed into the political arena. This debate was followed by: the capture of Jefferson Davis and his party on the 10th of May, the activation of the Freedmen's Bureau on the 12th of May, the opening of the Southern ports and the lifting of trade restrictions with Southern states on the 22nd of May, the movement of the loyal government of Virginia (which had been in residence in the Union-held portion of the state) to Richmond on the 23rd of May, and finally President Johnson's Proclamation of Amnesty. The Proclamation issued on the 29th of May granted amnesty and pardon to all who had participated in the rebellion if they took an oath supporting the Union and Emancipation. However a number of former Confederates, including those who owned more than $20,000 in property or who had held high rank either in the government or the military, had to individually apply for Presidential pardons. All property, with the exception of slaves, reverted back to the previous owners once pardoned. This last clause caused many blacks to lose property they had taken during the war.

During most of this period a great deal of attention was focused on the assassination and its aftermath. Booth was killed and his associate, David E. Herold, was finally caught on the 26th of April. Herold and the other seven incriminated in the plot were put on trial, resulting in the hanging of four of the plotters on June 30th and the imprisonment of the other four.

The main theaters of military operation were Virginia; the Carolinas; Mobile, Alabama; and isolated activity in the far West. The center of military attention, the Virginia Campaign, was rapidly moving to a close. The Battle of Five Forks on the 1st of April cut the last supply line into the siege area for the Confederates. After the breakthrough at Five Forks, Virginia, disaster continued to stalk the Confederates as they lost about one-third of their strength at the Battle of Sayler's Creek on the 6th of April. At this point, communications discussing the terms of surrender were frequent and specific between the two commanders, Grant and Lee. Grant wrote to Lee that his only criterion for surrender was "that the men and officers surrendered shall be disqualified from taking arms against the Government of the U.S. until properly exchanged."[4] Lee rejected the proposal and tried to break out of the Union stranglehold in the Battle of Appomattox. When that failed, he finally agreed to surrender his army.

In the Carolina Campaign, Sherman pressed forward toward Raleigh, North Carolina, and had skirmishes at Smithfield, Pikeville, and Beulah, North Carolina—all on the 11th of April. Raleigh fell on the 13th of April, and by the 14th General Johnston, seeing that he had no chance of joining his forces to those of General Lee, was seeking terms of surrender from Sherman. The Mobile Campaign, which was just getting underway in April, continued with siege actions at Fort Blakely, the fall of Spanish Fort on the 3rd of April, and finally the fall of Mobile on the 12th. On the 12th and 13th of May, the last land battle fought in the Civil War took place at Palmito Ranch, Texas.

After General Lee and his Army of Northern Virginia surrendered on April 10, 1865, the remaining Confederate Armies were not long in following his lead. They surrendered as follows: April 26—General Joseph E. Johnston, the Army of Tennessee; May 4—General Richard Taylor, Department of Alabama, Mississippi, and East Louisiana; May 10—General Samuel Jones, Department of Florida; May 11— General M. J. Thompson, Commander at Chalk Bluff, Arkansas; May 26—General E. Kirby Smith, Trans-Mississippi Department; and June 23—General Stand Watie, a Cherokee Indian and Brigade Commander, Indian Division, Cavalry Corps, Trans-Mississippi De-partment.                                   *Donald E. Markle*

*Sunday, April 2, 1865*

After days of sanguinary fighting near Petersburg, Gen. Grant telegraphs that Sheridan Comd'g Cavy & infy on the left has whipped the enemy & captured 3 brigades of Infy, several batteries of artillery & a wagon train & is now moving down towards Petersburg. Besides this the 6th Corps alone captured 3,000 rebels, & the 2d & 24th Corps have both taken forts, guns, pris, but it is not known how many. The rebel lines are broken in three places & at this time 10 a.m. the federal forces are enveloping the works defending Petersburg, which no doubt will fall into our hands.[5]

The Prest. still remains at City Point. Gen. Canby telegraphs from Mobile Bay Mar 23rd that he will move on Blakely [AL] the next day. He was delayed by storms which are unparalleled within 40 years.

Sherman reached Goldsboro [NC] Friday & is no doubt moving north at this time.

*Monday, April 3, 1865*

Today is one long to be remembered in the annals of our country, for today we have occupied Richmond the boasted stronghold of rebellion. Petersburg & Richmond were both evacuated last night. The enemy leaving in great haste. Genl. Weitzel[6] was the first to enter Richmond with his command at 8:15 a.m. He found many guns, the city on fire in one place. The people welcomed our forces with enthusiastic expression of joy. Lee with the remnant of the rebel army retreated towards Danville. Genl. Grant is already in pursuit & is on the inner line, it being farther from Richmond to Danville than from Petersburg. There is no doubt Lee will be intercepted & dispersed or captured.

Such a day of rejoicing has never been seen in this place. Very shortly after the news of our victory was rec'd a large crowd assembled in front of the War Dept. yard & speeches were made by Sec. Stanton, Seward, Senator Sherman,[7] Preston King, Jr.,[8] Johnson[9] & many others. Secy. Stanton's speech was splendid. He called for cheers for the brave soldiers of our armies who have by their valor & courage gained us this victory; for the heroic commander of the armies, Gen. Grant; for Comdr. of the U.S. forces by land & by sea, Abraham Lincoln; & for the gallant Sherman, the "great flanker." He then said, "Let us not forget to return thanks to our Heavenly Father for his kind care & protection over us, & let us remember also the wounded & dying who have purchased victory with their sufferings & with their blood. They deserve our deepest commiseration." God be praised for so great a triumph.

*Tuesday, April 4, 1865*

From all parts of the country we hear of great rejoicing over the fall of Richmond. Genl. Weitzel telegraphs that he found 28 Engines & 125 cars in Richmond & a great many supplies of different kinds. Gen. Grant telegraphs this eve'g from Sutherland's Station that the Enemy has destroyed a great deal of his transportation & munitions of war & his troops are leaving for home, some in large & some in small squads. The organized rebel force is on the north side of the Appomattox [River] apparently heading for Lynchburg. Mrs. Lee remains in Richmond.[10]

*Wednesday, April 5, 1865*

Gen. Grant teleghd last night from Wilson Station 27 miles from Petersburg that Sheridan with the Cavalry & 5th Corps was between that place & the Appomattox. Genl. Meade with the 2d & 6th Corps

President Lincoln's Last Telegram from City Point in reply to
Secretary Stanton's warning to be careful of himself

*(Courtesy of the Stern Collection, Library of Congress)*

following. Gen. Ord was following the line of the Southside Railroad. The prisoners captured on the 4th exceed 2,000. Gen. Grant's losses since Mar 28th in killed, wounded & missing will not exceed 7,000 of whom 1,500 to 2,000 are captured & a great many slightly wounded. The pursuit will be continued as long as there seems to be any use in it.

*Thursday, April 6, 1865*

Our telegraph line this eve'g is up to Gen. Meade's HdQrs at Jettersburg [Jetersville] near Amelia C.H.

Gen. Sheridan reports that his cavy yesterday captured 5 pieces of artillery, 200 wagons & several battle flags. The Army is near Jettersburg & Lee's army a little northwest. It is thought the two armies will come together soon.

Gen. Weitzel captured in Richmond 500 pieces of artillery, 5,000 small arms & a considerable amt of supplies & munitions of war.

*Friday, April 7, 1865*

As was supposed our army came up with Lee yesterday near Deatonville, & whipped him. Sheridan reports the battle as a rout. He captured 2,000 pris, among them Genls. Ewell, Custis Lee & three other Genls., 14 pcs of cannon, 200 wagons & 70 ambulances. Some 50 wagons were abandoned & destroyed by the enemy. Our forces are pressing the rebels closely.[11]

*Saturday, April 8, 1865*

Gen. Grant telegraphs from Farmville, Va. today at noon that he has thus far pushed Lee from the Danville road & is pressing him closely toward Lynchburg & is very confident of receiving the surrender of Lee & what remains of his army tomorrow.[12]

Genl. Thomas telegraphs that a scout in from Tupelo, Miss. near Corinth reports that Wilson's Cavalry drove Forrest out of Selma & captured that place.[13] News from Canby up to Mar 29. He was besieging Mobile closely & it is thought he will capture it very soon.

*Sunday, April 9, 1865*

Gen. Grant has telegraphed from Appomattox near Lynchburg that Genl. Lee surrendered the Army of Northern Va. to him today.

The following bulletin gives the details. [The following are newspaper articles pasted in the diary.]

USMTC Construction Crew Arrives at Richmond

*(Courtesy of the Massachusetts Commandery Military Order of the Loyal Legion and the U.S. Military History Institute, Carlisle, Pennsylvania)*

*Washington D.C., April 9, 1865, 9 p.m. Major General John A. Dix,*
*New York*

This Department has just received official report of the surrender, this day of General Lee and his army to Lieutenant General Grant. Details will be given as speedily as possible.

Edwin M. Stanton, Secretary of War

*Headquarters Armies Of United States, April 9, 9:40 p.m.*

Hon. Edwin M. Stanton, Secretary of War

General Lee surrendered the army of Northern Virginia this afternoon, upon terms proposed by myself. The accompanying additional correspondence will show the conditions fully.

U. S. Grant, Lieutenant General

*April 9, 1865*

Lieut. General U. S. Grant, Commanding United States Armies

General: I received your note of this morning on the picket line, whither I had come to meet you, and ascertain definitely what terms were embraced in your proposition of yesterday. With reference to the surrender of this army, I now request an interview in accordance with the offer contained in your letter of yesterday for that purpose.

Very respectfully, Your obedient servant

R. E. Lee, General

*April 9, 1865*

General R. E. Lee, Commanding Confederate States Army

Your note of this date is but this moment 12:00 a.m. received, in consequence of my having passed from the Richmond and Lynchburg road to the Farmville and Lynchburg road. I am at this writing about four miles west of Walter's Church and will push forward to the front for the purpose of meeting you. Notice sent to me on this road where you wish the interview to take place, will meet you.

Very respectfully, Your obedient servant,

U. S. Grant, Lieutenant General

*Appomattox C.H., April 9, 1865*

General R. E. Lee, Commanding C.S.A.

In accordance with the substance of my letter to you of the 8th inst. I propose the surrender of the Army of Northern Virginia on the following terms, to wit: Rolls of all the officers and men be made in duplicate, one copy to be given to an officer designated by me, the other to be retained by such officer or officers as you may designate. The officers to give their individual paroles not to take arms against the Government of the United States until properly exchanged and each company or regimental commander signs like parole for the men of their command. The arms, artillery, and public property to be packed and stacked, and turned over to the officers appointed by me to receive them. This will not embrace the side arms of the officers, nor their private horses or baggage. This done, each officer and man will be allowed to return to their homes, not to be disturbed by United States authority so long as they observe their parole and the laws in force where they may reside.

Very respectfully,

U. S. Grant, Lieutenant General

*Headq'rs Army Northern Virginia, April 9, 1865*

Lieut. Gen. U. S. Grant, Commanding United States Armies:

General: I have received your letter of this date containing the terms of surrender of the Army of Northern Virginia, as proposed by you. As they are substantially the same as those expressed in your letter of the 8th Inst. they are accepted. I will proceed to designate the proper officers to carry the stipulation into effect.

Very respectfully, Your obedient Servant.

R. E. Lee, General

The following previous correspondence between Lieutenant General Grant and General Lee, referred to in the foregoing telegraph to the Secretary of War, [is pasted into diary]:

*Clifton House, Va, April 9, 1865*

Hon. Edwin Stanton, Secretary of War

The following correspondence has taken place between General Lee and myself. There has been no relaxation in the pursuit during its pendency.

U. S. Grant, Lieutenant General

*April 7, 1865*

General R. E. Lee, Commanding C.S.A.

General: The result of last week must convince you of the hopelessness of further resistance on the part of the Army of Northern Virginia in this struggle. I feel that it is so, and regard it as my duty to shift from myself the responsibility of any further effusion of blood, by asking of you the surrender of that portion of the Confederate army known as the Army of Northern Virginia.

Very respectfully, Your obedient servant

U. S. Grant, Lieutenant General

*April 7, 1865*

To: Lieut. Gen. U. S. Grant, Commanding Armies of the U.S.

General: I have received your note of this date. Though not entirely of the opinion you express of the hopelessness of the further resistance on the part of the Army of Northern Virginia, I reciprocate your desire to avoid useless effusion of blood, and, therefore ask the terms you will offer on condition of its surrender.

R. E. Lee, General

*April 8, 1865*

General R. E. Lee, Commanding C.S.A.

General: Your note of last evening in reply to mine of same date, asking conditions on which I will accept the surrender of the Army of Northern Virginia is just received. In reply, I would say that peace being my first desire, there is but one condition I insist upon, [it] is: The men surrendered shall be disqualified from taking up arms again against the Government of the United States, until properly exchanged. I will meet you, or designate officers to meet any officers you may name for the same purpose, at any point agreeable to you, for the purpose of arranging definitely the terms upon which the surrender of the Army of Northern Virginia will be received.

Very Respectfully, Your obedient servant

U. S. Grant, Lieutenant General

*April 8, 1865*

General: I received at a late hour your note of today, in answer to mine of yesterday. I did not intend to propose the surrender of the Army of Northern Virginia, but to ask the terms of your proposition. To be frank, I do not think the emergency has arisen to call for the surrender of this army, but as the restoration of peace should be the sole object of all, I desire to know whether your proposals would lead to that end. I cannot therefore meet you with a view to surrender the Army of Northern Virginia but as far as your proposition may affect the Confederate State Forces under my command, and lead to the restoration of peace, I should be pleased to meet you at 10 a.m. tomorrow, on the stage road to Richmond, between the picket lines of the two armies.

Very respectfully, Your ob't serv't

R. E. Lee, General, Confederate States Army

*April 9, 1865*

General R. E. Lee, Commanding C.S.A.

General: Your note of yesterday is received. As I have no authority to treat on the subject of peace, the meeting proposed for 10 a.m. today could lead to no good. I will state, however, General, that I am equally anxious for peace with yourself, and the whole North entertains the same feeling. The terms upon which peace can be had are well understood. By the South laying down their arms they will hasten that desirable event, save thousands of human lives, and hundreds of millions of property not yet destroyed. Sincerely hoping that all our difficulties may be settled without the loss of another life, I subscribe myself, very respectfully,

Your obedient servant, U. S. Grant, Lieutenant General

*9:30 p.m. April 9, 1865*

Lieutenant General Grant:

Thanks be to Almighty God for the great victory with which he has this day crowned you and the gallant army under your command! The thanks of this department, and of the Government, and of the people of the United States, their reverence and honor have been deserved and will be rendered to you and the brave and gallant officers, soldiers of your army for all time.

Edwin M. Stanton, Secretary of War

*War Department, Washington, D.C. April 9, 10 p.m..*
Ordered: That a salute of two hundred guns be fired at the headquarters of every army and department, and at every post and arsenal in the United States, and at the Military Academy at West Point, on the day of the receipt of this order, in Commemoration of the surrender of General R. E. Lee and the Army of Northern Virginia, to Lieutenant General Grant and the army under his command. Report of the receipt and execution of this order to be made to the Adjutant General, Washington.

Edwin M. Stanton

*Wednesday, April 12, 1865*
We had an illumination of all the Depts. & some private residences last night & will have a general illumination tomorrow night.

Genl. Lee surrendered about 20,000 men. The previous captures amount to 21,000. Lee surendered 400 wagons, 50 cannons, 10,000 muskets, nearly half of his men having thrown their arms away in the flight.

Mrs. Gen. Lee is dying & her husband & Custis Lee have been sent for, to come to Richmond. Lee has sent to Johnston advising him to give up. Davis is supposed to be at Danville [VA] & to have with him the specie taken from Richmond. Breckinridge started for Lynchburg & has not since been heard of.

Lynchburg was surrendered yesterday to a Lieut,[14] with a scouting party.

Genl. Thomas teleghs that his scouts report Selma captured by Wilson's Cavy force. Forrest & Roddy [Roddey] with their forces were both taken.[15]

Mr. Lincoln returned to Wash. on the 10th from City Pt. Gen. Grant will be here tomorrow.

*Thursday, April 13, 1865*

Gen. Grant arrived here today. I was in the Secy's room with a message for him & to get one from him to put in cipher & saw him quite a while. He bears his honors meekly.

Tonight we have a grand illumination. Orders were issued tonight to stop all drafting & recruiting for Vols. in loyal states, to remove all restrictions upon trade & commerce so far as the public safety will permit, to reduce the number of Genl. & staff officers to suit the exigencies of the service & to curtail the expenses of the military establishment in all its branches. Purchases of arms, ammunition, QM & Comsy stores will be stopped. This will be glorious news for the people of the North.

Extra Billy Smith[16] sent a communication to Gen. Grant today dated Danville, Va. April 11. He asks if the Civil Govt of Va. will be molested by the Federal Govt. & if he & the others of the State Executive Dept. will be allowed to return to Richmond to exercise their functions. If not, if the United States will give them safe conduct to Europe. Genl. Grant has sent word to Genl. Meade by whom the communication was rec'd that he has no answer to make to Smith & if he does have any it will be forwarded by special messenger.

*Friday, April 14, 1865*

Genl. Canby telegraphs from near Mobile dated April 5 that he has completely invested Spanish Fort & Blakely. Gen. Steele moved up towards Montgomery & broke the RR[17] as far as Greenville [AL], capturing some locomotives & cars and 3 or 400 prisoners. Steele now invests Blakely from the North East.

Gen. Sherman telegraphs from Smithfield near Raleigh, N.C. that he'd be at the latter place April 13. He hopes to compel Johnston to surrender at Raleigh but if he don't he will follow him closely.

*Saturday, April 15, 1865*

It is my sad duty to chronicle the death of Abraham Lincoln our beloved President.

Last night he was assassinated at 10 p.m. in his private box at Ford's Theater in this city by a man named J. Wilkes Booth, an actor & brother of Edwin and Julius Brutus Booth also actors. Their father Julius Brutus Booth, now dead, was a celebrated actor.

It appears that while the play of *Our American Cousin* was going on, Booth came to the box from the dress circle and fired a pistol at Pres. Lincoln, the ball striking him in the back of the head three inches from the left ear and lodging back of his right eye. After firing, Booth jumped through the window of the box to the stage brandishing a dagger and exclaiming *"sic semper tyrannis*—now the south is avenged."* He then went out a side door before the audience had recovered from their stupefaction & mounting a horse he had ready, rode rapidly off & has not yet been caught.

About the same time the Prest. was assassinated a man rode up to Secy. Seward's house, where he was confined by injuries received in a fall from his carriage some weeks before, and dismounting entered the house saying to the servant he had a prescription to give to Mr. Seward.

He passed upstairs to the Secy's room and rushing upon him inflicted several severe wounds upon his face, which may not prove mortal. An attendant who was near & interfered was struck at most severely. The confusion brought in Frank W. Seward, the Secty's son, who was met at the door by the assassin and struck on the head with a slingshot & his skull fractured. His life is despaired of. The Secy's oldest son Major Clarence Seward was also slightly injured. The assassin then left the house & rode off & is supposed to have gone in the direction of Upper Marlboro [MD]. Cavalry has been sent in every direction and all precautions taken to capture the daring assassins.[18]

The Office of the President of the United States having devolved upon Andrew Johnson, Vice Prest., he was sworn in at 11 a.m. today and now performs the functions of the Presidential Chair. Wm. Hunter, Chief Clerk was appointed acting Secy. of State.

These occurrences have filled every heart with sorrow. The whole nation mourns the loss of one whose honesty of purpose have endeared him to all. He has deepened the love of all his friends & has challenged the respect of all his enemies.

During the last four years I have been in the War Dept Telegraph Office, I have seen him and conversed with him nearly every day and have learned to love him for his many virtues & his few faults. If he did err it was in being too lenient with the vile traitors seething the life of the nation, and perhaps in this we can see the hand of Providence. If he had lived his leniency may have given the rebels courage & power & at some future time caused another rebellion and more bloodshed. This however is avoided. The entire nation mourns his love. He is described as "first pure, then peaceable, gentle and easy to be entreated, full of mercy and good fruits, without partiality & without

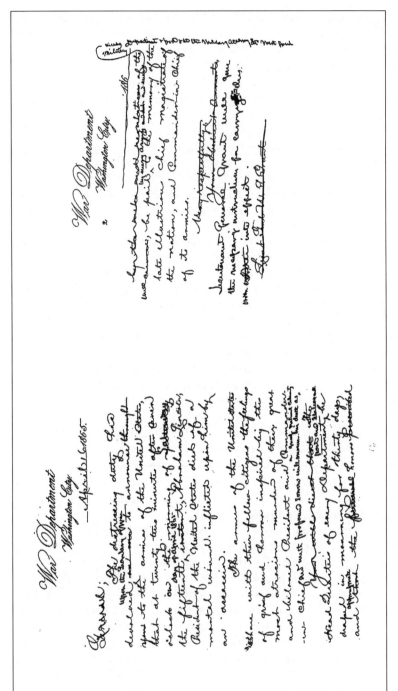

Draft of War Department Message Announcing the Assassination of President Lincoln

*(Courtesy of the Stern Collection, Library of Congress)*

APRIL, MAY, JUNE 1865                    217

hypocrisy." The people are all united in sentiment & there is no
sympathy whatever for treason or copperheadism.

Telegrams from all parts of the country proclaim the horror of the
most atrocious murder & show that the new Prest. has the most
cordial support of all.

May God help him to guide the ship of state thru the breakers.

*Sunday, April 16, 1865*

The excitement throughout the Country increases. Everybody is
wild with grief and rage.

Sherman occupied Raleigh on the 13th, Johnston retreating.
Johnston sent a communication to Genl. Sherman asking a suspension
of hostilities to enable the civil powers to arrange terms of peace.
Sherman replied that he had full powers to meet with Johnston & that
we would grant him the same terms as Lee rec'd from Gen. Grant.
Gov'n. Vance[19] & the civil authorities have been requested to return
and assume their official duties.

Genl. Wilson's official report of the capture of Selma on the 2d is
recd. He has 2,000 well & 2,000 sick prisoners & 20 guns & a large
amount of stores. Forrest, Dick Taylor, Adams,[20] Armstrong,[21] Roddy
[Roddey] escaped through the swamp.

Genl. Wilson has been directed to occupy Selma & operate from
there westward.

*Monday, April 17, 1865*

Moseby [Mosby] has offered to surrender to Genl. Hancock on
Wednesday on the same terms as were granted to Lee. Genl. Grant
has sent word to all the Commanders of Departments & Divisions to
offer these terms to the troops opposing them. It is thought that all of
the rebel armies will surrender.

Gen. Canby telegraphs that he took Spanish Fort by assault capturing 20 guns & some prisoners. Genl. Steele assaulted Blakely about
the same time & captured it with 3,000 prisoners & some Guns.[22] 3
Genl. officers were taken prisoner.

*Tuesday, April 18, 1865*

The body of the late lamented Prest. has laid in state in the East
Room all day today & the crowd has been very great endeavoring to
see it. At 3 p.m. I went over with the War Dept clerks to view it. He
looked very natural & had a sad expression. His whiskers being
shaven off made his face look small. We never shall know his like
again. His funeral takes place at 12 noon tomorrow & his body will

leave the next morning for Phila, there to lie in state, thence to N.Y. where it will lie in state, thence go via Albany, Buffalo, Erie, Cleveland & Toledo to Chicago.

We have official news of the occupation of Mobile on [the] 12th by Genl. Canby, the rebels having evacuated it.

Genl. Thomas forwards the report of Genl. Stoneman's expedition dated at Statesville, N.C. He reports his expedition as a complete success. One portion of his force captured Wytheville [VA] & another moved to within four miles of Lynchburg, whilst he with main force moved towards Salisbury, N.C. which was defended by 14,000 men with 14 pieces of Artillery. The place was taken by assault with 1,200 of the men & all of the artillery.[23] He destroyed the Bridge & railroad between Salisbury & Greensboro [NC] & between Charlotte [NC] & Salisbury[24] besides immense amounts of supplies of all kinds.

The authorities have captured several men supposed to be implicated in the President's murder. Names are Sam Arnold, Mike O'Flaherty, J. O'Laughlin, Payne & Celestino.[25] It is to be hoped they may be the right ones.

Mr. Seward and his son are both doing well & will probably recover. God grant they may be spared to us.

*Wednesday, April 19, 1865*

Today, the anniversary of the passage, 4 years ago, thro Balto, of Union troops & the assault upon them by the populace has been a sad day to the people of the North. The funeral obsequies of our late Prest. took place today. The procession was very long & the best of order prevailed. The body was taken to the Capitol where it remains until Friday when it leaves for Springfield, Ills.

*Thursday, April 20, 1865*

Genl. Tyler[26] at Relay House [MD] telegraphs that one of his scouting parties has captured Atzerodt,[27] one of the men implicated in the assassination of the President.

Genl. Halleck[28] leaves today to take command of the City of Richmond. Moseby will not surrender his command. They will all disperse. Gen. Echols[29] Comdg rebel forces at Christiansburg, Va., when he heard of the surrender of Lee, on the 12th inst. immediately disbanded his men, about 7,000 in all & started himself with a few followers to Trans-Miss.

*Friday, April 21, 1865*

Gen. Tyler at Relay House telegraphed last night that Sergt. Gannen had captured Atzerodt one of the assassins of the President. He is now confined on the Gunboat at the Navy Yard. The War Dept yesterday offered $50,000 for the apprehension of Booth & $25,000 for Atzerodt & $25,000 for Harrold [Herold],[30] Booth's accomplices.

Genl. Sherman has made an arrangement with Johnston which renders useless to the Confederacy his army. The details are not yet made public.[31]

*Saturday, April 22, 1865*

The arrangements made between Gen. Sherman and Johnston have not been ratified by the Prest. Sherman is ordered to renew hostilities. Genl. Grant leaves today for N.C. to assume command in person.

*Sunday, April 23, 1865*

The agreement made between Genl. Sherman & Johnston was in effect as follows: The rebel army was to be disbanded, the arms to be put in the State Arsenal & the men not to be interfered with so long as they obeyed the laws of the U. S. Sherman is very much censured for his assumption of authority & Grant will be there tomorrow to take personal charge.[32]

*Monday, April 24, 1865*

Genl. Canby telegraphs that he found 30,000 bales of cotton in Mobile & a large quantity of stores.

Information has been recd that Wilson occupied Macon [GA] on the 13th inst. with Howell Cobb & G. W. Smith,[33] prisoners, but they claimed to come under the amnesty agreement & Wilson has teleghed through rebel authorities for orders.

Lt. Col. Chapman[34] rebel, next in command to Moseby, has surrendered himself & all of his men to Gen. Hancock & our Cavy is now hunting Moseby. $2,000 reward is offered for his capture & his own [men] are engaged in the pursuit.

*Tuesday, April 25, 1865*

H. H. Atwater[35] operator at the Navy Yard made me a present Sunday of a handsome watch guard which he braided himself from my Mother's & Sister's hair. I am greatly obliged to him.

Genl. Grant arrived at Beaufort, N.C. on the evening of 23d. Our forces are advancing from Burkeville [VA] towards Danville.

The Telegraph Construction party captured 9 locomotives & 60 cars. The telegh line is intact to Danville & our operators have heard Danville working.

Wednesday, April 26, 1865

Gen. Grant reached Raleigh in the morning of 24th inst. Gen. Sherman was not surprised at the rejection & disapproval of his agreements with Johnston, but seemed rather to expect it. When he made the agreement he had before him Genl. Weitzel's call for the assembling of the Va. Legislature & supposed it was approved & sanctioned by the Prest. & the moment he learned that this permission to assemble was annulled, he sent word to Johnston, knowing it had a bearing on the negotiations. Gen. Grant sent notice to Johnston on the morning of 24th terminating the truce. Active operations will be begun immediately.

Thursday, April 27, 1865

J. Wilkes Booth & Jno C. Harrold [David E. Herold] were chased from the swamps in St. Mary's Co., Md. a few days ago & succeeded in crossing the Potomac & were pursued to near Pt. [Port] Royal on the Rappahannock. At 3 a.m. yesterday they were traced to a barn on Garrett's farm 3 miles beyond Pt. Royal on the Bowling Green road & the barn was fired. Booth was shot in the head, & after lingering a few hours died. Harrold was captured alive. Booth's body & Harrold are now on a monitor at the Navy Yd.

Col. Baker's men were the parties engaged in the capture.[36]

Friday, April 28, 1865

Genl. Grant telegraphs from Raleigh that Johnston on the 26th surrendered to Gen. Sherman, all the forces under his command on the same terms Gen. Grant gave Lee. Johnston's command embraces all this side of the Chattahoochie.

Jeff Davis is known to have with him a large amount of specie variously estimated from six to thirteen millions & is making for Texas. Everybody has been placed on the watch for him & it is thought he will be captured.

Saturday, April 29, 1865

The Secy. of War has issued a special order curtailing the expenses of the Mily [military] establishments. All enlisted men who have been prisoners of war & are on furlough or parole will be immediately discharged, also all men in hospitals who need no further medical treatment will be discharged. QM & Comsy Depts are to make no more purchases & to dispose of all needless stock on hand.

Mail routes, railroads & telegraphs are being opened, & trade with the South is being commenced. Truly peace is upon us. How grateful to Divine Providence should we be.

Genl. Grant arrived here today from N.C.

*Sunday, April 30, 1865*

The Army of the Potomac, Sheridan's Cavalry and Sherman's Army are ordered to march to Alexandria overland.

*Monday, May 1, 1865*

Every effort is being made to catch Jeff Davis who is supposed to be going towards the Miss. Weather clear but cool. Heavy raining yesterday.

*Tuesday, May 2, 1865*

Nothing of importance today.

*Wednesday, May 3, 1865*

The Prest. for apprehension of Jefferson Davis, Jake [Jacob] Thompson, Geo. N. Sanders,[37] & others, has offered a reward.

Davis, [Judah P.] Benjamin & others passed thro Yorkville S.C. on the 23rd of April & Col Palmer[38] was but one day behind & it was thought would capture the party. They had several wagon loads of specie with them.

*Saturday, May 6, 1865*

Genl. Canby & Dick [Richard C.] Taylor entered into an agreement similar to that of Sherman's & Johnston's, but it will probably be discontinued when the news of Johnston's surrender is rec'd.

Rebel Gen. Wofford[39] near Resaca, Ga. has surrendered himself & command, also several commands south of the Tenn. river near Decatur, Ala. & several in West Virginia.

Robert Ould the Confederate Agt. for Exchange of Prisoners & Hatch his asst have been arrested in Richmond on information that they diverted the money sent from the North for Federal Prisoners to other purposes.[40]

*Sunday, May 7, 1865*

A telegram from Genl. Canby dated Citronelle, Ala. May 4, states that Dick Taylor has surrendered himself & the forces under his command. Genl. Wilson telegraphs from Macon, Ga. May 6, that Jeff Davis was at Washington, Ga. on May 3d & the morning of 4th & that Upton's Div of Cavy[41] was at Atlanta & every precaution had been taken to capture Davis & his confederates & the specie with them.

Govr. Brown has called the legislature of Georgia to meet on the 22d inst. in view of the collapse of the currency & the consequent misery, woe & destitution among the poorer classes. The Secy. of War has teleghed him, that as this misery, woe, & destitution & the collapse of the currency were caused by Brown & his associates who incited & continued war against the U.S. Govt. which had been a blessing to them for half a century & made the state of Georgia a prosperous one, they would not be allowed to assemble as a legislature of the state & usurp its authority & franchise.

Genl. Wilson was directed to arrest Brown & send him to Washn under guard.[42] R. M. T. Hunter & J. A. Campbell[43] were tonight directed by Genl. Grant to be arrested & confined in prison.

Gen. Halleck telegraphs that one Speed, a relative of Atty. Genl. Speed,[44] has a written communication from Extra Billy Smith to the Prest. of the U.S. of vital importance to the people of the state of Va. & that he desires authority to come to Washn, to present it in person. Genl. Halleck has seen the communication & deems it inadmissible. The Secy. teleghed him that his action was approved & that Speed in recognizing Smith as Govr. of the state committed an act of treason & will be immediately arrested. Gen. Halleck is further directed to offer a reward of $25,000 for the apprehension of Smith that he may be brought to justice.

*Wednesday, May 10, 1865*

Weather damp and cloudy.

Capt. Gilmore[45] left for N.Y. today, on his way to S.C. to take charge of telegraph lines in that state & Ga. No news of interest.

*Saturday, May 13, 1865*

Genl. Wilson telegraphs from Macon [on the] 12th that Col. Pritchard[46] of 4th Mich Cavy captured Jeff Davis & family & staff on 10th at Irwinville, Irwin Co., Ga., 75 miles southeast of Macon.[47] He will be sent to Washn at once under strong guard. I wonder where the Southern Confederacy is at.

*Sunday, May 14, 1865*

It appears that Davis was captured in one of his wife's dresses & when first approached by our men brandished a bowie knife, but surrendered on seeing a revolver pointed at him.

He will be taken to Atlanta, thence to Augusta, Savannah & Ft. Monroe. C. C. Clay surrendered himself at Atlanta & will be sent with Davis.[48]

*Monday, May 15, 1865*

Sherman's Army crosses the Rappahannock tomorrow. Sheridan's Cavalry reached Fairfax [VA] today. [P.T.] Barnum has offered $500 for the dress in which Davis was captured.

*Tuesday, May 16, 1865*

Davis has passed Augusta safely. He goes thence to Savannah where he will be put on a gunboat & brot to Ft. Monroe.

The trial of the Conspirators progresses slowly. The evidence is very strong & conclusive.

*Wednesday, May 17, 1865*

Weather quite warm today. Line to Richmond via Fredksburg completed last eve'g & works prettily.

*Thursday, May 18, 1865*

It rained quite heavily this eve'g. Atmosphere is now quite cool.

Major Thos. T. Eckert was today appointed Asst. Secy. of War, vice Dana resigned.[49] He still retains his connection with the Telegraph, except that much of the details as far as regards the lines & the placing of operations will devolve upon me.

*Saturday, May 20, 1865*

Visited Alexandria today, was called on to attend the trial of the conspirators today but did not testify. I presume I will be called on next week. My testimony is in regard to the ciphers used by Jeff Davis, a key of which was found on Booth's body.[50]

Gen. Sheridan goes tomorrow to Texas to clean out Kirby Smith.[51]

*Tuesday, May 23, 1865*

The Army of the Potomac passed through Washington City today on review. There were probably 80,000 men. Sherman's Army passes tomorrow.

Gov. Letcher of Va.[52] has been arrested and is now in confinement at Winchester, Va. Permission has been given rebel Genl. Joe Johnston to pass thro the U.S. to Canada.

*Thursday, May 25, 1865*

Yesterday & the day before, the Army of the Potomac & Genl. Sherman's army passed in review up Penna. Avenue. It was a grand spectacle & the brave boys who have regained for us our liberties were joyously welcomed home. Long will the memories of those two days be cherished by all.

The rebel ram *Stonewall*[53] has been sold to the Spanish authorities at Havana.

General Brent[54] of the rebel Army has arrived at Baton Rouge to arrange terms for the surrender of Kirby Smith's forces.

*Friday, May 26, 1865*

The papers found on the person of Jeff Davis were yesterday brot to the War Dept & I have copied several. In a letter, dated Charlotte, N.C. Apl. 18, to his wife, Davis says that the terms between Sherman & Johnston though hard are very good, that they do not speak of slavery, but leave it as it was before the war, & that nothing is said of the rebel debt & he hoped to have a provision made to ensure the payment of the rebel debt in common with that of the U.S.

*Wednesday, May 31, 1865*

I have rented a house in Georgetown & am making arrangements to remove the family here. They will probably come about June 15. It will be delightful for me to live at home once more after an absence of over five years.

*Sunday, June 4, 1865*

There is very little news of importance. I leave for Pittsburgh tomorrow Monday & will return about the 15th or 16th inst. with the family.

## Notes

[1] John C. Hatter was a member of the USMTC.
[2] Bates, David Homer, *Lincoln in the Telegraph Office*, Pp. 370-371.
[3] Telegram from President Lincoln to General Grant, dated April 7, 1865.
[4] Smith, Jean Edward, *Grant*, p. 400.

[5]The Battles of Dinwiddie Court House and White Oak Road, Virginia, on March 31, 1865, were followed by the Battle of Five Forks, Virginia, on April 1, 1865.

[6]Union Brigadier General Godfrey Weitzel, Commander, 25th Corps, Army of the James, telegraphed the Secretary of War: "We entered Richmond at eight o'clock this morning." The message was received in Washington about an hour and a half later at approximately 9:30 a.m. It was the first telegraphic communication from Richmond in over four years.

[7]Senator John Sherman of Ohio was the brother of General Sherman. He was later noted for his authorship of the Sherman Anti-Trust Act.

[8]Preston King, Jr. was an ex-Senator from the state of New York and an active Republican Party member.

[9]Andrew Johnson, Vice-President of the United States.

[10]Mrs. Robert E. Lee had moved from the Custis family estate in Arlington, Virginia, to Richmond early in the war.

[11]The Battle of Sayler's Creek, Virginia, was fought April 6, 1865. The Confederate generals captured at Sayler's Creek were: Lieutenant General Richard S. Ewell, Commander, Department of Richmond, who was sent to Ft. Warren, Massachusetts, for incarceration and released on August 19, 1865: Major General George Washington Custis Lee (son of Robert E. Lee), Commander, Division, Department of Richmond, who was soon paroled to care for his sick mother in Richmond; Brigadier General Dudley M. DuBose, Commander, Wofford's old Brigade, Kershaw's Division, 1st Corps, Army of Northern Virginia, who was incarcerated in Fort Warren, Massachusetts, and released in July of 1865; Brigadier General Montgomery D. Corse, Commander, Brigade, Hoke's Division, Department of North Carolina, who was incarcerated in Fort Warren, Massachusetts, and released in August of 1865; Brigadier General Eppa Hunton, Commander, Garnett's old Brigade, Pickett's Division, 1st Corps, Army of Northern Virginia, who was incarcerated in Fort Warren, Massachusetts, and released in July of 1865; Major General Joseph B. Kershaw, Commander, Division, 1st Corps, Army of Northern Virginia, who was released in July of 1865.

[12]There was an engagement at High Bridge, Virginia, April 7, 1865.

[13]Selma, Alabama, fell to the Union April 2, 1865.

[14]Major William D. Branch officially surrendered the city of Lynchburg, Virginia, to Union Brigadier General Ranald S. Mackenzie on April 11, 1865.

[15]Confederate Brigadier General Philip D. Roddey, Commander, Cavalry Division (called Roddey's Brigade), Department of Alabama, Mississippi and East Louisiana and District of Alabama, surrendered his forces. Forrest and a few of his officers escaped.

[16]William Smith was inaugurated as the Governor of Virginia on January 1, 1864. He was known as "Extra" Billy Smith because while overseeing a postal route he had added on some questionable extra charges.

[17]The railroad in the Mobile area was the Mobile and Ohio Railroad.

[18]Lewis T. Powell, one of the Lincoln assassination conspirators, had tried to assassinate Seward. He was arrested on April 17, 1865, at the Surratt

Boarding House, tried, sentenced, and hanged on July 7, 1865. Secretary Seward suffered multiple knife wounds, as did his two sons. All three recovered from their injuries.

[19]Zebulon B. Vance was the governor of North Carolina during the Civil War.

[20]Confederate Brigadier General Daniel W. Adams, Commander, District of Alabama, Department of Alabama, Mississippi and East Louisiana.

[21]Confederate Brigadier General Frank C. Armstrong, Commander, Brigade, Chalmer's Division, Forrest's Cavalry Corps, Department of Alabama, Mississippi and East Louisiana.

[22]The siege of Fort Blakely, Alabama, began April 2, 1865. The fort was taken by assault April 9, 1865.

[23]There was an engagement at Salisbury, North Carolina, April 12, 1865.

[24]The railroad between Salisbury and Greensboro and between Salisbury and Charlotte was the North Carolina Railroad.

[25]Samuel B. Arnold was sentenced to life at Fort Jefferson on Dry Tartugas (off Key West, Florida). He was pardoned in 1869 by Andrew Johnson. Michael O'Laughlin was also sentenced to life at Fort Jefferson on Dry Tartugas and died there of Yellow Fever in 1867. (The original telegram reporting transfer of two prisoners to the Navy Yard lists one name as O'Flaherty, but it is crossed out and the name O'Laughlin handwritten in. Since Bates would have received the original telegram in the War Department Telegraph Office, he included the name in his diary entry.) "Payne" refers to Lewis T. Powell, who was known to his co-conspirators as Lewis Paine or Payne. Joao (John) Celestino, an itinerant Cuban sea captain, was later released. (National Archives, *War Department Records*, File R, Document 1916 JAG.)

[26]Union Major General Erastus B. Tyler, Commander, 1st Separate Brigade, 8th Corps, Middle Department.

[27]Lincoln assassination conspirator, George A. Atzerodt, had the assigned task of killing the Vice President. Captured and tried, he was eventually hanged on July 7, 1865.

[28]Union Major General Henry W. Halleck, Commander, Department of Virginia and Army of the James, Military District of the James.

[29]Confederate Brigadier General John Echols, Commander, Department of West Tennessee.

[30]Lincoln assassination conspirator, David E. Herold, was captured, tried and hanged July 7, 1865.

[31]The agreement between Sherman and Johnston was signed April 18, 1865.

[32]Grant's trip to North Carolina was in response to Sherman's terms of surrender for Johnston's army. Sherman violated the instructions given to Grant by Lincoln by discussing political matters, such as recognition of state governments, the establishment of Federal Courts, and the guarantee of political rights for citizens. The Secretary of War rejected the agreement and sent General Grant to Sherman to correct his actions. The old agreement was

negated, and a new surrender agreement in line with Lincoln's instructions was signed by Johnston and Sherman on April 26, 1865.

[33]Confederate Major General Howell Cobb, Commander, District of Georgia, Department of Tennessee and Georgia, and Confederate Major General Gustavus W. Smith, Commander, 1st Division, Georgia Militia, Department of South Carolina, Georgia and Florida.

[34]Confederate Lieutenant Colonel William H. Chapman, Second-in-Command, Mosby's Raiders, surrendered and was paroled on April 22, 1865.

[35]H. H. Atwater was a member of the USMTC.

[36]Union Colonel Lafayette Baker, self-proclaimed head of the Secret Service in Washington, DC, during the Civil War, was in charge of the pursuit of the assassins. His cousin, Luther B. Baker, was one of the agents who made the capture.

[37]George Nicholas Sanders of Kentucky was founder of the nationalistic expansionist "Young America" movement in the 1850's. During the Civil War he became a Confederate agent in both Canada and the Union.

[38]Probably Union Brigadier General William Jackson Palmer.

[39]Confederate Brigadier General William T. Wofford, Commander, Department of Northern Georgia.

[40]Judge Robert Ould was Chief of the Confederate Commission for the Exchange of Prisoners until early 1864. Confederate Captain William M. Hatch was assistant to Judge Ould for the exchange of prisoners of war. Both men were cleared of all charges after the war.

[41]Union Brigadier General Emory Upton, Commander, 4th Division, Cavalry Corps, Military District of the Mississippi.

[42]Joseph E. Brown was the wartime governor of the state of Georgia. Although arrested, he was held only briefly.

[43]Hunter and Campbell, Confederate Peace Commissioners at the Hampton Roads Peace Conference, were both imprisoned at Fort Pulaski for six months.

[44]James Speed had replaced Edward Bates as President Lincoln's Attorney General December 1, 1864.

[45]James Gilmore, an ex-USMTC telegraph operator, was commissioned as a Captain and Assistant Quartermaster in November of 1864 to serve with the USMTC.

[46]Union Lieutenant Colonel Benjamin D. Pritchard, Commander, Detachment, 4th Michigan Cavalry, Wilson's Cavalry Corps.

[47]The Davis party captured consisted of President Davis; his wife, Varina; four Davis children; a white and a black servant; John M. Reagan, C.S.A. Postmaster General; Colonel Francis R. Lubbock (ex-Governor of Texas); Colonel Burton N. Harrison (Davis's private secretary); Colonel William P. Johnston; Colonel John T. Wood, who later escaped to Cuba; a brother and sister of Mrs. Davis; and a small force of cavalry. The huge amount of specie, rumored to be between $6,000,000 and $13,000,000, turned out to be silver and gold coins with a total value of between $8,000 and $10,000. President Davis was sent to Fort Monroe, Virginia, where he was held for over two years

awaiting trial for treason. He was released in 1867 and returned to his native Mississippi. (Wilson, James H., How Jefferson Davis was Overtaken. In *The Annals of the War Written by Leading Participants, North and South.* Pp. 554-589.)

[48]Davis claimed that he mistakenly donned his wife's raglan and that she threw a shawl over his shoulders before he was confronted by a Union soldier leveling a carbine at him. (Hanna, A. J., *Flight into Oblivion.* Pp. 100-101.) Clement C. Clay, Jr., who had worked with Jacob Thompson in the Confederate operation in Canada, was confined to Fort Monroe for a year without a trial.

[49]Thomas T. Eckert was not appointed Assistant Secretary of War at this time but was brevetted through grades to Brigadier General in May of 1865. He did not serve as Assistant Secretary of War until July 27, 1866, when he held the position for seven months. Bates may have confused Charles A. Dana, Assistant Secretary of War from January 12, 1864, until August 1, 1865, with Brigadier General Napoleon Jackson Tecumseh Dana who resigned his commission in May of 1865.

[50]Major Eckert, Bates's supervisor, testified that the alphabet square cipher found in Booth's Washington hotel room was identical to the two cipher keys found on April 6, 1865, by Dana in the Richmond office of Judah Benjamin, Confederate Secretary of State. (Pitman, Benn., *The Assassination of President Lincoln and the Trial of the Conspirators*, p. 41.) Bates considered it to be "inconceivable that Booth was not supplied with this cipher-code by the Confederate government, although it does not follow that President Davis or any of his cabinet had any previous knowledge of the assassination plot." (Bates, David Homer., *Lincoln in the Telegraph Office.* p. 85.)

[51]Confederate General E. Kirby Smith, Commander, Trans-Mississippi Department, surrendered his Army on May 26, 1865, the last major Confederate Army to do so.

[52]John Letcher was the governor of the state of Virginia at the time of secession. He served until the end of 1863 and was imprisoned for six weeks after the war.

[53]The *CSS Stonewall*, an ironclad, had been built in France due to the efforts of James Bulloch. When finally turned over to the Confederates, it arrived in Cuba in the Western Hemisphere in May of 1865 after the war had ended. It was sold to the Spanish Captain General in order to pay off the crew.

[54]Confederate Brigadier General G. W. Brent served with General E. Kirby Smith's Trans-Mississippi Command.

# Appendix A

## Civil War Cipher Systems

### The Route System

The Union Route System for encryption basically involved the reordering of the words of a plain text message by first putting the words of the original message into a matrix horizontally and extracting (enciphering) them vertically from the same matrix—to be transmitted in the order extracted.

The steps involved in ciphering or deciphering a message were:

1. The telegraph operator was given a message to transmit. His first job was to count the number of words in the message. Example: "For Colonel Ludlow: Richardson and Brown, correspondents of the *Tribune* captured at Vicksburg, are detained at Richmond. Please ascertain why they are detained and get them off if you can. The President. 4:30 p.m."[1] Word count=32. ("The President" was enciphered as one word.)

2. After the word count was established, the operator went to the cipher clerk, usually a telegraph operator, who held the Route Book and told him how many words were in the message to be transmitted. The cipher clerk gave the operator a specific route to employ in enciphering the message as well as the cover name for the route. In the example below the cover name is GUARD; that word was sent first, indicating a route based on a 5 column matrix containing spaces for 35 words. The operator's job was then to copy the original message into the 5 column matrix, putting the first word into column 1, line 1, the second into column 2, line 1, and so forth until the matrix was filled. In the case of the example, three filler words have been added to the end of the message and placed in column 3, line 7; column 4, line 7; and column 5, line 7.

3. The words were then extracted using the route for a GUARD message; *i.e.,* up the first column, down the second column, up the fifth column, down the fourth column, and finally up the third. The message was transmitted in this sequence to the receiving operator.

4. The receiving telegrapher carried out the steps in reverse. He went to his cipher clerk and told him he had a message with a specific route cover name. The cipher clerk gave him the route, and by reversing it, the plain text was easily read.

5. Long messages could contain several different routes in order to accommodate the total number of words. When the route changed, a new cover name was used and a new route employed. (By the end of the war, some of the routes for extraction of messages went through the matrix on the diagonal.)

Example Of Union Message Using Route System

Original Message: For Colonel Ludlow: Richardson and Brown correspondents of the *Tribune* captured at Vicksburg are detained at Richmond. Please ascertain why they are detained and get them off if you can. The President. 4:30 p.m.

Inserted in the GUARD Matrix:

| (kissing) | | (commissioner) | | (times) |
|---|---|---|---|---|
| for | venus | ludlow | richardson | and |
| brown | correspondents | of | the | tribune |
| wayland | at | odor | are | detained |
| at | neptune | please | ascertain | why |
| they | are | detained | and | get |
| them | off | if | you | can |
| adam | nelly | this | fills | up |
| | (turning) | | (belly) | |
| ↑ | ↓ | ↑ | ↓ | ↑ |
| First | Second | Fifth | Fourth | Third |

The words in parentheses are *turning words* indicating when to change columns.[2] Code words: The President=Adam, Nelly=4:30 p.m., Neptune=Richmond, Venus=Colonel, Wayland=Captured, Odor=Vicksburg.[3]

Message or division of ...7... lines.

COMMENCEMENT WORDS.

| Grayson / Giles / Grafton } 6 COLUMNS | Guard / Henry / Harbor } 5 COLUMNS | Kelly / Lucky / Mobile } 4 COLUMNS |
|---|---|---|

Six Column

ROUTE:—Up the .... column—down the 4 —up the 3 —
down the 5 —up the 2 —down the 1 —up the 6

*Four Column Route*

Down the 2nd
Up the 1st
Down the 3d
Up the 4th

*Five Column Route*

Up the 1st
Down the 2nd
Up the 5th
Down the 4th
Up the 3d

| Code | Meaning | Code |
|---|---|---|
| Adam | President U.S. | Asia |
| Abel | Secretary of State | Austria |
| Aaron | " " War | Arabia |
| Amos | " a Treasury | Africa |
| Anthon | " " Navy | America |
| Acton | " a Interior | Alba |
| Abner | Postmaster General | Alpha |
| Alden | Attorney General | Andover |
| Alvord | Adjutant General | Antwerp |
| Abbot | Quarter Master Genl | Aragon |
| Agnew | | Aurora |
| Adonis | | Ashland |
| Abacus | | Avon |
| Argus | | Advent |
| Argyle | | Adverb |
| Arno | | Ague |
| Adrian | Jno G Nicolay | Alloy |
| Apollo | Fred W. Seward | Altar |
| Alps | Peter H. Watson | Amber |
| Andes | Jno G Tucker | Anchor |
| Arctic | C. P. Wolcott | Angel |
| Appian | Geo Harrington | Animal |
| Atlas | Gen U. Fox | Annal |
| Alamo | J. Dahlgren | Armada |
| Akron | H. A. Wise | Anvil |
| Adair | E. D. Townsend | Apple |

GUARD Route Cipher Page and Example of Code Word Page

*(Courtesy of the George C. Marshall Research Library, Lexington, Virginia, William F. Friedman Cryptologic Collection)*

The message, as sent from the War Department Telegraph Office on June 1, 1863, was:

GUARD
ADAM THEM THEY AT WAYLAND BROWN FOR KISSING VENUS CORRESPONDENTS AT NEPTUNE ARE OFF NELLY TURNING UP CAN GET WHY DETAINED TRIBUNE AND TIMES RICHARDSON THE ARE ASCERTAIN AND YOU FILLS BELLY THIS IF DETAINED PLEASE ODOR OF LUDLOW COMMIS-SIONER.

## The Vicksburg Square

The Confederate Vicksburg Square System was a variation on a 16th Century French system known as the *Vigènere* System. It was based on a 26 x 26 matrix comprised of the alphabet repeated 26 times in 26 different orders, each order on a slide of one from the one preceding. A key phrase was used as the basis for enciphering. The Confederacy in general used only three key phrases during the war: *Come Retribution, Manchester Bluff,* and *Complete Victory.* To use the system, the operator took the following steps:

1. He chose one of the three phrases as the key.
2. He wrote out the message in plain text.
3. He wrote the key phrase under the plain text, repeating the phrase as required, as shown in the following example:

| Plain | T | h | e | | e | n | e | m | y | | w | i | l | l | | a | t | t | a | c | k |
|--------|---|---|---|---|---|---|---|---|---|---|---|---|---|---|---|---|---|---|---|---|---|
| Key | c | o | m | | p | l | e | t | e | | v | i | c | t | | o | r | y | c | o | m |
| Cipher | v | v | q | | t | y | i | f | c | | r | q | n | e | | o | k | r | c | q | w |

4. He used the 26 x 26 matrix shown below as follows: The vertical coordinate shows the plain letter; the horizontal coordinate shows the key letter; the intersection of the two is the cipher letter.

5. To decipher the message, the procedure was reversed.

## *Vicksburg Square*

|   | A | B | C | D | E | F | G | H | I | J | K | L | M | N | O | P | Q | R | S | T | U | V | W | X | Y | Z |
|---|---|---|---|---|---|---|---|---|---|---|---|---|---|---|---|---|---|---|---|---|---|---|---|---|---|---|
| A | A | B | C | D | E | F | G | H | I | J | K | L | M | N | O | P | Q | R | S | T | U | V | W | X | Y | Z |
| B | B | C | D | E | F | G | H | I | J | K | L | M | N | O | P | Q | R | S | T | U | V | W | X | Y | Z | A |
| C | C | D | E | F | G | H | I | J | K | L | M | N | O | P | Q | R | S | T | U | V | W | X | Y | Z | A | B |
| D | D | E | F | G | H | I | J | K | L | M | N | O | P | Q | R | S | T | U | V | W | X | Y | Z | A | B | C |
| E | E | F | G | H | I | J | K | L | M | N | O | P | Q | R | S | T | U | V | W | X | Y | Z | A | B | C | D |
| F | F | G | H | I | J | K | L | M | N | O | P | Q | R | S | T | U | V | W | X | Y | Z | A | B | C | D | E |
| G | G | H | I | J | K | L | M | N | O | P | Q | R | S | T | U | V | W | X | Y | Z | A | B | C | D | E | F |
| H | H | I | J | K | L | M | N | O | P | Q | R | S | T | U | V | W | X | Y | Z | A | B | C | D | E | F | G |
| I | I | J | K | L | M | N | O | P | Q | R | S | T | U | V | W | X | Y | Z | A | B | C | D | E | F | G | H |
| J | J | K | L | M | N | O | P | Q | R | S | T | U | V | W | X | Y | Z | A | B | C | D | E | F | G | H | I |
| K | K | L | M | N | O | P | Q | R | S | T | U | V | W | X | Y | Z | A | B | C | D | E | F | G | H | I | J |
| L | L | M | N | O | P | Q | R | S | T | U | V | W | X | Y | Z | A | B | C | D | E | F | G | H | I | J | K |
| M | M | N | O | P | Q | R | S | T | U | V | W | X | Y | Z | A | B | C | D | E | F | G | H | I | J | K | L |
| N | N | O | P | Q | R | S | T | U | V | W | X | Y | Z | A | B | C | D | E | F | G | H | I | J | K | L | M |
| O | O | P | Q | R | S | T | U | V | W | X | Y | Z | A | B | C | D | E | F | G | H | I | J | K | L | M | N |
| P | P | Q | R | S | T | U | V | W | X | Y | Z | A | B | C | D | E | F | G | H | I | J | K | L | M | N | O |
| Q | Q | R | S | T | U | V | W | X | Y | Z | A | B | C | D | E | F | G | H | I | J | K | L | M | N | O | P |
| R | R | S | T | U | V | W | X | Y | Z | A | B | C | D | E | F | G | H | I | J | K | L | M | N | O | P | Q |
| S | S | T | U | V | W | X | Y | Z | A | B | C | D | E | F | G | H | I | J | K | L | M | N | O | P | Q | R |
| T | T | U | V | W | X | Y | Z | A | B | C | D | E | F | G | H | I | J | K | L | M | N | O | P | Q | R | S |
| U | U | V | W | X | Y | Z | A | B | C | D | E | F | G | H | I | J | K | L | M | N | O | P | Q | R | S | T |
| V | V | W | X | Y | Z | A | B | C | D | E | F | G | H | I | J | K | L | M | N | O | P | Q | R | S | T | U |
| W | W | X | Y | Z | A | B | C | D | E | F | G | H | I | J | K | L | M | N | O | P | Q | R | S | T | U | V |
| X | X | Y | Z | A | B | C | D | E | F | G | H | I | J | K | L | M | N | O | P | Q | R | S | T | U | V | W |
| Y | Y | Z | A | B | C | D | E | F | G | H | I | J | K | L | M | N | O | P | Q | R | S | T | U | V | W | X |
| Z | Z | A | B | C | D | E | F | G | H | I | J | K | L | M | N | O | P | Q | R | S | T | U | V | W | X | Y |

The encryption/decryption process using the Vicksburg Square was very time consuming and cumbersome for the operators. In order to make it more efficient, the Confederates adopted a procedure similar to that of Napoleon's, whereby they only enciphered what were considered to be the important words.

Early in the war the Confederates converted the Square into a cipher disc that was easier to use and less cumbersome for the cipher clerk to carry.

In the cipher below, the letter:

A becomes: ⌐|     B becomes: ⊡

H becomes: V     K becomes: ⋖

And so forth.

---

**Pigpen Cipher Chart**

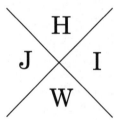

---

Thus the message, "the enemy will attack," was encoded as:

## THE ENEMY WILL ATTACK
⊓V⊐  ⊐⊏•⊐⊏⌐|  Λ⋖V̇V̇  ⌐|⊓⊓⊓⌐|□⋖

The Pigpen Cipher

The Pigpen Cipher

The Confederate Pigpen Cipher was a cipher system that George Washington taught his agents to use during the Revolutionary War. Four symbols were drawn: a tic-tac-toe figure, a tic-tac-toe figure with a dot in each space, a large X, and a large X with a dot in each space. The cipher was then created by placing the letters of the alphabet in the spaces of the figures in a sequence known to both the encoder and the decoder of the message.

## Notes

[1]Kahn, David, *The Codebreakers*, p. 215.

[2]The turning words were inserted by the telegraph operator. The words employed made no sense in the context of the message. Their use was purely a safeguard as the Route cover name indicated the length of each column.

[3]The code words employed came from a list created and supplied by the cipher clerk in the Telegraph Office in Washington, DC. The list included persons, times to 14 minutes, geographic locations including rivers, and other sensitive military terms.

# Appendix B

## Commemorative Plaque of USMTC Operators from Allegheny County, Pennsylvania

The plaque commemorating the residents of Allegheny County, Pennsylvania, who served in the U.S. Military Telegraph Corps during the Civil War is displayed in the Soldiers' and Sailors' Monument in Pittsburgh, Pennsylvania. The bronze plaque is approximately six feet in length with a width of four feet and depth of four inches. It was presented to commemorate the 50th anniversary of the founding of the USMTC. The men who served and their units (when known) are as follows:

Thomas Armor, Army of the Potomac
Bennett R. Bates
David Homer Bates, War Department
Joseph W. Boyd, Peninsula Eastern Shore of Virginia
Nicholas H. Brady
Warren Brockett
Samuel M. Brown, War Department
Jesse H. Bunnell, Army of the Potomac
A. H. Caldwell, Army of the Potomac
Andrew Carnegie, Assistant General Manager
Albert B. Chandler, War Department
Captain Thomas B. A. David, Army of the Potomac
David R. Ecker
Benjamin W. Flack, Army of the Potomac
George Holmes
Charles W. Jaques, Army of the Potomac
John S. Kerbey, Army of the Potomac
Major Joseph O. Kerbey, Army of the Potomac
Henry King
Thomas M. King
Henry Knowland
George A. Low, War Department
L. D. McCandless, Army of the Potomac
J. P. McIlvaine, Army of the Potomac

E. W. McKenna, Army of the Potomac
John A. L. McKenna, War Department
Theodore E. Moreland, Army of the Potomac
David Morse
J. Anderson Munson, Army of the Potomac
Martin Murray
J. Hervey Nichols, Army of the Potomac
John L. O'Niell, Army of the Potomac
J. Theodore Paisley, Army of the Potomac
George W. Perkins, Army of the Potomac
Thomas S. Perkins
J. William Pope, Army of the Potomac
Jesse H. Robinson, Army of the Cumberland
Augustus Steinmyer
F. A. Stumm
John A. Torrence
Robert F. Weitbrec, Army of the Potomac
Thomas D. Williams, Western Army
Benjamin P. Woodward, War Department

This Information was supplied by David Doell, Archivist, Historical Society of Western Pennsylvania, Pittsburgh, Pennsylvania.

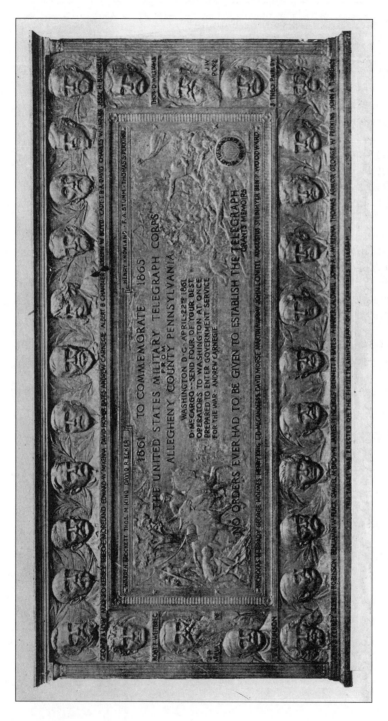

USMTC Plaque Erected on the Fiftieth Anniversary of Andrew Carnegie's
Telegram Summoning Operators to Washington, DC

*(Courtesy of David Hoell, Archivist, Historical Society of Western Pennsylvania, Pittsburgh, Pennsylvania)*

From a photograph by Davis and Eickemeyer, taken in May, 1907

**Charles Almerin Tinker**
Cipher-operator, War Department
telegraph office, 1861–1869

**David Homer Bates**
Manager and cipher-operator, War Department telegraph office, 1861–1866

**Thomas Thompson Eckert**
Chief of the War Department Telegraph
Staff, 1861–1866

**Albert Brown Chandler**
Cashier and cipher-operator, War Department telegraph office, 1863–1866

*(1907 photograph from Lincoln in the Telegraph Office, p. 393)*

# Bibliography

## Primary Materials

Bates, David Homer. Unpublished diary. Washington, DC: Library of Congress, Rare Book Collection.

## Documents

National Archives. *War Department Records*, File R, Document 1916 JAG.

U.S. War Department. (1880-1901) *The War of the Rebellion: A Compilation of the Official Records of the Union and Confederate Armies.* 128 Vols. Washington, DC: U.S. Government Printing Office.

## Atlases and Maps

Adams, James T. (Ed.) (1943) *Atlas of American History.* New York: Scribner's & Sons.

Davis, George B., Perry, Leslie J., & Kirkley, Joseph W. (1983) *The Official Military Atlas of the Civil War.* New York: Arno Press. (Reprint of U.S. Government Printing Office 1891 edition.)

McPherson, James M. (Ed.) (1994) *The Atlas of the Civil War.* New York: MacMillan.

## Magazines and Articles

Bates, David Homer. Lincoln in the Telegraph Office, Part I, Recollections of the United States Military Telegraph Corps. *Century Magazine*, Vol. 74, No. 1, May, 1907, Pp. 123-140.

Bates, David Homer. Lincoln in the Telegraph Office, Part II, His Special Interest in the Work of the Cipher Operators. *Century Magazine*, Vol. 74, No. 2, June, 1907, Pp. 290-306.

Bates, David Homer. Lincoln in the Telegraph Office, Part III, Lincoln in Everyday Humor. *Century Magazine*, Vol. 74, No. 3, July, 1907, Pp. 364-371.

Botelho, Michael A. Albert Pike and the Confederate Indians. *Heredon, Transactions of the Scottish Rite Research Society,* Vol. 2., 1993, Pp. 41-56, 137-138.

O'Brien, John Emmet. Telegraphing in Battle. *Century Magazine,* Vol. 38, 1889, Pp. 782-793.

Wilson, James H. (1988) How Jefferson Davis was Overtaken. In *The Annals of the War Written by Leading Participants, North and South.* Dayton, OH: Morningside. Pp. 554-589.

*New York Times Index,* Vol. II, 1863-1864.

## Books

Adjutant General's Office, U.S. Army. (1865) *Register of the Volunteers, U.S. Army, 1861-1865.* Washington, DC: Adjutant General's Office.

Baker, L. C. (1867) *History of the United States Secret Service.* Philadelphia: L. C. Baker.

Bates, David Homer. (1907) *Lincoln in the Telegraph Office: Recollections of the United States Military Telegraph Corps during the Civil War.* New York: The Century Co.

Boatner, Mark M., III. (1959) *The Civil War Dictionary.* New York: David McKay.

Bowman, John. (1983) *The Civil War Almanac.* New York: Gallery Books.

Bristwhistle, A. C. (1997) *75 Years of Service: Royal Engineers.* Dorset, UK: Royal Signals Museum.

Davis, William C. & Wiley, Bell I. (Eds.) (1994) *Photographic History of the Civil War, Vicksburg to Appomattox: Fighting for Time/the South Besieged/the End of an Era.* New York: Black Dog & Leventhal.

Donald, David Herbert. (1995) *Lincoln.* New York: Simon & Schuster.

*Encyclopaedia Americana.* (1986) Danbury, CT: Grolier.

Foner, Eric. (1988) *Reconstruction: America's Unfinished Revolution, 1863-1877.* New York: Harper & Row.

Freeman, Douglas S. (1998) *Lee's Lieutenants: A Study in Command.* New York: Simon & Schuster.

Geary, James W. (1991) *We Need Men: The Union Draft in the Civil War.* DeKalb, IL: North Illinois Press.

Gibbons, Tony. (1989) *Warships and Naval Battles of the Civil War.* New York: Gallery Books.

Grant, Ulysses S. (1982) *Personal Memoirs of U. S. Grant.* New York: Da Capo Press.

Hancock, Harold B. (1961) *Delaware during the Civil War: A Political History.* Wilmington, DE: Historical Society of Delaware.

Hanna, A. J. (1938) *Flight into Oblivion.* Richmond, VA: Johnson.

Heitman, Francis B. (1903) *Historical Register & Dictionary of the US Army, 1789-1903.* Washington, DC: Congressional Printing Office.

Johnson, Robert U. & Buel, Clarence C. (Eds.) (1887) *Battles and Leaders of the Civil War.* New York: The Century Co.

Kahn, David. (1967) *The Codebreakers.* New York: The MacMillan Company.

Kane, Joseph N., Anjonen, Steven, & Powell, Janet (Eds.) (1993) *Facts about the States.* New York: H. W. Wilson.

Krick, Robert. (1991) *Lee's Colonels: A Biographical Register of the Field Officers of the Army of Northern Virginia.* Dayton, OH: Morningside.

Marquis Who's Who Staff. (1967) *Who Was Who in America, Historical Volume 1707-1896.* (Revised Edition) New Providence, NJ: Marquis Publishing.

McClure, Alexander K. (Ed.) (1988) *The Annals of the War Written by Leading Participants North and South.* Dayton, OH: Morningside.

Naval History Division, Department of the Navy. (1971) *Civil War Naval Chronology, 1861-1865.* Washington, DC: U.S. Government Printing Office.

O'Brien, John Emmet. (1910) *Telegraphing in Battle: Reminiscences of the Civil War.* Scranton, PA: Reader.

Osborn, Thomas W. (1993) *No Middle Ground: Thomas Ward Osborn's Letters from the Field, 1862-1864.* Hamilton, NY: Edmonston.

Perret, Geoffrey. (1997) *Ulysses S. Grant: Soldier and President.* New York: Random House.

Pitman, Benn. (1954) *The Assassination of President Lincoln and the Trial of the Conspirators.* New York: Funk & Wagnall.

Plum, William R. (1882) *The Military Telegraph during the Civil War in the United States.* (Vols. I & II) Chicago: Jansen, McClurg & Co.

Ritchie, Norman L. (Ed.) (1997) *Four Years in the First New York Light Artillery: The Papers of David F. Ritchie.* Hamilton, NY: Edmonston.

Roscoe, Theodore. (1959) *The Web of Conspiracy.* Englewood Cliffs, NJ: Prentice-Hall.

Sheridan, P. H. (1888) *Personal Memoirs of P. H. Sheridan.* New York: Charles L. Webster.

Sherman, William T. (1892) *Memoirs of Gen. W. T. Sherman Written by Himself.* New York: Charles L. Webster.

Sifakis, Stewart. (1983) *Who Was Who in the Civil War.* (Vol. I) *Who Was Who in the Union.* New York: Facts on File.

Sifakis, Steward. (1988) *Who Was Who in The Civil War.* (Vol. II) *Who Was Who in the Confederacy.* New York: Facts on File.

Smith, Jean Edward. (2001) *Grant.* New York: Simon & Schuster.

Smith, Raymond W. (1998) *Out of the Wilderness: The Civil War Memoir of Cpl. Norton C. Shepard.* Hamilton, NY: Edmonston.

Standage, Tom. (1998) *Victorian Internet.* New York: Walker.

Thompson, Robert L. (1947) *Wiring a Continent: The History of the Telegraph Industry in the United States, 1832-1866.* Princeton, NJ: Princeton University Press.

Urban, Mark. (2001) *The Man Who Broke Napoleon's Codes.* New York: Harper Collins.

Van Sickle, R. (Ed.) (1987) *General Index to Official Army Register of the Volunteer Forces of the US, 1861-1865.* Gaithersburg, MD: R. Van Sickle.

Wall, Joseph Frazier. (1970) *Andrew Carnegie.* New York: Oxford University Press.

Weber, Ralph E. (1993) *Masked Dispatches: Cryptograms and Cryptology in American History, 1774-1900.* Ft. Meade, MD: Center for Cryptologic History, National Security Agency.

West, Richard S., Jr. (1957) *Mr. Lincoln's Navy.* New York: Longmans, Green & Co.

Woodward, C. Vann. (1981) *Mary Chesnut's Civil War.* New Haven, CT: Yale University Press.

# Index

Abingdon, VA, 39; burial of Morgan, 139; attack on Salt Mines at, 156; Stoneman at, 166

Acworth, GA, attack of, 96-97; arrival of cavalry, 100-101, 103

Adams, Charles F., Jr., 129

Adams, Daniel W., 217

Adamson, Mr., 61

Adamstown, MD, 125

Adamsville, TN, 91

*Adelaide, USS*, 107

Adjutant General, USA, 3, 69, 121, 184, 213

Alabama, 20, 68, 131, 185, 187, 203

Alabama & Mississippi RR, 66

Albany, NY, 218

*Albemarle, CSS*, 88, 160

Aldie, VA, 121

Alexandria, LA, 68, 93

Alexandria, VA, 20, 66, 68, 82-83, 85, 154, 157, 221, 223

Alexandria RR, 68

Allatoona, GA, 92, 95, 97, 99, 101, 152, 155-156

Allatoona Pass, GA, 100, 102

Allegheny County, PA, 236

Altoona, PA, 23

Amelia CH, VA, 201-202, 207

American Telegraph Company, 3-4, 13, 20, 33

Anderson Cavalry, 184

Anderson, Charles D., 131

Andersonville Prison, GA, 59, 124

Annapolis, MD, 23, 80, 82, 184; Thomas sends troops to, 180; Farragut departs from, 187

Antietam Ford, MD, 128

Appomattox, VA, 203, 207

Appomattox CH, VA, 207

Appomattox River, 107, 205

Appomattox Station, VA, 91

Arapahoe Indians, 152

Argyle Island, GA, 167

Arkansas, 58, 83, 95, 116-117; ratified pro-Union constitution, 76; A. J. Smith ordered to, 139

Arlington, VA, 122

Armor, Thomas (USMTC operator), 236

Armstrong, Frank C., 217

Army of Northern Virginia, 78, 153, 180, 187, 202, 204, 209-213; surrender of, 207

Army of the Cumberland, 155

Army of the Ohio, 43

Army of the Potomac, 29-30, 34, 39-41, 45, 58, 60, 65, 67, 69, 71, 76-79, 83, 85, 88-90, 92, 95, 100-101, 104, 118, 153-154, 188, 196; ordered to Alexandria, VA, 221; Grand Review, 223-224

Army of the Tennessee, 29, 124-125, 128, 204

Army of Western Mississippi, 93

Arnold, Samuel B., 218

Asboth, Alexander S., 16

Ashepoo River, 190

Ashland Station, VA, 89-90

Associated Press, 202

Atchafalaya River, 79

Athens, TN, 42

Atlanta, GA, 14, 33, 153, 155-158, 222-223; campaign of, 78, 85-86, 89-95, 97-106, 116-118, 121-125, 128; Sherman's plan to encircle, 132, 134-136; CSA troops from Valley rumored moved to, 137; fall of, 138-139, 152; Sherman prepares for March to Sea at, 159; Sherman departs for Savannah from, 160-161

Atlanta & West Point RR, 122, 124, 128, 137, 139, 142

*Atlanta, CSS*, 119

Atlantic & Ohio Telegraph Co., 81

Atwater, H. H. (USMTC operator), 219

Atzerodt, George A., 218-219

Augur, Christopher C., 120, 127

Augusta, GA, 161; Sherman south of, 163, 189; Jefferson Davis sent to Ft. Monroe via, 223

Austria, 3

Averasborough, NC, 183; Battle of, 195

Averell, William W., 103; march to Elroy, VA, 46; ordered to Staunton, 93; defeats enemy at Winchester, 123; drives McCausland out of Chambersburg, PA, 127; defeats CSA at Battle of Moorefield, WV, 130; defeats Vaughn's cavalry, 138

AX2 (telegraph line terminus), 63

Badeau, Adam, 12

Baird, Absalom, 38

Baker, Lafayette B., 220

Bald Hill, GA, Battle of, 118

Baldwin, G. I. (USMTC operator), 33, 130, 160, 204; translating Confederate ciphers, 158

Baltimore, MD, 1, 3, 13-14, 33, 61, 78, 93, 102, 107, 116, 120-121, 158, 160; Sheridan sends troops to, 184, 218

Baltimore & Ohio RR, 1, 61-62, 121, 127

Baltimore & Ohio Telegraph Company, 24

Banks, Nathaniel P., 12, 68; commencement of Red River Campaign, 79, 81-82

Barlow, Francis C., 99-100

Barnum, P. T., 223

Barnum Museum, NY, 152

Bates, Bennett R. (USMTC operator), 236

Bates, David H., 13, 16-18, 20, 23-26, 28, 57, 59-61, 76-77, 116, 119, 131, 136, 138-139, 151, 153, 158, 160, 162, 166, 180, 185, 189, 192-193, 219, 236; recollections of First Bull Run, 6-7; deciphers Confederate messages, 45-47, 49; attends President's levee, 67; temporary duty with Grant and Army of the Potomac, 107; on duty in Telegraph Office night when Lincoln was assassinated, 201-202, 214; called to testify at conspirators' trial regarding ciphers, 223; moves family to Washington, DC, 224

Bates, David H. (son), 24

Bates, Jennie (sister), 185

Bates, Sallie J. Raphael Kenny (wife), 24, 191, 193

Baton Rouge, LA, 81, 167; Brent surrenders at, 224

Battery Parsons, 187

Battery Wagon, 83

Bealeton, VA, 30

Bean's Station, TN, 40, 162

Beardslee Telegraph Equipment, 77

Beatty's House (near Petersburg, VA), 105

Beaufort, NC, 62; breaking of RR line at, 163; Porter sails from, 185; Grant arrives at, 219

Beauregard, Pierre G. T., 7, 86, 88, 100; announces fall of Savannah, 171; in Charleston, SC, 173; evacuates Columbia, SC, 191

Beaver Dam Station, VA, 79, 89

Beckwith, Samuel H., 17

Bell's Landing, TN, 163

Belle Plain, VA, 89-90, 94

Bellefield, VA, 189

Benjamin, Judah P., 45-47, 221

Benjamin, Samuel W., 100

Bentonville, NC, 183

Bermuda, 45, 47

Bermuda Hundred, VA, 103-107

Berryville, VA, 131, 139, 170

Bethesda Church, VA, Battle of, 97

Beulah, NC, 204

Beverly, WV, 46

Bidwell, Daniel D., 159

Big Black River, 167

Big Shanty, GA, 155

Birney, David E., 144, 155; at Battle of Harris Farm, 92; at Battle of Cold Harbor, 99; Tenth Corps under attack, 135; on New Market Road, 143

Black and White Station, VA, 92

Blackhawk, USS, 101

Blain's Cross Roads, TN, 40

Blair, Francis P., Jr., ordered from Rome to Allatoona, GA, 97; arrives at Allatoona Pass, 102; attacked near Atlanta, 123

Blair, Frances P., Sr., 152, 181, 185

Blair, Montgomery, 143

Blakely, AL (See Fort Blakely)

Blockading Fleet, 160

Blue Ridge Mountains, 162

Booth, Edwin, 214

Booth, John Wilkes, assassinates Lincoln, 202-203, 214-215; reward offered for, 219; killed, 220; CSA ciphers of, 223

Booth, Julius, 214

Bosquet, A. J. (USMTC operator), 122

Bottom's Bridge, VA, 89-90

Bowers (Confederate agent), 47

Bowling Green, VA, 92-94, 220

Bowman, Thomas, 166

Boyd, Joseph W. (USMTC operator), 236

Boyd's Landing, SC, 163

Brady, Nicholas H. (USMTC operator), 236

Bragg, Braxton, 4, 29-33, 37-39, 58, 171; resigns, 40; reported to be en route to Augusta, GA, 161; at Battle of Kinston, NC, 195

Branchville, SC, 189-190

Brandy Station, VA, 39, 85

Bratton, John, 155

Breckinridge, John C., 103, 162; at Battle of New Market, 91; losses at Battle of Cold Harbor, 100; in Shenandoah Valley, 119; defeat of Gillem in east Tennessee, 161; reported to be appointed CSA Secretary of War, 187; moving toward Lynchburg, 213

Brent, G. W., 224

Brice's Cross Roads, MS, Battle of, 79, 104

Bridgeport, AL, 28, 30-31, 36

Bridgewater, VA, 153

Briggs (Confederate agent), 47

Bristol, TN, 161, 166

Bristol, VA, 41

Broad River, 163

Brockett, Warren (USMTC operator), 236

Brook Turnpike, VA, 90

Brooke, John R., 100

Brooks, William T. H., 121

Brookville, MD, 120

Brown (correspondent of *The Tribune*), 229-230

Brown, Joseph E., 222

Brown, Mr. & Mrs., 33

Brown, Samuel M. (USMTC operator), 23, 236

Brown's Gap, VA, 154

Brownlow, James R., 128

Buchanan, Franklin, 130

Buckner, Simon B., 97

Buffalo, NY, 218

Buford, John, 43, 45

Bull Run, First Battle of, 4, 6-7

Bull's Gap, TN, 31, 161-162

Bunnell, Jesse H. (USMTC operator), 236

Burbridge, Stephen C., engagement with Morgan in KY, 103-104; reports on activity in Kentucky, 136; arrives at Garrettsburg, KY, 156; in pursuit of Breckenridge, 161-162; enters Bristol, TN, 166

Burkeville, VA, 219-220

Burnside, Ambrose E., 29, 80-81, 85-86, 94-95; in Knoxville campaign, 30-32, 34, 38-39, 42; turns over command to Foster, 43; departure from Annapolis, 82-83; at Battle of Cold Harbor, 99-100; at Petersburg, 106, 127

Butler, Benjamin F., 12, 43, 63, 65-66, 77, 79, 85-86, 88-93, 95, 102-103, 106-108, 130, 132, 153, 155, 164, 167, 169, 171, 173, 184; reports on New Berne, 61-62; attack

on Ft. Fisher, 173; relieved of command, 184; testifies before Committee on Conduct of the War, 186

Buzzard Roost, GA, 65

Byrne, Richard, 100

Cabinet, Confederate, 202

Cabinet, Union, 58, 181

Cairo, IL, 14, 60, 104, 130

Calcium Light, 136

Caldwell, A. H. (USMTC operator), 236

Camden, AR, 85

Cameron, Simon, 4, 6

Cammack, J. H., 45, 47

Camp Stoneman, 65

Campbell, John A., 188, 222

Campbell's Station, TN, 31

Canada, 18, 122, 151-152, 158, 224

Canby, Edward R. S., 95, 104, 131, 174, 192, 204; takes command of Division of West Mississippi, 93; reports on Mobile Bay, 132; destruction of Hood's RR communications, 167; in Mobile campaign, 183, 187-188, 207, 214, 217-219; Taylor surrenders to, 221-222

Canty, G. F., 49

Cape Charles, VA, 13-14

Cape Fear River, 164, 171-172, 191; Porter and Butler at, 167; Grant deploys troops for attack on Ft. Fisher, 174; Porter moves fleet up, 187; Schofield departs for, 189

Capitol, U.S., 186, 193, 218

Carnegie, Andrew, 23, 236; called to Washington, 4; suffers heat stroke during First Bull Run, 6; supports USMTC widows after war, 8; offers Bates a position, 162

Catlett, VA, 83

Cedar Creek, VA, Union retreat to, 91; Sheridan's position at, 131; Battle of, 153, 158-159

Cedar Point, NC, 132

Celestino, Joao, 218

*Century Magazine*, 24

Cesnola, Colonel, 100

Chaffin's Bluff, VA, 118

Chaffin's Farm, Battle of, 143, 154

Chalk Bluff, AR, 204

Chambersburg, PA, 118, 125, 127

Chambliss, John R., Jr., 134

Chancellorsville, VA, 85

Chandler, Albert, B., 20, 24, 28, 154, 158, 236; deciphering Confederate messages, 45-46, 49, 61; participates in calcium light experiment, 136

Chandler, Mrs. William, 81

Channing, William E., 185

Chapman, George H., 142

Chapman, William H., 219

Charles City, VA, 43, 105, 125

Charleston, SC, 30, 35, 42, 159, 183-185; breaking of RR line with Savannah, 163, 165; Beauregard at, 173; evacuated by Beauregard, 191

Charleston, TN, 39, 42

Charleston & Savannah RR, 163, 190

Charlestown, WV, 128, 135

Charlotte, NC, 192, 218, 224

Charlottesville, VA, 102, 154, 194

Charlottesville Station, VA, 101

Chase, Samuel P., 58, 78, 81; resignation of, 119; appointed Chief Justice, 166

Chattahoochee River, 92-93, 105-106, 122, 132, 220; Fourth Corps entrenched at, 136; Hood crosses, 156

Chattanooga, TN, 4, 28-29, 69, 79, 83, 156-158, 161; campaign of, 30-31, 33-39, 42; telegraph communications broken, 132

Chattanooga Creek, TN, 36

Cheraw, NC, 195

Cherokee Indians, 204

Cherrystone, VA, 65-67, 104

*Chesapeake*, 43

Chesapeake Bay, 14; cable broken, 69, 104; new cable across bay at Ft. Monroe operational, 137

Cheyenne Indians, 152

Chicago, IL, 138, 152; Democratic Convention, 117; Presidential funeral route, 218

Chickahominy River, 86, 90, 97, 100, 105-106

Chickamauga Valley, TN, 36

*Chickamauga, CSS*, 187

*Chicora, CSS*, 191

Christiansburg, VA, 218

Cincinnati, OH, 69, 80, 83, 102

Cipher systems, 17, 33, 48, 61, 202, 229-230; Confederate, 45-48, 50, 157-159, 202; Route system, 16-18, 23, 229; Pigpen cipher, 18, 235; Vicksburg Square, 18, 202, 232-233; Vigènere, 232

*Circassian, USS*, 42

Citronelle, AL, 222

City Point, VA, 12-13, 17, 85, 96, 106-107, 119, 121, 125, 127, 129, 154-155, 165, 173, 180, 183, 187-188, 195-196; telegraph line to, 14; becomes Grant's Headquarters, 105; telegraph line constructed to, 105; line to Ft. Monroe operational, 108, 116; boat explosion at, 130; direct telegraph communications with Washington, 116, 138; Sixth Corps ordered to,

161; F. P. Blair, Sr. arrives at, 185; Lincoln at, 202, 204; Lincoln returns to Washington from, 214

Clay, Clement C., Jr., 20, 223

Clendenin, David R., 127

Cleveland, OH, 33, 77, 100, 218

Cleveland & Dalton RR, 33

Clifton, TN, 155

Clifton House, VA, 211

Clinch Mountain, TN, 40

Clinch River, 39

Clingman, Thomas L., 98

Clinton, GA, 128

Coalfield Station, VA, 91-92

Cobb, Howell, 219

Coggins Point, VA, 139

Cold Harbor, VA, Battle of, 78, 98, 101, 106

Colfax, Schuyler, 41

Collierville, TN, 104

Colored Troops, 43, 86, 95, 105, 108, 182; at Ft. Pillow, 78, 81; with Tenth Corps, 135

Colt (Samuel) Pistol Factory, 62

Columbia, SC, 183, 190; Sherman enters, 191; arsenals destroyed, 195

Columbia, TN, 171-172

Columbia, VA, 194

Columbus, GA, 124

Columbus, KY, 81

Columbus, OH, 35

Columbus RR, 124

Combahee River, 190

Committee on Conduct of the War, 186, 190

Conant, J. E., 49

Congress, Confederate, 57-58, 182, 191

Congress, U.S., 1, 4, 41, 58, 66-67, 117, 163, 188; receives President's annual message, 47; approves

rank of Lt. General for Grant, 66-67; passes amendment abolishing slavery, 188

Connor, Charles O. (USMTC lineman), 68

Convers, GA, 124

Coosa River, 157

Coosawhatchie River, 165

Copperheads, 117, 152, 216

Corcoran, Michael, 45

Corinth, MS, 174, 184, 207

Corse, John M., 156

Corse, Montgomery D., 207

Couch, Darius N., 125

Covington, GA, 124

Cox, Samuel S., 157

Crater, Battle of, 118, 127

Crawford, Samuel W., 97

Crimean War, 3

Crook, George, 12, 77, 93, 99, 103, 165; at Staunton, 96; moving toward Aldie, VA, 121; defeats Early near Winchester, 122; at Second Battle of Kernstown, 123; evacuates Martinsburg, 124; at Battle of Fisher's Hill, 142; captured at Cumberland, MD, 192

Croxton, John T., 128

Culpeper, VA, 31, 83, 85, 100

Culpeper Ford, VA, 85

Cumberland, MD, 61, 127, 192

Cumberland Gap, TN, 30-32, 34, 42; Morgan in area of, 135; Burbridge at, 162; Stoneman reports from, 166

Cumberland River, 171

Curtis, Samuel R., 69, 160

Cushing, William B., 160

Custer, George A., 65, 129

Cynthiana, KY, 102-103

Dahlgren, John A. B., 153, 163

Dahlgren, Ulric, 59, 66-67

Dahlonega, GA, 42, 66-67

Dallas, GA, 95, 97, 128, 152, 157

Dalton, GA, 38, 65, 79, 86, 90, 99, 128, 155; Johnston evacuates, 89; Wheeler attacks, 132; Hood at, 157-158

Dana, Charles A., 42, 50, 86, 89, 102, 107, 184; preparation of cipher books for, 33; as Asst. Secretary of War, 223; visit to front, 96

Dana, Napoleon J. T., 98, 174, 223

*Dandelion, USS,* 168

Danenhower, Mrs., 61

Danville, VA, 201, 207, 219; Sheridan heads toward, 196; Lee retreats toward, 205; Jefferson Davis reported at, 213; Extra Billy Smith communicates with Grant from, 214; telegraph connected to, 220

Darby Road, VA, 144, 155

Darbyville, VA, 153

Darience, D. H., 68

Darnestown, MD, 120-121

Dauphin Island, AL, 129, 131-132

David, Thomas B. A. (USMTC operator), 236

Davis, Charles H., 136

Davis, Henry W., 117

Davis, Jefferson, 18, 29, 57, 152, 159, 180-183, 202-203, 212; correspondence with Thompson in Canada deciphered, 158; advised of fall of Ft. Fisher, 171; recommends arming slaves, 190; appoints Lee General-in-Chief, 187; flight of 213, 220-224; capture of, 222

Davis, Jefferson C., 42, 57-59, 92; recommended to command Fourteenth Corps, 129

Dean, Professor, 65

Deatonville, VA, 207

Decatur, AL, 123, 172, 192; Thomas moves troops toward, 171; Wofford surrenders near, 221

Decatur, GA, 122

Deep Bottom, VA, 118, 127, 132

Delaware, 31, 160, 190

Democratic National Convention, 117, 138

Demopolis, AL, 66

Dennison, William, 16, 143

Department of Alabama, Mississippi and East Louisiana, 204

Department of Florida, 204

Department of Kentucky, Tennessee and Mississippi, 10

Department of Maryland, 129

Department of Mississippi, 83

Department of Missouri, Kansas, and Arkansas, 10

Department of North Carolina, 189

Department of Ohio, 29, 184

Department of Pennsylvania, 129

Department of Tennessee, 29

Department of the Cumberland, 29, 167, 184

Department of the Gulf, 10, 119

Department of the Potomac, 10, 82

Department of the South, 10

Department of Virginia and North Carolina, 184

Department of Washington, 129

Department of West Virginia, 10, 93, 129

Devereux, VA, 85

Dictionary Code, 18

Dimick, Justin, 136

Dinwiddie CH, VA, 183; Battle of, 196

Dix, John A., 93, 168, 202, 209

Dodge, Grenville, 123, 135

Dover, DE, 14

Draft, Military (Union), 58, 61, 123, 152; ends, 214

Drewry, CSS, 187

Drewry's Bluff, VA, 143; Second Battle of, 79, 91

DuBose, Dudley M., 207

Duck River, 171

Duke, Basil W., 166

Dunbar, CSS, 35

Dunn, William A. (USMTC operator), 66

Dutch Gap, VA, 164

Dutch Gap Canal, VA, 162, 164

Dwight, J. H. (USMTC operator), 120

Early, Jubal A., 46, 79, 89, 122, 124, 131, 134-136, 157, 159; raid on Washington, 116, 118-120; in Shenandoah Valley, 137; defeat at Winchester, 139, 142; Battle of Fisher's Hill, 142; escapes capture at Charlottesville, 194

East Pascagoula, FL, 174

East Point, GA, 128, 138

East Tennessee & Georgia RR, 160-161

Eastport, MS, 186

Eastport, TN, 174

Eastville, VA, 66

Eatonton, GA, 128

Echols, John, 46, 91, 218

Ecker, David R. (USMTC operator), 236

Eckert, Thomas T., 7, 28, 46, 49, 59, 69, 81, 108, 119, 136, 162, 201; gives raise to Bates, Chandler and Tinker for cipher work, 49; sends Bates to Major Dana as cipher clerk, 107; at Ft. Monroe, 138; carries instructions to Grant regarding CSA peace commissioners, 188; reported appointed Asst. Secretary of War, 223

Eckert, Mrs., 59

Edisto River, 190

Edward's Ferry, 120

Eighteenth Corps, USA, 100, 106, 143-144

Eighteenth SC Regt., 127

Eighteenth VA Mounted Infantry, 46

Eighth NY Heavy Artillery, 100

Electoral College, 152, 181

Eleventh Corps, USA, 37, 42

Elk River, 156

Ella & Annie, USS, 43

Ellicott's Mills, MD, 120

Elroy, VA, 46

Ely's Ford, VA, 83, 85

Embosser, 1

Emerick, J. H. (USMTC operator), 68

Erie, PA, 218

Escambia River, 174

Etowah River, 101

Everett, Edward, 185-186

Ewell, Richard S., reinforcing Longstreet, 34; attacks Union at Harris Farm, 92, 97; at Malvern Hill, 105; captured at Battle of Snyder's Creek, 207

Ewing, Hugh B., 31

Ezra Church, GA, Battle of, 118

Fairburn, GA, 137

Fairfax, VA, 223

Fairfax CH, VA, 6, 45

Fairfax Station, VA, 83

Falmouth, KY, 102

Farmville, VA, 207, 209

Farragut, David G., 129, 187

Fayetteville, NC, 183, 195

Federal Point, NC, 190

Fenton, R. E., 160
Fessenden, William P., 119
Field, Charles W., 155
Fifteenth Corps, USA, 42, 123, 125, 166, 168
Fifth Corps, USA, 69, 101, 205
Fifty-third PA Regt., 100
First Brigade, Third Division, Ninth Corps, 196
First Corps, USA, 69
First NY Regt., 100
First VT Regt., 100
Fisher's Hill, VA, 157, 159; Battle of, 118, 142-143
Fitch, Leroy, 163
Five Forks, VA, Battle of, 202-204
Flack, Benjamin W. (USMTC operator), 236
Florence, AL, 156, 171-173
Florence, SC, 191
Florence, TN, 156, 171
Florida, 30, 47, 57-58, 64
Flusser, W. W., 82
Ford's Theater, Washington, DC, 201-203, 214
Forrest, Nathan B., 118, 155; at Battle of Paducah, KY, 71; at Battle of Ft. Pillow, 78, 81; at Brice's Cross Roads, 104; reported death of, 130, 168; escapes across Tennessee River, 156; rumored to have replaced Hood, 172; driven through Pulaski,172; Grierson defeats, 185; driven out of Selma, AL, 207; reported captured, 213; escapes, 217
Fort Anderson, NC, 190, 192
Fort Blakely, AL, 204, 214, 217
Fort Caswell, NC, 187
Fort Darling, VA, 90-91
Fort Delaware, DE, 89

Fort Fisher, NC, 153; Battle of, 171-173; campaign of, 182, 184-186; Grant visits, 187
Fort Gaines, AL, 130-132
Fort Gilmer, VA, 118
Fort Harrison, TN, 118; Battle of, 143, 154
Fort Holly, VA, 153
Fort Larned, KS, 182
Fort Lafayette, NY, 49, 93
Fort Leavenworth, KS, 69
Fort Loudon, TN, 29
Fort McAllister, GA, 151, 153; capture of, 166, 168-169
Fort Monroe, VA, 13-14, 16, 30, 57, 80-81, 83, 105, 107, 136, 163, 172, 174, 184, 187; cable broken at, 65; telegraph line completed to City Point, 108, 116, 127; cable across Chesapeake Bay to, 137-138; military preparations at, 162; Butler arrives at, 173; Sheridan's troops depart from, 186; Seward and Lincoln travel to, 188; Presidential party returns from, 189; Jefferson Davis on way to, 223
Fort Morgan, AL, 130-132; falls to Union, 137-138
Fort Pillow, TN, Battle of, 78, 81
Fort Powell, AL, 130, 132
Fort Powhatan, VA, 119; attack on, 94; disruption of telegraph line at, 108; possible cable from Jamestown Island to, 138
Fort Reno, DC, 120
Fort Sanders, TN, Battle of, 29, 39
Fort Stedman, VA, 183; attack by John Gordon, 196
Fort Stevens, DC, 120
Fort Sumter, SC, 30, 186, 192
Fort Totten, NC, 62
Fort Washington, MD, 68

Foster, John G., 39-40, 42-43, 60, 151, 165, 168, 171-172; destroys RR bridge over the Pocotaligo, 163; meets Sherman at Ft. McAllister, 166; at Hilton Head, 189

Four Mile Creek, VA, 153

Fourteenth AL Regt., 105

Fourteenth Corps, USA, 92, 129

Fourteenth PA Regt., 46

Fourth Corps, USA, 125, 136, 159

Fourth MI Cavalry, 222

Fourth NY Mounted Rifles, 21

Fourth US Cavalry, 167

France, 3

Franklin, Ben (NY detective), 49

Franklin, TN, 153; Battle of, 161; report of Thomas from, 166-168

Franklin, William B., 120-121

Frederick, MD, 121, 127

*Fredericksburg, CSS,* 187

Fredericksburg, VA, 88, 100, 194, 201; removal of wounded to, 86, 90; opening of Union telegraph office to, 90; telegraph line to Richmond via, 223

Freedmen's Bureau, 203

Frémont, John, 16, 78; nomination for president, 100; resigns commission, 100; withdraws from presidential race, 117

French, Samuel G., 155

French, William H., 69, 155

Front Royal, VA, rebels retreat to, 123; fighting at, 142; Sheridan moves to, 154; artillery fire at, 158

Gaines, CSS, 130

Galesville, GA, 159-160

*Galina, CSS,* 130

Gannon, Sgt., 219

Garrard, Kenner, 90, 99, 124

Garrett's Farm, VA, 220

Garrett's Station, VA, 92

Garrettsburg, TN, 156

Gauley Bridge, VA, 65

*General Lyon, USS,* 163

Gentry, W. D. (USMTC operator at ATC), 33

Georgetown, DC, 202, 224

Georgia, 21, 38, 59, 77, 152, 157, 159, 167, 222

Georgia RR, 163, 190

Germanna Ford, VA, 84-85

Gettysburg National Cemetery, 31

Gibbon, John, 99-100

Giesboro Point, DC, 65

Gillem, Alvan C., 191; surprises Morgan, 139; in east Tennessee, 154; defeated, 161

Gillmore, Quincy A., reports on Florida expedition, 64; with Butler at Ft. Darling, 90; at Petersburg, 102-103; at Charleston, SC, 191

Gilmore, James R., 222

Girardey, Victor, J. B., 134

Globe Tavern, VA, Battle of, 118

Gold, price of, 32, 80-81, 96, 143, 157-158, 161, 169, 195

Goldsboro, NC, 160, 196, 204

Gonsalves, Mrs., 61

Gonsalves, Will, 64

Goochland CH, VA, 194

Goodman (Confederate agent), 47

Gordon, GA, 161

Gordon, George W., 162

Gordon, James B., 100, 142

Gordon, John B., 196

Gordonsville, VA, 96, 103, 129, 194

Gordonsville & Charlottesville RR, 96

Graham, Alexander, 39

Grand Squirrel Bridge, VA, 89

Granger, Gordon, goes to relief of Burnside at Knoxville, 34, 39-40,

42; lands troops on Dauphin Island in Mobile Bay, 129; moves to invest Ft. Morgan, 132; lands troops at Grant's Pass, AL, 138; at Huntsville, AL, 172; near East Pascagoula, MS, 174

Grant, Ulysses S., 12-14, 16-17, 20-21, 29-30, 58-60, 66, 68-69, 71, 76-77, 80, 83, 85-86, 88-98, 103-105, 116-118, 121-122, 124-125, 132, 134, 138, 151-152, 159, 162-163, 165, 171, 180-183, 185, 188-189, 191-192, 194-196, 201-205, 217, 221, 224; Chattanooga campaign, 31-39, 41-42; Battle of Orchard Knob, 35-38; Battle of Lookout Mountain, 29, 31, 33, 36, 38-39; Battle of Missionary Ridge, 29-33, 35-38; goes to Knoxville to drive out Longstreet, 49; commissioned Lieutenant General in command of all U.S. armies, 67; initiation of Grand Strategy, 78-79; at Battle of Cold Harbor, 99-100; corresponds with Lee to arrange removal of wounded from battlefield, 102; reports on recent movements, 106-107; meets Lincoln at Ft Monroe, 127; goes to Valley, 129; reports explosion at City Point, 130; reports fighting at Weldon RR, 134-136; reports on Battle of Reams' Station, 137; reports fighting at Chaffin's Farm, 143-144, 154; visits Washington, 155; approves Sherman's March to the Sea, 157; directs removal of Rosecrans, 160; dissatisfaction with Thomas's failure to attack Hood, 164; sends 8,000 men to Cape Fear River for attack on Ft. Fisher, 174; replaces Butler with

Ord, 184; visits Ft. Fisher, 187; testifies before Committee on Conduct of the War, 190; correspondence with Lee regarding terms of surrender, 193; reports on fighting at Ft. Stedman, 196; telegraphs surrender of Lee's army, 207, 209; correspondence with Lee, 209-212; details of surrender terms, 212; receives congratulations from Stanton, 213; arrives in Washington, 214; takes charge of Johnston's surrender to Sherman, 219-220; orders arrest of Hunter and Campbell, 222

Grant's Pass, AL, 130, 138
Great Britain, 18, 20, 42-43, 78; use of telegraph in Crimean War, 3
Greensburg, PA, 23
Greensboro, NC, 218
Greenville, AL, 214
Greenville, TN, 104, 139
Gregg, David M., temporary command of cavalry, 69; moves to north side of James River to threaten Richmond, 132; captures Stony Creek Station, 162
Gregg, John, 155, 184-185
Grierson, Benjamin H., 184-185
Griffin, Charles, 98, 124, 154
Grover, Cuvier, 159
Guinney's Station, VA, 92
Gulf of Mexico, 187-188
Gunpowder Bridge, MD, 120
Guntown, MS, 104
Guthridge, Jules F. (USMTC operator at ATC), 33
Gutta-percha, 1

H. L. Hunley, CSS, 58
Habeas Corpus (CSA), 58

Halifax, NS, 43, 45, 47, 143; Tinker sent to on special duty, 137

Halleck, Henry W., 7; replaced by Grant, 68; asked by Grant to take command of Mississippi Dept., 83; disagrees with Grant on relieving Thomas, 164; takes command of Richmond, VA, 218; in Richmond, 222

Hampton, Wade, 195

Hampton Roads, VA, 119, 167

Hampton Roads Peace Conference, 152, 181, 188-189

Hancock, Winfield S., 69, 94-95, 97, 101, 127; at Battle of The Wilderness, 85; in Spotsylvania CH campaign, 88-89, 91; at Battle of Cold Harbor, 99-100; advances on Petersburg, 105-106; at Battle of Reams' Station, 136-137; Mosby offers to surrender to, 217; Mosby's troops surrender to, 219

Hanover CH, VA, 97-98

Hanover Ferry, VA, 95

Hanover Junction, VA, 98

Hanovertown, VA, 96

Hardee, William J., 190, 195; replaces Bragg, 40; defeat by Sherman, 139; commands in Savannah area, 169; escapes from Sherman at Savannah, 172

Hardwicksville, VA, 194

Harper's Ferry, WV, 69, 129-131, 142, 156; opening of RR to, 121; reconnection of telegraph lines to, 122; CSA movement to, 128; fighting at Opequon Creek, 139

Harrisburg, PA, 43, 93

Harris Farm, VA, Battle of, 92

Harrisonburg, VA, 154, 156

Hartford, CT, 62

Hartranft, John F., 196

Haskell, Frank A., 100

Hatch, Edward, 167-168

Hatch, William M., 221

Hatcher's Run, VA, 153; Battle of, 183, 189

Hatter, John C., 201

Havana, Cuba, 224

Havre de Grace, MD, 195

Hays, Alexander, 86

Hazen, William B., 166, 168

Herold, David E., 203, 219-220

Heth, Henry, 100

Hicksford, VA, 163, 165

Hill, Ambrose P., 88, 105

Hill, Benjamin H., 47

Hilton (engraver of Confederate plates), 47, 50

Hilton Head, SC, 163, 165, 189

Hiwassee River, 34, 39

Hobson, Edward H., 46, 103, 136

Hollow Tree Gap, TN, 166

Holmes, George (USMTC operator), 236

Holston River, 40, 166

Hood, John B., 123, 128, 152-153, 156, 163-165, 167-169, 171-172, 184-185; relieves Johnston, 122; in Atlanta, 132; reported killed, 137; defeated by Sherman at East Point, GA, 138; evacuates Atlanta, 139; retreats from Lovejoy's Station, 142; at Dalton, GA, 157-158; retreats south, 158-159; threatens Chattanooga, 161; attacked by Thomas, 166; crosses the Tennessee River, 173; replaced by Taylor, 187

Hooker, Joseph M., 28; at Battle of Lookout Mountain, 31, 33, 36, 38; at Allatoona Pass, 99; asks to be relieved of command, 125

Housatonic, USS, 58

House of Representatives, U.S., 77, 181-182

Howard, Joseph, 93

Howard, Oliver O., 35, 37, 165; at Battle of Resaca, GA, 90; command of Army of the Tennessee, 125

Howe, Albion P., 121

Howlett Battery, 187

Huff's Ferry, TN, 31

Hull, Joseph B., 184

Hungarian Language, 16

Hunter, David, 79, 102, 121, 123-124; command of Department of WV, 93, 96, 99; ordered to join Sheridan, 101; reports on fight at Piedmont, WV, 103; at Frederick, MD, 127; reports enemy advances on Harper's Ferry, 128; asks to be relieved of command, 129

Hunter, Robert M. T., 188-189, 222

Hunter, William, 215

Hunton, Eppa, 207

Huntsville, AL, 172

Illinois, 66, 182, 188; rebel movement into, 132; Grant requests 30-day men from, 164; ratifies Thirteenth Amendment, 189

Imboden, John D., 46, 91

Independent Telegraph Company, 93

Indiana, 41; elections in, 157; Grant requests 30-day men from, 164

Indians, American, 152, 182, 204

India Rubber (See Gutta-percha)

Ingalls, Rufus, 86

Irwinville, GA, 222

Iverson, Alfred, 128

Jackson, MS, 167

Jackson, William L., 46

Jaques, Charles W. (USMTC operator), 6, 236

James River, 77, 79, 81, 91, 102, 104-106, 119, 163, 187, 194; Second and Tenth Corps moved to north side of, 132, 134; Second Corps withdrawn from north bank of, 135; beef raid near, 139; Sheridan's Sixth Corps moves to, 156; Butler's force crosses at Dutch Gap, 164

James River Canal, VA, 194

Jamestown Island, VA, 14, 108, 138; construction of telegraph line to City Point from, 105

Jenkins, Micah, 86

Jericho Bridge, VA, 94-95

Jetersville, VA, 201, 207

*Jno A. Warner, USS*, 107

Johnson, Adam R., 136

Johnson, Andrew, 58, 78, 205, 217, 219, 221-222; nomination for Vice President, 102; sworn in as President, 203, 215

Johnson, Edward, 88-89

Johnson, Mr., 191

Johnson, Richard, 168

Johnston, Joseph E., 79, 203-204, 221; Commander of Department of TN, 29; faces Sherman, 85-86, 88-92, 95, 97, 103-105; relieved of command, 122; reported as replacing Lee in command of Army of Northern VA, 187; advised by Lee to surrender, 213; at Raleigh, NC, 214; requests cease-fire to discuss peace, 217; negotiates with Sherman, 219; Grant advises truce terminated, 220; surrenders to Sherman, 220; given permission to go to Canada, 224

Jones, John M., 46, 86

Jones, Samuel, 204
Jones, William E., 39, 102-103
Jones' Bridge, VA, 104
Jonesborough, GA, 136, 139
Julesberg, CO Territory, 182

Kalorama Hospital, DC, 64
Kautz, August V., 89, 91-92; departs Suffolk, VA, on special service, 85-86; at Petersburg, 102-103; in sight of Richmond, 144
Keith, Alexander J., Jr., 45, 47, 137
Kelley, Benjamin F., 130; at Cumberland, MD, 127; possible replacement for Hunter, 129; captured, 192
Kelley's Ferry, TN, 36
Kennesaw, GA, 104-105, 156
Kennesaw Mountain, GA, 105; Battle of, 79
Kenny, Sallie J. Raphael, 24, 191, 193
Kentucky, 38, 156; Burbridge reports from, 136; Lincoln fails to carry in election, 160; Breckenridge threatens, 161; Lyon defeated, 171
Kerbey, Joseph O. (USMTC operator), 236
Kerbey, John S. (USMTC operator), 236
Kernstown, VA, Second Battle of, 123
Kershaw, Joseph B., 137, 207
Killingsworth, Mr., 65
Kilpatrick, Hugh J., 59, 67, 83; raid on Richmond, 65-66; breaks Macon RR near Jonesborough, GA, 134-136; attacked by Hampton, 195
King, Henry (USMTC operator), 236
King, Preston, 205

King, Thomas M. (USMTC operator), 236
Kings and Queens CH, VA, 67
Kingsbridge, GA, 169
Kingston, GA, 90; Sherman's arrival at, 91; evacuation of, 92; Sherman's departure for Atlanta from, 94, 98, 102
Kinston, NC, 62; Battle of, 183, 194-195
Kitching, John H., 159
Knipe, Joseph F., 167
Knowland, Henry (USMTC operator), 236
Knoxville, TN, 60, 173, 192; campaign (Confederate), 29-34, 39-40, 42, 49

Lafayette, TN, 158
La Fayette, GA, 152
Lamar (Confederate agent), 47
Lamb, William, 186
Lamb's Ferry, AL, 172
Laurel, MD, 116, 120-121
Laurel Hill, NC, 195
Law, George (USMTC), 80
Lee, Fitzhugh, 46, 135; attack on Ft. Powhatan, VA, 94; at Battle of Cold Harbor, 98; wounded, 142
Lee, G. W. Custis, 207, 213
Lee, Robert E., 30-31, 57, 78, 86, 88-90, 93-95, 97, 100-101, 105, 135-136, 144, 153, 169, 181, 183, 187, 201-204, 217-218, 220; corresponds with Grant about removal of wounded from battlefield, 102; suggests arming slaves, 182; appointed General-in-Chief of CSA armies, 182; reports Pegram killed, 189; asks Grant for interview, 193; retreats toward Danville, VA, 205; surrenders, 207,

209, 213; correspondence with Grant, 209-212; wife's illness, 213

Lee, Mrs. R. E., 205, 213

Lee, Samuel P., 107, 171, 173

Lee, Stephen D., 122

Lee, William Henry Fitzhugh ("Rooney"), 136

Leetown, WV, 137

Leggett's Hill, VA, 118

Leonardstown, MD, 69, 80

Letcher, John, 224

*Levi, CSS*, 62

Lewes, DE, 13-14

Lexington, KY, 104

Libby Prison, 58-59, 63-64

Lincoln, Abraham, 4, 6, 8, 12, 17, 20, 24, 58-59, 63, 66, 76-77, 91, 93, 107, 117-118, 123, 127-129, 143, 158, 160, 180-181, 184-185, 194, 201-205, 214; Gettysburg Address, 31; illness, 41; message to Congress (1863), 41; congratulates Grant for Chattanooga victory, 42; nominated for second term, 78, 102; witnesses calcium light test, 136; reelected, 152; establishes Thanksgiving as national holiday, 152; draft calls, 61, 152, 169; message to Congress (1864), 163; in Richmond, 183; at Hampton Roads Peace Conference, 188-189; instructions to Grant regarding conference with Lee, 193; re-inauguration, 193; assassination, 214-219; funeral route of, 217-218; trial of conspirators, 202, 223

Lincoln, Mary Todd, 194

Lincoln, William Wallace (Willie), 63

*Lincoln in The Telegraph Office*, 24, 201

Little Rock, AR, 85, 95

Lockwood, Henry H., 98

Lomax, Lunsford L., 157

Long Bridge, DC, 62

Long Bridge, VA, 104

Longstreet, James, 97, 123, 132, 159; transferred to TN, 29; in Knoxville campaign, 30-34, 39-43, 46, 49; retreats from TN, 66; wounded at Battle of The Wilderness, 86; at Battle of Cold Harbor, 98; falsely reported to have replaced Hood in Atlanta, 137; meets with Ord, 193

Lookout Creek, TN, 36

Lookout Mountain, TN, Battle of, 29, 31, 33, 36, 38-39

Loring, William W., 125

Lost Mountain, GA, 105-106

Loudon, TN, 29-31

Louisiana, 58, 77-78, 117; adopts new constitution, 105

Louisville, KY, 60, 80, 96

Lovejoy, Owen, 69

Lovejoy's Station, GA, 118, 139, 142

Lovett, A. A., 80

Low, George (USMTC operator), 80, 236

Lowell, Charles R., 159

Lowell, MA, 184

Ludlow, Colonel, 229-230

Lugur, Dr., 49

Luray Valley, VA, 142-143

Lynchburg, VA, 101, 106, 195, 205, 209, 218; Lee's movement toward, 90; Sheridan moves to, 192; RR destroyed to, 194; Grant pushes toward, 207; surrenders, 213

Lynchburg RR, 92

Lyon, Hylan B., 171

Macbeth, Mayor, 191

MacIntosh, William (USMTC operator), 83
Mackenzie, Ranald S., 159
Macon, GA, 124-125, 128, 134, 161, 163, 222
Macon & Western Central RR, 122, 128, 134-137, 139
Magahick Church, VA, 96
Maine, 66; ratifies Thirteenth Amendment, 189
Malvern Hill, VA, 105
Manassas, VA, 83
Manassas Gap RR, 155
Manassas Junction, VA, 7
Mansfield, LA, Battle of, 78, 81
Marais des Cygnes River, 152
March to the Sea, 151, 153, 157, 159-160, 163, 165-169, 171, 180
Marcy, Alfred T., 185
Marietta, GA, 95, 98-103, 116, 124, 128; telegraphic communications with Washington established from, 138; Sherman moves army to, 156
Marion, VA, 166
Marmaduke, John S., 104
Martinsburg, WV, 119, 124
Maryland, 119, 124, 129, 152; election results, 157; ratifies Thirteenth Amendment, 189
Maryville, TN, 135
Massachusetts, ratifies Thirteenth Amendment, 189
*Massachusetts, USS*, 30, 184
Mattapony River, 94
Mattingly, Mr. (ATC), 33
Maury, Dabney H., 130
Maynardsville, TN, 40
McCandless, L. D. (USMTC operator), 236
McCargo, David, 23
McCausland, John, 119, 127, 161

*McClellan, USS*, 66
McClellan, George, 138; observer at Crimean War, 3; uses telegraph in Civil War, 3; nominated for President, 117
McClives, Mr., 125
McCook, Alexander D., 121, 124, 128-129
McCook, Daniel, 121
McCook, Edward M., 128
McDowell, Irvin, 4, 6-7
McIlvaine, James P. (USMTC operator), 236
McIntosh, John B., 142
McKenna, E. W. (USMTC operator), 237
McKenna, John A. L. (USMTC operator), 237
McKnight, Mr., 33
McLaughlin, Napoleon B., 196
McMahon, James P., 100
McPherson, James B., at Villanow, 86, 88, 97, 99, 101, 104; at Kennesaw Mountain, 105
Meade, George G., 12, 30-33, 35, 60, 63, 65-67, 78, 81-83, 119, 127, 137, 214; rumored to be replaced by Sedgwick, 40; Lincoln visits, 107; in pursuit of Lee, 205, 207
Meadow Bluff, WV, 99
Meadow Bridge, VA, 90
Meagher, Thomas F., 187
Meigs, Montgomery C., 39
Memminger, Christopher G., 47
Memphis, TN, 68, 81, 95, 104; Dana reports from, 174
Memphis & Charleston RR, 160
Meridian, MS, 57-58, 66
Merritt, Wesley, 162
Mexican War, 1
*Miami, USS*, 82
Mifflin, PA, 23

Milford Station, VA, 92, 94

Milledgeville, GA, 157, 161, 163

Millen, GA, 157, 161, 163

Mine Run, VA, Battle of, 29

*Minna* (British), 42

Missionary Ridge, TN, Battle of, 29-31, 33, 35-38

Mississippi, 29, 58, 68, 95, 104, 221

Mississippi Central RR, 185

Mississippi River, 60, 81, 104, 132

Missouri, 95, 139, 152, 160; outlaws slavery, 185; ratifies Thirteenth Amendment, 189

Mobile, AL, attack on, 34, 66, 82, 129-130, 134-135, 139, 183, 187-188, 203, 207; surrender rumored, 143; Canby on road to, 174; Spanish Fort and Ft. Blakely, AL, invested, 214; occupied by Canby, 218-219

Mobile Bay, AL, 116, 118, 132, 204; report of battle, 130; fall of Ft. Morgan confirmed, 137-138

Mobile & Ohio RR, 64, 68, 157, 167, 174, 184-185, 214

*Monitor-Merrimac*, Battle of, 7

Monocacy, MD, Battle of, 120

Monocacy River, 124-125, 128

Monroe's Cross Roads, SC, 183; Battle of, 195

Montgomery, AL, 34, 187, 192; destruction of RR, 123-124; Steele moves toward, 214

Montgomery & Atlanta RR, 122-124

Montgomery, Richard, 18, 151

Moorefield, WV, 62; skirmish near, 130

Moreland, Theodore E. (USMTC operator), 237

*Morgan, CSS*, 130-131

Morgan, John H., 64, 104, 166; escapes from Columbus, OH, prison, 35; fighting in Kentucky, 102-104; reported in Cumberland Gap area, 135; death of, 139

Morgan, Colonel (brother of John Hunt Morgan), 166

Morris, Orlando W., 100

Morristown, TN, 66

Morse, David (USMTC operator), 237

Morse Code, 1, 7-8

Morton's Ford, VA, 62

Mosby, John S., 125, 127; attacks at Salem, VA, 155; offers to surrender to Hancock, 217; disperses command, 218; his troops surrender while he flees, 219

Mount Crawford, VA, 153, 183

Mount Jackson, VA, 143, 153, 159

Mount Pleasant Hospital, DC, 122

Mount Sterling, KY, 102

Mullarkey, Patrick (USMTC operator), 96

Munson, J. Anderson (USMTC operator), 237

Murfreesboro, TN, 168

Murphy, NC, 42

Murray, Martin (USMTC operator), 237

Murray, P. J. (USMTC operator), 80

Murray, Robert, 45, 50

Myer, Albert J., 77

Napoleon, 233

Nashville, TN, 60, 68, 153, 157, 168; Thomas reports from, 155-156; threatened by Hood, 161-163; Battle of, 166

Nassau, 47

National Hotel, DC, 202

National Union Convention, 78

Navy Yard, DC, 23, 219-220

Negroes, 62, 95, 169, 180-181, 185; soldiers, 43, 78, 81, 86, 105, 108, 135, 182; prisoners of war, 182

Neuse River, 61, 195

Nevada, 152

New Berne, NC, 61-62, 82, 88

New Castle, VA, 97-98

New Creek, WV, 61, 161

New Hope Church, GA, campaign of, 79

New Kent CH, VA, 65, 92

New Market, VA, 79, 91, 125, 143, 153

New Market Heights, VA, 118

New Market Road, VA, 143

New Orleans, LA, 16, 34, 76, 101, 120, 129, 132; Page sent to, 138; Canby at, 188

New Orleans & Jackson RR, 68

New River, 173

New York, 85-86, 138, 157, 160; ratifies Thirteenth Amendment, 189

New York, NY, 1, 24, 28, 43, 50, 60, 69, 80-81, 86, 93, 168, 202, 209, 222; Confederate cipher letters sent from, 45-47; arrests in, 49; burning of Barnum Museum, 152; Presidential funeral route, 218

*New York Herald*, 163

*New York Journal of Commerce,* 93

*New York Times*, 93

*New York Tribune*, 3, 77, 85

*New York World*, 93

Newport Barracks, NC, 62

Newton, John, 69

Nichols, J. Hervey (USMTC operator), 107, 237

Nicodemus, William J. L., 136

Nineteenth Corps, USA, 121, 124-125, 154, 186

Ninth Corps, USA, 30, 101, 106, 120, 128, 142, 154, 188, 196

Norfolk, VA, 71

North Anna River, 89, 100; Battle of, 78, 94-95

North Carolina, 12, 57, 78, 153, 164, 182, 192, 219-221

North Carolina RR, 218

Nottoway, VA, 165

Nova Scotia, 43, 45, 47, 137, 143

Ny River, 94

O'Brien, Richard (USMTC operator), 23, 107, 197, 236

Oconee River, 163

Ogeechee River, 166-167, 169

Ohio, 6, 16, 66, 119, 138, 143, 151; election results, 157; Grant requests 30-day men from, 164; ratifies Thirteenth Amendment, 189

Ohio River, 62, 132

Okolona, MS, 122, 184

O'Laughlin, Michael, 218

Old Capitol Prison, DC, 20

Olustee, FL, Battle of, 58

One Hundred Thirty-ninth NY Regt., 43

O'Niell, John L. (USMTC operator), 237

Oostanaula River, 90

Opelika, AL, 123-124

Opequon, VA, 139

Orange & Alexandria RR, 30, 88, 194

Orange CH, VA, 33

Orangeburg, SC, 190

Orchard Knob, TN, Battle of, 35-38

Ord, Edward O. C., 144, 171, 186; assigned to Tenth Corps, 121; replaces Butler, 184; notifies Washington of arrival of peace commissioners, 188; meets with Longstreet, 193; following line of Southside RR, 207

Ossabaw Sound, GA, 166, 168-169

Ould, Robert, 221
*Our American Cousin*, 215

Paducah, KY, Battle of, 71
Page, Richard L., 138
Paine, Lewis (See Powell, Lewis T.)
Paisley, J. Theodore (USMTC operator), 237
Palmer, Innis N., 62, 164
Palmer, John M., 129
Palmer, Solemen (USMTC), 68-69
Palmer, W. J., 184, 221
*Palmetto State, CSS*, 191
Palmetto Station, GA, 142
Palmito Ranch, TX, 204
Palo Alto, Mexico, Battle of, 1
Pamunkey River, 95-96
Pascagoula Bay, MS, 34
*Patapsco, USS*, 186
Patterson Creek, MD, 61
Payne, Lewis (See Powell, Lewis T.)
Peace talks (See Hampton Roads Peace Conference)
Peach Tree Creek, GA, Battle of, 118
Peeble's Farm, VA, Battle of, 153
Pegram, John, 189
Pendleton, George H., 138
Pennsylvania, 157; ratifies Thirteenth Amendment, 189
Pennsylvania RR, 4, 23, 162
Pensacola, FL, 174
People's Line Telegraph, 43, 63, 80
Perez, Joseph, 49
Perkins, George W. (USMTC operator), 237
Perkins, Thomas S. (USMTC operator), 237
Petersburg, VA, 17, 119, 134-135, 153, 161, 183, 189, 202; campaign of, 78-79, 88-89; assault on, 102-103, 105-106; seige of, 118, 121, 124, 204; explosion of mine and

Battle of the Crater, 118, 127; two CSA divisions leave to reinforce Early in the Valley, 131; evacuated, 205
Petersburg & Weldon RR (See Weldon RR)
Philadelphia, PA, 60, 69, 81, 93, 191, 193, 195; Presidential funeral route, 218
Philadelphia Navy Yard, 184
Pickett, George E., 103
Piedmont, VA, 79, 103
Pigpen Cipher System, 18, 234-235
Pikesville, NC, 204
Pine Bluff, AR, 85
Pine Hill, GA, 105
Pine Mountain, GA, 79
Piney Branch Church, VA, 86
Pittsburgh, PA, 16, 23, 80-81, 86, 93, 160, 162, 195, 202, 224, 236
Pleasant Hill, LA, Battle of, 78
Pleasonton, Alfred, 69
Plum Creek Station, Nebraska Territory, 152
Plymouth, NC, 78, 82
Po River, 94
Pocahontas County, WV, 46
Pocotaligo, SC, 163, 165, 189
Pocotaligo River, 163, 165
Point Lookout, MD, 68-69, 80-81, 89
Point of Rocks, MD, 107, 119, 125
Point Pleasant, WV, 62
Polignac, Camille A. J. M., Prince de, 95
Polk, Leonidas, 104-105
Pollard, AL, 174
Pollard, James, 157
Pomeroy Circular, 58
Pomeroy, Samuel C., 58
Poolesville, MD, 127
Pope, William (USMTC operator), 237

Port Republic, VA, 143
Port Royal, SC, 165
Port Royal, VA, 94, 220
Port Tobacco, MD, 68
Porter, David D., 153, 167, 171, 173; fire on flagship, 101; at Ft. Fisher, 185-186; on Cape Fear River, 187; bombards Ft. Anderson, 192
Porter, Peter A., 100
Potomac River, 66, 119-120, 124-125, 127; Booth crosses, 220
Potter, Robert B., 154
Powder Springs, TN, 156
Powell, Lewis T., 218
Powhatan Station, VA, 92
Preston, James D., 100
Price, Sterling, 152, 160
Prisoner of War Exchanges, Grant's denial of, 78; CSA policy for captured colored troops, 182; Longstreet discusses with Ord, 193
Pritchard, Benjamin D., 222
Proclamation of Amnesty, 203
Pugh, George E., 157
Pulaski, TN, 172
Purcellville, VA, 121-122

Quartmaster Corps, U.S., 3, 10
Quitman, MS, 64

Radical Republican Presidential Convention, 77, 100, 117
Raleigh, NC, 204; Sherman approaching, 173, 214; captured by Sherman, 217; Grant reports surrender of Johnston from, 220
Ramseur, Stephen D., 142, 159
Ransom, Robert, Jr., 40
Ransom, Thomas E. G., 107
Rapidan River, 33, 39, 62-63, 78, 85
Rappahannock Bridge, VA, 86

Rappahannock River, 33, 39, 220, 223
Rappahanock Station, VA, 85-86
Reams' Station, VA, 163; Battle of, 118, 136-137
Red Clay Station, GA, 33
Red River Campaign, LA, 68, 76, 78-79, 95
Red Oak, GA, 137
Relay House, VA, 218-219
Relay Sounder, 63
Republican Party, 118
Resaca, GA, 88, 152; Battle of, 79, 89-91; McPherson's arrival at, 86; Sherman south of, 158; Wofford surrenders near, 221
Resaca de Palma, Mexico, Battle of, 1
Revolution, American, 20, 78, 235
Rhode Island, ratifies Thirteenth Amendment, 189
Richardson, Mr., 229-230
Richmond, VA, 17-18, 20, 28, 58-59, 63-64, 79, 86, 88-91, 94-95, 100, 104, 118, 123-124, 128, 131, 137-138, 144, 151, 153, 161-162, 171, 181-182, 185, 187-189, 192, 194, 196, 201-203, 207, 209, 212-214, 229-230; cipher letters sent to, 45, 47, 159; telegraph lines destroyed to, 46; Kilpatrick's raid on, 65-67; RR tracks to Petersburg destroyed, 106; Grant threatens from north, 132; Lincoln visits, 183; inflation in, 190; occupied, 205; Halleck in command, 218; Ould arrested in, 221; telegraph line completed to, 223
Richmond & Danville RR, 89, 92, 165
Richmond Enquirer, 130
Richmond Examiner, 29, 102; reports on Battle of Mobile Bay, 130;

reports evacuation of Charleston, SC, 191

Richmond, Fredericksburg, & Potomac RR, 86, 100, 106, 194-195

*Richmond Sentinel*, 130

Ricketts, James B., 159

Ricksford, VA, 86

Rifes Point, VA, 94

Ringgold, GA, 29, 66, 85

River's Bridge, SC, 189

*Roanoke, USS*, 119

Roanoke River, 164

Robertson's (Robinson's) Tavern, VA, 34

Robinson, Jesse H. (USMTC operator), 237

Rockville, MD, 120-121, 124

Rocky Face Ridge, GA, 88

Roddey, Philip D., 213, 217

Rodes, Robert E., 142

Rome, GA, 90, 97, 152, 157; arrival of Union forces in, 92

Rosecrans, William S., 4, 69; replaced, 29; Grant directs removal of, 160

Rosser, Thomas L., 157, 161

Rossville Gap, TN, 36, 38

Round Mountain, AL, 152-153

Rousseau, Lovell H., destroys RR in AL, 123; arrives at Marietta, GA, 124; Forrest eludes, 156; at Murfreesboro, TN, 168

Route Cipher System, 16-18, 23, 229-230

Rucker, Edmund W., 168

Russell, David A., 142

Rutledge, TN, 40, 43

Rye River, 106

Sabine Cross Roads, LA (See Mansfield, LA, Battle of)

Sacred Three, 20

St. Albans, VT, 152

St. John's Church, DC, 191

St. John's River, 30

St. Louis, MO, 69

St. Mary's County, MD, 220

Salem, VA, 46, 155

Salisbury, MD, 13-14

Salisbury, NC, 218

Salkehatchie River, 189

Sampson, J. T. (USMTC operator), 33

Sand Creek Massacre, 152

Sanders, George N., 221

Sanderson (Chief Clerk), 7

Sandusky City, OH, 69

Sanford, Edward S., 4

Savannah, GA, 151, 153, 157, 159; Sherman marches toward, 159-161, 163, 165-167; false rumor of capture, 166; capture of, 169, 171-172; Meagher's troops arrive in, 187; Jefferson Davis moved to on way to Ft. Monroe, 223

Savannah Canal, GA, 165

Savannah River, 169

Sayler's Creek, VA, Battle of, 203, 207

Scammon, Eliakim P., 62

Schenck, Robert C., 33

Schimmelfennig, Alexander, 191

Schofield, John M., 66, 128, 154, 158, 180, 186; at Allatoona Pass, GA, 99; advance on Lost Mountain, GA, 105; at Battle of Franklin, 161; recommended by Grant to replace Thomas, 164; sent to Annapolis, 184; troops arrive in DC for deployment to Ft. Monroe, 187; commands Department of NC, 189; at Federal Point, NC, 190; captures Wilmington, 192; at

Kinston, NC, 194-195; occupies Goldsboro, NC, 196

Scott, Thomas A., 4, 6, 162

Scott, Winfield, 6

Scottsville, VA, 194

Second Corps, USA, 69, 106, 125, 127, 132, 134-135, 204-205

Second Division, Sixth Corps, USA, 142

Second VA Mounted Infantry, 46

Seddon, J. A., 130, 187

Sedgwick, John, 62, 69; rumored to replace Meade, 40; temporary command of the Army of the Potomac, 60

Selma, AL, 34, 187, 189; Thomas's cavalry moves toward, 192; Forrest driven out of, 207; captured by Wilson, 213, 217

Senate, Confederate, 191

Senate, U.S., 77, 82, 166, 181

Seventeenth Corps, USA, 123

Seward, Clarence, 215

Seward, Frank, 215

Seward, William H., 67, 93, 205; leaves for Ft. Monroe, 188; attacked by assassin, 215; recovers, 218

Seymour, Horatio, 138, 160

Shawneetown, IL, 132

Shelby, Joseph O., 95

Sheldon, George D. (USMTC operator), 67

Shenandoah River, 143

Shenandoah Valley, VA, 12, 16, 77, 79, 119, 125, 139, 143, 152-153, 156, 183, 193; Sheridan's victory in, 118; burning of, 154

Sheperdstown, WV, 128, 136

Sheridan, Philip H., 69, 78-79, 88, 91-92, 97, 101-104, 118, 125, 128, 137-138, 143, 151-153, 155, 158, 165, 180, 183-184, 192, 195, 204-205, 207, 221; at Yellow Tavern, 89-90; at Battle of Cold Harbor, 98; at Deep Bottom, 127; takes command of Middle Military Division and Army of the Shenandoah, 127, 129; prepares to advance toward Winchester, 129-130; presses enemy at Winchester, 131-132; reports on Early's movements and reinforcements, 134-136; skirmish near Charlestown, WV, 135; at Third Winchester, 139, 142; promoted to Brigadier General in Regular Army, 142; at Fisher's Hill, VA, 142; burns crops and stores of food in Shenandoah Valley, 154, 156; moves Sixth and Nineteenth Corps to Army of the Potomac, 154; refugees with, 156; at Tom's Brook, VA, 157; at Cedar Creek, 159; sends Sixth Corps to City Point, 161; reports on Merritt's expedition east of the Blue Ridge, 162; sends troops to reinforce Terry at Wilmington, 186; reported to enter Staunton, 193; reported to capture Charlottesville, VA, 194; at Waynesboro, VA, 194; raid toward Danville, VA, 196; sent to Texas, 223

Sherman, John, 205

Sherman, William T., 12, 14, 29-34, 57, 64, 66, 68, 71, 76-77, 79, 83; commends value of telegraph, 21; at Missionary Ridge, 35-40, 42; Atlanta campaign, 78, 85-86, 88-95, 97, 99-106, 116-118, 121-125, 128-129, 132, 134-139, 152; reports resignation of Palmer, 129; encircles Atlanta, 132, 134-136; in area of Fairburn and Red Oak, GA, 137; defeats Hood and captures Atlanta, 138-139, 152; March to the Sea, 151, 153, 157, 159-160, 163, 165-169, 171, 180; captures Savannah, 169, 171-172; Carolina campaign, 186-188, 190-192, 194-196, 203-205, 214, 217; captures Columbia, SC, 191; visits Grant at City Point, 196; Johnston's army surrenders to, 219-220; in Grand Review, 224

Ships Gap, GA, 158

Shoal Creek, AL, 156

Shreveport, LA, 68, 81-82

Sigel, Franz, 77, 79, 81, 85, 91, 93, 103; at Martinsburg, 119

Signal Corps, CSA, 18

Signal Corps, U.S., 20, 77, 105, 151

Signal Instruments, 82

Simpson, Bishop, 193

Singleton, James, 181

Sixteenth Corps, USA, 123

Sixth Corps, USA, 69, 90, 98, 120-121, 124, 142, 154, 156-157, 161, 204-205

Sixty-sixth NY Regt., 100

Slaves, 224; CSA arming of, 180-182, 190

Slidell, John, 47

Slocum, Henry H., 139, 156, 158; command of Twentieth Corps, 125; drives Stewart's Corps out of Atlanta, 138

Smith, Andrew J., attacked by S. D. Lee, 122; ordered to Arkansas, 139; arrives at Nashville, 161; sent to Eastport, TN, 174; sent to assist Canby, 187

Smith, Edmund Kirby, battle near Shreveport, 81; moves forces to assist against Sherman, 131; attempts movement east of Mississippi, 132; surrender of, 204; Sheridan sent to Texas to face, 223

Smith, Gustavus W., 219

Smith, John E., 95, 134

Smith, Morgan L., 123

Smith, Orlando, 100

Smith, William (Extra Billy), 214, 222

Smith, William F., 90; reinforces Grant, 95-97; at Battle of Cold Harbor, 98-100; ordered to advance on Petersburg, VA, 105; at Petersburg, 106

Smithers, Nathaniel B., 31

Smithfield, NC, 204, 214

Smithfield, WV, 137

Smithsonian Institution, 136

Soldiers' and Sailors' Monument, 236

Soldiers' Home, DC, 136

Solemn Grove, SC, 183; Battle of, 195

Sounder, 1

South Anna River, 88, 94-95; Grant's position near, 101; destruction of bridge over, 195

South Carolina, 162, 183, 222

South Central RR, 190

South Mountain, MD, 124

Southern Telegraph Company, 3, 13

Southfield, USS, 82

Southside RR, 91, 189, 195, 207

Spain, 3

Spanish Fort, AL, 183, 204, 214; Canby captures, 217

Speed (relative of James Speed, U.S. Attorney General), 222

Speed, James, 222

Spotsylvania CH, VA, 65, 94, 137; Battle of, 78, 88

Spring Creek, NE Territory, 152

Spring House, TN, 40

Spring Place, GA, 134

Springfield, IL, 218

Springfield, VA, 6

Stafford, Leroy B., 86

Stager, Anson, 16-17, 23, 60, 191; report to Quartermaster, 10; purchase of Western Union stock from, 81

Stanley, David S., 125

Stannard, George J., 100

Stanton, Edwin M., 35, 41, 45, 59, 67, 81, 91, 192, 194, 201, 205, 210-211; issues bulletin on Battle of Nashville, 167; visits Grant at City Point, 195; issues statement on Lee's surrender, 209; praises Grant for his actions, 213; commences military drawdown, 220; denies GA legislature right to assemble, 222

Statesville, NC, 218

Staunton, VA, 81, 96, 99, 102-103; arrival of Union troops, 93; Sheridan's forces enter, 143; destruction of government shops and supplies in, 154; Sheridan enters, 193; bridges and RR destroyed at, 194

Steedman, James B., 134, 172

Steele, Frederick, 82-83, 85, 95, 139; moves toward Montgomery, 214; assaults Ft. Blakley, AL, 217

Steinmyer, Augustus (USMTC operator), 237

Stephens, Alexander E., 188-189

Steubenville, OH, 23, 121

Stevensburg, VA, 67

Stevenson, AL, 171

Stevenson, John D., 139

Stevenson, Carter L., 139, 166-167

Steuart, George H., 89

Stewart, Alexander P., 89, 138

Stewart, Frank (USMTC operator), 130

Stone Mountain, GA, 122

Stoneman, George, 98, 129; relief of Foster, 60; at Battle of Resaca, 90; at Allatoona Pass, 99; tries to free Union prisoners at Andersonville, 124; captured by Iverson, 128; routs Basil Duke's command, 166; reports on raid into southwestern VA, 173; Thomas's report of raid in NC and VA, 218

*Stonewall, CSS*, 224

Stony Creek, VA, 85, 189; breaking of RR at, 86, 91

Stony Creek Station, VA, 162

Strasburg, VA, 142, 158; Union withdrawal from New Market, 91; CSA retreat from Winchester in July, 1864, 123; CSA falls back to in August, 1864, 131

Strawberry Plains, TN, 42

Streight, Abel D., 63

Strouse, David (USMTC operator), 23, 236

Strouse, John (USMTC operator), 6, 236

Stuart, James E. B., 89

Stumm, F. A. (USMTC operator at ATC), 33, 237

Sturgis, Samuel D., 104

Suffolk, VA, 85-86

Summerville, GA, 159

Sunbury & Erie RR, 162

Surrender, 207, 212; exchange between Grant and Lee on, 210; Stanton issues statement on, 213

Sussex CH, VA, 165

Sutherland's Station, VA, 205

Swan's Point, 108

Sykes, George, 69

*Tallahassee, CSS*, 187
Taylor, Richard, 79, 217; relieves Hood in Alabama, 187; surrenders army, 204, 221-222
Taylor's Bridge (North Anna River), VA, 94
Taylor's Ridge, GA, 158
Tazewell, TN, 31-32, 39-40
*Tecumseh, CSS,* 130
Telegraph Lines, 13-14, 40-41, 45, 60-65, 71, 80, 103, 120, 164; between DC and City Point, 180; opened to Warrenton Village, VA, 42; down west of Harrisburg, PA, 43; torn up to Richmond, 46; failed at Ft. Monroe, 65; not working to Alexandria, VA, 66; under construction at Point Lookout, MD, 68; completed to Ft. Washington, MD, 68; complete to Pt. Tobacco, MD, and Pt. Lookout, MD, 68; broken at Chesapeake Bay, 69, 104; down at Pt. Lookout, 80; extended to Winchester, 81; reestablished at Pt. Lookout, 81; construction to Port Royal, VA, 94; operational between Rifes Pt. and Pt. Royal, 94; to White House, VA, 96; between Yorktown and White House, VA, 97; between DC and White House, VA, 97; at West Point, VA, 98; being constructed between Jamestown, VA, and City Point, 105; operational between City Point and Ft. Monroe, 108; attacked at Ft. Powhatan, VA, 108; attacked near Laurel, MD, 116; down at Point of Rocks, MD, 119; repaired at Point of Rocks, 121; repaired to Harper's Ferry, 122; disrupted at Adamstown, MD, 125, 127; broken between Kingston, GA, and Chattanooga, 132; laid to Ft. Monroe, 136-137; between Ft. Powhatan and Jamestown Island, 138; operational to Allatoona, GA, 155; disrupted near Big Shanty, GA, 155; open to Allatoona and Atlanta, 156; broken between DC and Philadelphia and Philadelphia and Pittsburgh, 195; extended to Meade's Headquarters at Jetersville, near Amelia CH, 207; intact to Danville, 220; open to Richmond via Fredericksburg, 223
Telegraph Offices, opened at Brandy Station, VA, 39; attacked at Cherrystone, VA, 66; reopened at Cherrystone, VA, 67; evacuated between Brandy Station, VA, and Devereux, VA, 85; open at Rappahannock Bridge, VA, 86; open at Mid Point, VA, Belle Plain, VA, and Fredericksburg, VA, 90 (See also War Department Telegraph Office)
Tellico Plains, TN, 42
Tenallytown, MD, 120
Tennessee, 4, 28-29, 34, 38-39, 58, 67, 78, 102, 104, 152-153, 155, 158, 166, 195; abolishes slavery, 185
*Tennessee, CSS*, 130
Tennessee River, 36, 174, 221; Burnside crosses, 31; Sherman crosses, 35; Forrest escapes across, 156; Hood's army south of, 161; efforts to prevent Hood from crossing, 171-172; Hood crosses, 173

Tenth Corps, USA, 121, 132, 134-135, 143

Terry, Alfred H., 186-187, 196

Terry, Henry D., 69

Terry, William, 142

Texas, 82, 220, 223

Texas Brigade, CSA, 93

Thala Station, VA, 92

Thanksgiving, Declaration of, 152

Third Brigade, Third Division, Ninth Corps, 196

Third Corps, USA, 69

Third Division, Sixth Corps, 142

Third NY Cavalry, 100

Third VA Mounted Infantry, USA, 46

Thirteenth Amendment, 77, 181-182, 188-190

Thirty-sixth WI Regt., 100

Thoburn, Joseph, 159

Thomas, George H., 30, 65-66, 129, 151, 157, 159, 162-163, 169, 172, 180, 192, 207, 213, 218; succeeds Rosecrans in Chattanooga campaign, 29; in Chattanooga campaign, 32, 35, 37-38; in Atlanta campaign, 105; sent to drive Forrest out of TN, 155; Battle of Franklin, TN, 161; Grant orders to attack Hood, 164; Grant recommends replacement by Schofield, 164; at Battle of Nashville, 165, 167-168; reports defeat of Lyon in KY, 171; pursues Hood, 173-174, 184; sends troops to Canby in New Orleans, 187-188

Thompson, Jacob, 152, 158, 221

Thompson, Maj., 127

Thompson, Meriwether J., 204

Tinker, Charles A., 17, 20, 24, 28, 46, 49-50, 59-60, 130-131, 135, 158; deciphers Confederate messages, 45; sent to Halifax on special service, 137; ordered home from Halifax, 143

Tod, David, 119

Toledo, OH, 218

Tom's Brook, VA, 153

Torbert, Alfred T. A., 92, 134, 143

Toronto, Canada, 35

Torrence, John A. (USMTC operator), 237

Totopotomoy Creek, VA, 96

Totten, Joseph G., 82

Trans-Mississippi Department, 83

Trenton Station, GA, 30-31

Trent's Reach, 106

Trevilian Station, VA, 79

Trowbridge (Confederate agent), 47

Tullifinney River, 165

Tunnel Hill, GA, 85

Tupelo, MS, Battle of, 122, 207

Turkey, 3

Turkey Bend, VA, 91

Twentieth Corps, USA, 125, 139, 156-157

Twenty-eighth MA Regt., 100

Twenty-first AL Regt., 131

Twenty-fourth Corps, USA, 204

Twenty-second SC Regt., 127

Twenty-third MA Regt., 100

Tyler, Erastus B., 218-219

Tyler, Robert O., 92, 100

Underwater Cable, 10, 13-14, 41, 65-66, 69, 104, 116, 136-139, 181, 195

*Underwriter, USS*, 61

Union City, TN, 71

Union Mills, VA, 85

United States Military Telegraph Corps (USMTC), 23, 28, 57, 63, 76-77, 83, 116-117, 151, 180, 201-202; established, 3-21; annual report to Quartermaster, 10;

plaque, 236 (See also War Department Telegraph Office)

United States Telegraph Company, 20

Upper Marlboro, MD, 215

Upton, Emory, 142, 222

Utoy Creek, GA, 118

Vallandingham, Clement, 117

Valley Station, CO Territory, 182

Van Duzer, J. C., 116, 132, 138

Van Wert, GA, 157

Vance, Zebulon B., 217

Varioloid, 61

Vaughn, John C., 138

Vermont, 152, 154

*Vibbard* (locomotive engine), 62

Vicksburg, MS, 34, 68, 93, 104, 192, 229-230, 232; Canby at, 167; Grierson reaches after raid, 185

Vicksburg Square Cipher System, 18, 202, 232-233

Vigènere Cipher System, 232

Villanow, GA, 86

Virginia, 4, 12, 14, 21, 28, 40, 46, 57, 66, 68, 78, 152, 156, 173, 181, 183, 187, 203; permission requested for state government to assemble, 214, 220, 222; Governor Letcher arrested, 224

*Virginia, CSS* (ram), 187

Virginia & Tennessee RR, 46, 166

Virginia Central RR, 86, 100-101, 194

Voorhees, Daniel, 157

Waagner, Gustav, 16

Wade, Benjamin, 117

Wade-Davis Manifesto, 117

Wade-Davis Reconstruction Bill, 77, 117

Wadsworth, James S., 86

Wakeman, Abraham, 45

Walker, William S., 93

Walker, William H. T., 125

Wallace, Lewis, 120

Walter's Church, VA, 209

War Department (CSA), 189

War Department (U.S.), 6-8, 17, 23, 43, 66, 151, 168, 192-193, 205, 213, 217; offers reward for capture of assassins, 219, 222; papers found on Jefferson Davis arrive at, 224

War Department Telegraph Office, 7-8, 16-18, 23-24, 28, 45, 57, 201-202, 215

Ward, John H. H., 88

Warren, Gouverneur K., 69, 85, 92, 94-95, 97, 144, 154; at Battle of Cold Harbor, 99, 106; at Weldon RR, 134-136, 163-164; advance on Petersburg, 134; attacked near Petersburg, 135; destroys Richmond & Danville RR, 165

Warrenton Village, VA, 42

Washburne, Cadwaller C., 104, 155

Washington, DC, 1, 3-4, 6-8, 12-14, 16-18, 20, 23-24, 28-30, 33, 57-58, 61, 69, 76-77, 80, 83, 93, 108, 117, 121, 151, 155, 158-160, 165, 180-181, 185-186, 188, 190, 193, 202-203, 209, 213-214, 221-222; telegraph line complete from White House, VA, to, 97; Early's raid on, 116, 118-120; defense of, 123, 129; direct telegraphic communications with City Point, 137-138;, Grand Review, 223

Washington, GA, 222

Washington, George, 20, 64, 235

Washington Road, AR, 85

Watie, Stand, 204

Watson, Peter H., 50

Waynesborough, VA, 154, 183; Battle of, 194

Webb, Alexander S., 86

Webster County, KY, 136

*Weehawken, USS*, 42

Weitbrec, Robert F. (USMTC operator), 237

Weitzel, Godfrey, 205, 207, 220

Weldon, VA, 86, 196

Weldon RR, 92, 162, 164, 189; Warren's Corps crosses, 134; under Union control, 135-136; reconnaisance by Gregg, 162; Warren's men move down, 163; Sherman moves toward, 196

Wellville Station, VA, 92

Wesley Chapel, DC, 166

West, William C., 184

West Point, GA, 124

West Point, MO, 160

West Point, NY, (U.S. Military Academy), 213

West Point, VA, 14; telegraph line within ten miles of, 97; line completed to, 98; destruction of RR toward, 124

West Point Road, GA, 128; Sherman's army in area, 137; Hood at Palmetto Station on, 142

West Virginia, 31, 41, 46, 77, 221; ratifies Thirteenth Amendment, 189

Western & Atlantic RR, 66, 90, 92, 122, 155-156, 158, 160-161

Western Union, 3, 16, 20, 24, 81

Wheaton, Frank, 69

Wheeler, Joseph, 39-40; falsely reported wounded at Atlanta, 125; repulsed in attack on Dalton, 132, 134; moves to east Tennessee, 134; artillery attack on Maryville, TN, 135

White House, VA, 14, 95, 101, 103-104, 106; becomes Union base of supplies, 96; completion of telegraph line to West Point, 97-98; Sheridan heads toward, 194

White House, DC, 7-8, 181; fire in stable at, 63; President's levee, 67; illumination of, 192

White Oak Road, VA, 183; Battle of, 196

White Oak Swamp, VA, 105

White Plains, VA, 155

Whiteside Station, TN, 30

Whiting, William H. C., 171, 186

Wickham, William C., 143, 157

Wicksford, VA, 91

Wigwag Flag System, 77, 151

Wilcox Wharf, VA, 104

Wild, Edward A., 94

Wilderness, Battle of the, 76-78, 85, 88

Willcox, Orlando B., 31-32, 188

Willcox & Gibbs Sewing Machine Co., 24

Williams, Lt. Colonel, 130

Williams, Thomas D. (USMTC operator), 237

Williamsburg, VA, 14, 63, 66, 86

Williamsport, MD, 119, 124-125

Willis (Confederate agent), 47

Wilmington, DE, 13-14

Wilmington, NC, 118, 160-161, 164, 167, 171, 173, 182, 184-185, 187, 190-192, 196; report of capture, 186

Wilmington & Weldon RR, 120, 196

Wilson, James H., 105-106, 129, 134, 162, 172, 222; destruction of RR by and skirmishing at Hanover CH, 98; at Battle of Cold Harbor, 100; at Front Royal, VA, 142; assigned as Cavalry Chief for Sherman, 154; at Battle of Nashville, 167-168; drives Forrest out of Selma, 207, 213, 217; occupies Macon, GA, 219

Wilson, Mr. (Telegraph operator at ATC), 33

Wilson, William B., 6

Wilson Station, VA, 92, 205

Winchester, VA, 122-123, 132, 143, 192; extension of telegraph line to, 81; Sheridan moves troops toward, 130; CSA retreats from, 131; Torbert driven out of, 134; Early retreats toward, 137; Third Battle of, 118, 139, 142; Governor Letcher of VA confined at, 224

Wistar, Isaac J., 43

Wofford, William T., 221

Wood's Redoubt, 36-37

Woodstock, VA, 93, 96, 156

Woodward, Benjamin P. (USMTC operator), 237

Wright, Horatio G. M., 89, 91, 94-95, 121-124; at Battle of Cold Harbor, 98-99, 101; wounded at Cedar Creek, 159

Wytheville, VA, 218

Yellow River, 123

Yellow Tavern, VA, Battle of, 79, 89

York, Zebulon, 142

York River, 81-82, 123

Yorktown, VA, 63, 66, 195; telegraph line to White House, VA, completed, 97

Yorkville, SC, 221

Young, Pierce, 98

Zollicoffer, TN, 154

**Donald E. Markle** spent 34 years in the U.S. Intelligence Service of the Department of Defense where he worked as a cryptologist, predominantly at the National Security Agency. His interest in all aspects of communications in military environments is unabated in retirement. A graduate of the University of Maryland, Markle has lectured on the telegraph at the Smithsonian Institution and the National Archives. He now teaches in the Elderhostel Program at Gettysburg, Pennsylvania, where he resides. His first book, *Spies and Spymasters of the Civil War*, was a selection of the Military Book Club.

*The text of this book is set in 10 point
New Century Schoolbook typeface.
A neutral pH recycled paper has been used to assure
the future permanence of the book; the binding is a vermin proof,
moisture resistant, impregnated Arrestox B cloth.
The printing and binding was done by McNaughton & Gunn, Inc.
Composition and design are by Edmonston Publishing, Inc.
Jacket design and illustration design are by
Ellen L. Walker.*

Also of Interest from Edmonston Publishing:

## Civil War

*While My Country is in Danger: The Life and Letters of Lt. Col. Richard S. Thompson, 12th NJ Volunteers* by Gerry Harder Poriss & Ralph G. Poriss

*No Middle Ground: Thomas Ward Osborn's Letters from the Field (1862-1864)* edited by H. S. Crumb & K. Dhalle

*Unfurl the Flags: Remembrances of the American Civil War* edited by W. E. Edmonston

*Personal Recollections of the War of 1861* by Charles A. Fuller

*Out of the Wilderness: The Civil War Memoir of Cpl. Norton C. Shepard* edited by Raymond W. Smith

*Four Years in the First New York Light Artillery: The Papers of David F. Ritchie* edited by Norman L. Ritchie

*Memoirs of the 149th New York Volunteers* by George K. Collins

*A History of the 117th Regiment, New York Volunteers (Fourth Oneida)* by James A. Mowris

## Hypnosis

*Mesmer and Animal Magnetism. Biography of Franz Anton Mesmer* by Frank A. Pattie

## Mystery

*The Strange Case of Mr. Nobody* by Owen Magruder